White Women's Work

Examining the Intersectionality of Teaching, Identity, and Race

A Volume in
Contemporary Perspectives on Access, Equity, and Achievement

Series Editor:
Chance W. Lewis, *University of North Carolina, Charlotte*

Contemporary Perspectives on Access, Equity, and Achievement

Chance W. Lewis, Series Editor

White Women's Work: Examining the Intersectionality of Teaching, Identity, and Race (2017)
Edited by Stephen D. Hancock and Chezare A. Warren

Cultivating Achievement, Respect, and Empowerment (CARE) for African American Girls in Pre-K–12 Settings: Implications for Access, Equity and Achievement (2016)
Edited by Patricia J. Larke, Gwendolyn Webb-Hasan, and Jemimah L. Young

Reaching the Mountaintop of the Academy: Personal Narratives, Advice and Strategies From Black Distinguished and Endowed Professors (2015)
Edited by Gail L. Thompson, Fred A. Bonner, II, and Chance W. Lewis

School Counseling for Black Male Student Success in 21st Century Urban Schools (2015)
Edited by Malik S. Henfield and Ahmad R. Washington

Exploring Issues of Diversity within HBCUs (2015)
Edited by Ted N. Ingram, Derek Greenfield, Joelle D. Carter, and Adriel A. Hilton

Priorities of the Professoriate: Engaging Multiple Forms of Scholarship Across Rural and Urban Institutions (2015)
Edited by Fred A. Bonner, II, Rosa M. Banda, Petra A. Robinson, Chance W. Lewis, and Barbara Lofton

Autoethnography as a Lighthouse: Illuminating Race, Research, and the Politics of Schooling (2015)
Edited by Stephen Hancock, Ayana Allen, and Chance W. Lewis

Teacher Education and Black Communities: Implications for Access, Equity and Achievement (2014)
Edited by Yolanda Sealey-Ruiz, Chance W. Lewis, and Ivory Toldson

Improving Urban Schools: Equity and Access in K–16 STEM Education (2013)
Edited by Mary Margaret Capraro, Robert M. Capraro, and Chance W. Lewis

Black Males in Postsecondary Education: Examining Their Experiences in Diverse Institutional Contexts (2012)
Edited by Adriel A. Hilton, J. Luke Wood, and Chance W. Lewis

Yes We Can! Improving Urban Schools through Innovative Educational Reform (2011)
Edited by Leanne L. Howell, Chance W. Lewis, and Norvella Carter

White Women's Work

Examining the Intersectionality of Teaching, Identity, and Race

Edited by

Stephen D. Hancock
University of North Carolina, Charlotte

and

Chezare A. Warren
Michigan State University

IAP

Information Age Publishing, Inc.
Charlotte, North Carolina • www.infoagepub.com

Library of Congress Cataloging-in-Publication Data

CIP data for this book can be found on the Library of Congress website:
http://www.loc.gov/index.html

Paperback: 978-1-68123-647-6
Hardcover: 978-1-68123-648-3
E-Book: 978-1-68123-649-0

Printed in the United States of America

CONTENTS

INTRODUCTION

White Women's Work? Unpacking Its Meaning and Significance for the Contemporary Schooling of Diverse Youth

Chezare A. Warren
Michigan State University

Stephen D. Hancock
University of North Carolina, Charlotte

Utilizing social media networks to gauge public appeal around ideas of broad significance could almost be considered imperative in today's world. Social media provides a platform for which to pilot new concepts with the explicit aim of naming the utility of a project to achieve a specific goal. In that spirit, a Facebook inquiry was posted with questions including, "If you were to pick up a book about White women teachers, what would you expect or want to learn more about? If you are a White woman, what if anything would you expect to read in such a text?" The responses centered on wanting to better understand White women's perspectives on race, the intersections of White racial identity and teaching, and the implications of whiteness for negotiating humanizing interactions with diverse youth.

White Women's Work: Examining the Intersectionality of Teaching, Identity, and Race
pp. vii–xiii

One friend responded asking that the book foreground the significance of whiteness for how White women do their work specific to their capacity to comprehend the needs of others from historically oppressed racial groups. Another friend insisted the book explore how White women's understanding of race influences their ability to "nurture students of color." Other friends hoped the book would critically examine the not-so-easy to recognize complications posed by the kind-hearted hyperprivileged White woman teacher trope (e.g. Erin Gruwell of *Freedom Writers*), as well as spotlight how good intentions facilitate the persistence of racism. Finally, a White woman respondent thought it would be important for the book to touch on the diversity within White womanhood, or the "impact of intersectionality within that group, and the implications for students of color." We can say with confidence that the contributions to this volume cover each of these topics and more.

UNPACKING THE MEANING AND SIGNIFICANCE OF *WHITE WOMEN'S WORK*

White Women's Work is born out of years of teaching next door to White women who labored (some with burgeoning racial consciousness) at being the best teachers they could for their diverse students. These are women teaching as racial minorities in communities of color, or women in university settings who we believe to be smart, and also articulate a commitment to the aims of social justice. On the contrary, far too many of our White women colleagues in K-12 and college classrooms toil under the guise of good intentions while simultaneously failing to be critically aware of the influence whiteness has on their professional decision-making. Not recognizing or choosing to acknowledge this racial blind spot poses significant threats to establishing and maintaining culturally affirming learning environments for all students.

Historically, White women have had a tremendous influence on establishing the ideological, political, and cultural scaffold of American public schools (Anderson, 1988; Leonardo & Boas, 2013). Racialized pedagogical orientations, school policies, and classroom practices are underwritten by White, cisgender, feminine, and middle to upper class social and cultural norms. One response to the disproportionality of White women teachers, and the increasing multiethnic and multilingual public school population, is to increase the number of racially, ethnically, and linguistically diverse classroom teachers. We agree that a more multicultural teacher workforce can have a tremendously important impact on the field of education. However, a more immediate response might be to unveil the unique challenges faced by White women who teach, and to coordinate resources for responding to such challenges. Supporting White women in-service and preservice teachers requires providing access to opportunities and knowledge that broadens their perspectives on race and teaches them to recognize and subvert whiteness (Hancock, 2011; Warren, 2015; Warren & Hotchkins, 2015). Doing so better positions them to arrange more equitable schooling experiences for an increasingly multicultural public school student demographic.

White Women's Work hinges on our contention that White women teachers, and those preparing or providing them professional development, must increase White women's racial literacy (Stevenson, 2014) and their capacity to raise "race questions" (Michael, 2015). These issues are of particular significance for White teachers because of the longstanding implications of race on schooling outcomes and the history of racism in the United States. Discussing race out loud and knowing how to recognize its operation in a school can be stressful and bewildering largely because of the fear White people have for appearing racist or culturally incompetent (Stevenson, 2014). Explicitly naming how and why race and whiteness matter in the professional teaching context forges alternative intellectual pathways for disrupting oppressive schooling arrangements. The title of this book is reminiscent of segregationist language, yet our intention here is to emphasize the unique factors shaping the professional practice of White women teaching in the United States. This book underscores the struggle they may experience learning to navigate diverse epistemologies as the race and gender majority in the teaching profession. Comprehensive texts that place the intersection of race, identity, and teaching in its appropriate social, cultural, political, and historical perspective are essential in today's education marketplace. *White Women's Work* is one such text.

CONTEMPORARY SCHOOLING IN A DIVERSE SOCIETY

The chapters in this volume emphasize a number of themes that broadly examine how White women's teaching dispositions (i.e. teacher knowledge, beliefs, and skills) intersect with their racial identity development, their awareness of whiteness, institutional racism, and their cultural perspectives of racial difference. All of which, as the authors in this book argue, matter for nurturing a teaching practice that leads to more equitable schooling outcomes for youth of color. The chapters in this volume are also critical of the roles White women occupy for disrupting (or perpetuating) White supremacy, and manifestations of racism in multiple facets of American society. Contributors scrutinize how whiteness and racial illiteracy significantly impair a White woman's efforts to communicate with and respond effectively to culturally diverse students. The book is comprised of critical literature reviews, empirical studies, and personal narrative. Each chapter is written with the intention of foregrounding theoretical perspectives needed to help White women teachers resist and undo racist schooling policies and practices. The authors also describe pragmatic approaches to establishing learning environments that ensure efficacious cross-cultural and cross-racial teaching.

White Women's Work is divided into three sections. Each section of the book offers important considerations for thinking about the contours of White women's work—physical actions, behavioral habits, and professional decisions—in diverse teaching contexts. Part I explores how White women navigate interpersonal relationships with students attending multiethnic schools. In Chapter 1, Benterah Morton and his colleagues put forward the concept "cultural disability of whiteness" (CDW) based on examination of one White woman's teaching experience. They use CDW to demonstrate how whiteness disables White teachers by reducing their capacity to see and overcome the barriers posed by a racial mismatch. Their work provides recommendations for grappling with and disrupting whiteness while at the same time working to establish a classroom environment that values and affirms cultural diversity.

Chapter 2 is a rich exploration of White culture as seen through the eyes (and personal life experiences) of a White woman, a Korean woman, a Latina woman, and two Black women. The chapter, "Naming the Unnamed: White Culture in Relief" acknowledges how schools are constructed around the norms of White culture, and the significant role White women play in the maintenance of these oppressive cultural habits and expectations. They use personal narrative to demonstrate the threat of White culture on the schooling experiences of culturally diverse youth. Chapter 3 is the final manuscript in Part I. It is a moving expression of one White woman's memory of an illness she experienced while teaching predominantly Black students. Coffee, Stutelberg, Clements, and Lensmire draw on the methodological approach "collective memory work" to examine how race, gender, and authority interact to form the burden experienced by White women when making critical professional decisions regarding their own vulnerability. The chapter reminds readers of the genuine care students of color may possess for their teacher as demonstrated through their own acts of selflessness, and the responsibility teachers have to recognize and appreciate that effort when negotiating classroom interactions.

Part II explicates the impact of White image, whiteness, and White racial identity formation on the capacity of White women teachers to be effective educators of diverse students. Chapter 4 grapples with the intersectionality of White teacher identity and academic relationships. Through insightful narratives, Stephen D. Hancock demonstrates the role of "double image" consciousness to help White women better understand their academic relationship with youth of color and resist deficit perspectives of them and their families. Chapter 5 inquires whether a self-proclaiming liberal White woman teacher can also be truly antiracist. Brown and Reed use data from a critical ethnography conducted in an urban high school to provide an incisive critique of White subjectivities that mediate how teachers interact with youth of color, and the neoliberal market ideals/agendas that contextualize those interactions. The two researchers emphasize the tensions and possibilities for utilizing qualitative research to help participants, and in this case a White woman teacher, to become aware of whiteness and a brand of liberalism they identify as "neoliberal multiculturalism."

Chapters 6 and 7 focus primarily on White women's developmental understandings around issues of race and whiteness in their preparation to teach. In Chapter 6, Matias and Nishi cleverly share stories and poetry to "illuminate how the dynamics of whiteness" operate among White teacher educators and White women preservice teachers. "Becky Please ..." elucidates common rhetorical, emotional, intellectual, and professional moves made by White women in teacher education. The two authors emphasize the fallibility of White women's understanding of whiteness when unraveling the complexities of teaching in communities of color. They insist on the imperative for White women to see their whiteness as an impediment to their professional preparation to teach. In Chapter 7, Erin Miller authored a fascinating study of her own White daughter's engagement with whiteness and White images. Miller shows how White women, who were once White girls, come to know what it means to be White, and the significance of these realizations for shaping how they eventually conceptualize their place in the world of teaching. She offers a set of recommendations for teacher education that specifically take up the task of helping White women preservice teachers recognize they are in a "continual state of becoming White through discourse messages that dichotomize whiteness and Blackness."

Part III explores the practical reality of race in a teacher's quest to demonstrate evidence of culturally responsive teaching. Warren and Talley's "Nice White Ladies" chapter is a review of extant literature for examples of practicing White women who grapple with issues of race and whiteness to eventually achieve success educating Black and Latino/a youth in urban school settings. The authors aimed to identify specific challenges associated with being a White woman teacher, and strategies that may become particularly useful to this group in developing the skills necessary to be culturally responsive. Chapter 9 explores the salience of race in White women teacher's discipline practices. New Orleans is a case study that Henry and Warren use to draw parallels between White supremacy and acts of "spirit murder" experienced by youth of color at the hands of good-intentioned White women teachers. Recommendations for how to utilize culturally relevant teaching to reframe discipline practices that lead to more effectual interactions with Black youth are provided.

CONCLUSION

White Women's Work takes an intellectually rich and critically astute approach to understanding the nature of White women teachers' behavioral habits, physical actions, and professional teaching decisions in the classroom. This book is concerned with how their work looks, why it looks the way it does, and the factors shaping the effectiveness of this work for producing high academic and social outcomes for diverse youth. The premise underlying much of the research and theory put forward in this text is that no teacher is effective without being able to recognize the intersections of race, teaching, and identity. *White Women's Work* does not demonize or exceptionalize White women who choose to teach. Instead, our aim is to challenge the reader to courageously consider examinations of race for naming the real-life consequences of racial illiteracy. We invite White women teachers, and those who interact with them in schools, to do their part in dismantling racist systems and institutional norms that ultimately end up oppressing all teachers and students. It is our ambition that this book not only offers practical support and a strong critique of whiteness for reducing one's teaching effectiveness, but that it also offers hope.

REFERENCES

Anderson, J. D. (1988). *The education of Blacks in the South, 1860–1935*. Chapel Hill, NC: The University of North Carolina Press.

Hancock, S. D. (2011). White women's work: On the front lines of urban education. In J. G. Landsman & C. W. Lewis (Eds.), *White teachers/diverse classrooms: Creating inclusive schools, building on students' diversity, and providing true educational equity* (2nd ed., pp. 93–109). Sterling, VA; Stylus.

Leonardo, Z., & Boas, E. (2013). Other kids' teachers: What children of color learn from White women and what this says about race, whiteness, and gender. In M. Lynn & D. Dixson (Eds.), *Handbook of critical race theory in education* (pp. 313–324). New York, NY: Routledge.

Michael, A. (2015). *Raising race questions: Whiteness & inquiry in education*. New York, NY: Teachers College Press.

Stevenson, H. C. (2014). *Promoting racial literacy in schools: Differences that make a difference*. New York, NY: Teachers College Press.

Warren, C. A. (2015). Conflicts and contradictions: Conceptions of empathy and the work of good-intentioned White female teachers. *Urban Education, 50*(5), 572–600.

Warren, C. A. & Hotchkins, B. K. (2015). Teacher education and the enduring significance of "false empathy." *The Urban Review, 47*(2), 266–292.

PART I

WHITE WOMEN AND THE CULTURALIZATION OF THE SCHOOL ENVIRONMENT

CHAPTER 1

ROADBLOCK IN THE MIRROR

Recommendations for Overcoming the Cultural Disability of Whiteness in Non-White Educational Spaces

Benterah C. Morton, Melvin J. Jackson, Marcie E. Frazier, and Kenneth J. Fasching-Varner
Louisiana State University

FRUSTRATED BEYOND BELIEF

Exploring the contradictions between White female teachers' good intentions, and their often-misinformed cultural perspectives of the students in their classrooms that are culturally and linguistically different from themselves, poses both challenges and opportunities for educational researchers and teachers alike. One method of exploring these incongruities is to first examine the experience of a White female teacher as he/she prepares and interacts with students in situations of racial mismatch. This chapter begins with a brief illustration of one such case that will be revisited in later sections as a tool to assist us in describing the cultural disability of whiteness.

White Women's Work: Examining the Intersectionality of Teaching, Identity, and Race
pp. 3–17

A brief story about Marcie, a White middle-class teacher, written in her words.

> I first answered my calling to education in Springfield, Illinois. This city was shrouded in the history and legacies of presidents Abraham Lincoln and Barack Obama. It was also the setting of the 1908 race riots that were a catalyst in the creation of the National Association for the Advancement of Colored People (NAACP). The city of Springfield remains staunchly segregated, as indicated by the common references that the "bad part of town"' is (figuratively and literally) situated on the opposite side of the "tracks."
>
> As an educator, I worked in three different schools on the east side of town, which was considered the bad part of town, before relocating to Baton Rouge, Louisiana. Sadly, I did not ascertain the necessary skills of being a good teacher until after I left the school system. At times I look back with disappointment, thinking of how much better I could have been for my students if I would have known then what I know now.
>
> My traditional training in a teacher education program looked like most other traditional trainings. I excelled in my coursework, received Illinois Future Teacher Corps scholarships and served on the education forum. I did well in every observation experience and was even told it appeared as if I had been teaching for a while by cooperating teachers. Looking back, all of my placements were "easy" schools. I was placed in parochial, rural, and urban schools. My urban school placement was the gifted school, and it did not have much diversity in race or socioeconomic status (Ford, 1998). That school placement was little preparation for the schools and communities in which I would later serve. Although my cooperating teacher had been Teacher of the Year and was an excellent mentor, I needed additional experiences to prepare for the challenges of urban education. With excellent references and grades, I was placed in an urban school within Springfield public schools for my student teaching assignment. We were told that this urban district was the ideal placement for all of us because it improved our chances for employment after student teaching. I was beyond thrilled to start this leg of my teacher preparation.
>
> At the school where I did my student teaching, 90% of the students received free and reduced lunches. My classroom was disproportionately populated with African American and mixed race students, although the school statistics at this time were 60.2% White and 32.9% African American. Although my background differed greatly from the students I was teaching, I believed that I would be able to handle any situation that came my way because I was "trained very well and I felt prepared." I had "great mentor teachers" along the way and was ready for the challenge. I could not wait for January.
>
> My first week of student teaching, we caught a student taking her leftover cafeteria food and putting it into her book bag, and she was also taking extra food from other student's plates to take home with her. From the school's perspective, this was a major infraction because there was a rodent

problem in the school, especially in the wintertime. Through prodding and questioning, we learned that my student was recently homeless. She was taking the food to feed her brothers and sisters because there was no consistency of when they would eat at home. Immediately we asked the cafeteria for more food to sneak into her book bag. After we shared the situation with the cafeteria staff, they were more than willing to help, giving us extra food every day. My heart was broken for this 10-year-old that did not know where she would sleep that night nor when she and her family would eat again. I felt helpless, what could I do? My mentor teacher was also unaware of methods we could employ to assist the student.

Later that month we had our first cohort meeting with our university supervisors. At this meeting, we were learning about classroom management and used the time as a sounding board for concerns and problems. As our instructional leaders were asking about our first month as student teachers, I boldly raised my hand and shared about my homeless student. I asked what measures we could take to help the homeless student and her family. The individuals, college professors and university supervisors, who I assumed would have gems of advice, resources, or at least ideas, were speechless. They stammered as they tried to communicate that we will run into many different situations and that sometimes this will happen. They did not have any clues as to how to handle working with the student through her struggles. I pushed with more questions and tried reframing the way I was asking. Eventually they told me that this was just a hard situation and everyone handles it differently. What does that mean? How do I know how to handle it if I have never been in it before?

I was frustrated beyond belief. How can the university teach me anything about being a teacher in urban schools if they do not know how to teach in urban schools? Why did my mentor teacher not know what to do? Why could no one help me think through best practices to engage the student? Questions continuously ran through my mind throughout student teaching. The next year, my first year of teaching, I learned that there were a variety of resources to utilize to help students in similar situations. There was a parent educator who took the initiative to assist students and families in these situations, and there were school social workers that met with students about a variety of troubling situations. There was even a list of homeless students that my student could have been added to so that she and her family could receive additional benefits and resources from our district. Why neither my university mentor teacher nor my school did not utilize these resources or know about them is mind numbing. This experience was just the first of many that semester that would bring to light that I had not been adequately prepared to work in urban schools.

This chapter explores the journey of Marcie, a White female teacher working in a setting that predominately serves students with black and brown faces. It uses Marcie's experience from her undergraduate teacher training program to her first few years of teaching to illustrate several examples of the cultural disability of whiteness. We begin by framing the problem with public education. Then we use the problem of public education to posit the idea of a cultural disability of whiteness. Finally, we provide a list of recommendations that may assist teachers in wrestling with the contradictions of participating with and obtaining experience in diverse cultures while not imposing a standard of whiteness on their non-White students (Fasching-Varner et al., 2014).

THE DANGERS OF RACIAL MISMATCH IN PUBLIC EDUCATION

Looking at the *Profile of Teachers in the U.S. 2011* published by The National Center for Education Information (NCEI), we see that in 2011, 84% of U.S. teachers were White (Feistritzer, Griffin, & Linnajarvi, 2011). That same year the National Center for Education Statistics published data showing that 48% of the U.S. public school student population was non-White (National Center for Education Statistics, 2014). The general trend is that the population of teachers remains mostly White and mostly female, while the student population increased in racial and ethnic variability (Hayes & Fasching-Varner, 2015). Examining trends of racial mismatch with a predominantly White female middle-class educational workforce teaching a disproportionately large population of non-White students proves to be quite problematic. We agree with Leonardo and Boas (2013) and Leonardo (2009) that the disproportionately high numbers of White female teachers in the current education system places these teachers in a prime position to proselytize for White supremacy through the illusion that whiteness is good and well intentioned. As Fasching-Varner (2012) suggested, this position is not simply about disconnects between White teachers and Black students; White teachers are teaching White, Black, and brown students about the value of whiteness as they have cornered the identity market within educational settings. Whiteness not only shapes and informs acceptable blackness and brownness in the American educational system, but it also begets whiteness. This idea of the educational "replication of whiteness" is echoed in the work of McGrady and Reynolds (2013) and Warren (2015), who evaluate the role racial mismatch plays in putting non-White students at a disadvantage to their White peers.

Fasching-Varner et al. (2014) apply the critical race theory tenant, racial realism, to the current educational system (Bell, 1995) to posit a theory of educational and penal realism. The theory of educational and penal realism put forth by Fasching-Varner et al. implies that the current systems are "functioning per their design and the demands of the society," with the educational system serving as a driving force in the creation "of an economic imperative of free-market capitalism" (p. 411). This free market approach, consequently, reifies the standard of whiteness described by Sue (2006) and Jay (n.d.) where Whites benefit from whiteness at the expense of non-Whites. Teacher education programs consciously and unconsciously support this design by teaching preservice teachers to focus on "the intentionally nebulous illusion of change" (Fasching-Varner et al., 2014, p. 411) instead of educating teachers to embrace the educational realism that the current system is not broken, but part of a capitalist design that requires a stratified class system whereby the poor service the rich. As long as the system is seen as broken, we will continue to pour money into an irreparable system where the investments yield no return to anyone except for those who profit from reform (Fasching-Varner et al., 2014; Irizarry & Raible, 2014).

Through the lens of educational realism (Fasching-Varner et al., 2014), we see racial mismatch as intentional. McGrady and Reynolds (2013), working toward the understanding that "both students' and teachers' racial/ethnic statuses are important" (p. 7), were able to confirm that racial/ethnic statuses and racial stereotypes were contributing factors to the effects of racial mismatch. These effects include teacher bias, complicated classroom interactions that undermine academic achievement, and the reproduction of inequality across generations (McGrady & Reynolds, 2013). Further, McGrady and Reynolds (2013) report that there was never a gain or advantage for Black or Hispanic students, in their study, to having White instead of non-White teachers. In fact, they found that Hispanic and Black students "never receive[d] worse ratings from non-White or same-race teachers, and in some cases they [were] rated more positively" (p. 14) by non-White teachers. There is a stark difference in the experience of students of color with non-White teachers versus students of color with White teachers. The lack of gains and advantages to non-White students being taught by White teachers can, in effect, be interpreted as a result of the replication of whiteness. What is the problem with public education: nothing! It is functioning just as it was designed: for the benefit of Whites (Fasching-Varner et al., 2014).

THE CULTURAL DISABILITY OF WHITENESS

Warren (2015) explains, "There are likely fundamental differences in the social and cultural perspectives of White teachers and the students and families of color they serve" (p. 3). From this understanding, Warren (2015) moves the literature of racial mismatch further, and illustrates what we are calling the cultural disability of whiteness. Despite good intentions, White female teachers' lack of prolonged interactions with people of color often causes them to develop misinformed cultural perspectives of racially, ethnically, and linguistically diverse students. The cultural disability of whiteness hinders the ability of White female teachers to engage non-White students and families in educational excellence. We believe good intentions carried out with misinformed cultural perspectives are a cultural disability of whiteness. Outcomes are far more interesting and important than good intentions. The cultural disability of whiteness, like other disabilities, limits a person's movements, senses, or activities. In this instance it limits the teachers' ability to see past racial stereotypes (McGrady & Reynolds, 2014), acknowledge fundamental differences in social and cultural perspectives (Warren, 2015), engage in their own identity construction (Fasching-Varner, 2012), and at times causes them to unintentionally and even intentionally devalue non-White students (Kjolseth, 1983; McCollum, 1999).

Further Understanding the Cultural Disability of Whiteness

Benterah's brother was born deaf. Although he had some visible birth defects, it was not until later that the prognosis of deafness was given. Benterah's parents went to doctors, surgeons, audiologists and the like seeking remedies for his brother's disability. In an effort to find ways to accommodate his brother's condition, the family began learning sign language. The brother was also sent to a local school that focused on working with deaf children with the goal of producing productive members of society.

Now, more than 30 years later, Benterah's brother lives a normal life: he has a job, a family, friends, and is respected in his community. He has not overcome the disability of deafness and never will. He is at peace with his auditory condition and considers hearing people, not deaf people, to be at a disadvantage. He says he would rather people learn sign language to communicate with him than for him to be able to hear and speak. Although Benterah's brother is at peace with his deafness, there are often reminders of his inability to hear. Most often these reminders come in the form of hearing people trying to limit his potential because of their view of how he should live. Another reminder occurs every time he writes or tries to use his voice to communicate. There are clear syntactic inconsistencies in his writing, and his words—though audible—sound muted.

The disability of whiteness and the disability of deafness are similar in that they both can be accommodated, but not completely overcome. No matter how much accommodation is provided for deafness (cochlear implants, hearing aids, sign language, or reconstructive surgery) there are still remnants of disconnects that can be observed. Similarly with whiteness, no matter the accommodations a teacher learns, there are characteristics of disconnects in identity that will always be present when the identity of the teacher and her students is distanced. Additionally, as an integral and beneficial part of a fully functioning system (Fasching-Varner et al., 2014) that privileges whiteness, it becomes extremely difficult for teachers to change and transform the world into something different (Gordon, 1990; Milner, Pearman, & McGee, 2013), something more mutually beneficial to all students, as that appears not to be the goal of public education.

Marcie and the Cultural Disability of Whiteness

After her initial experience in student teaching, Marcie continued to work in urban schools. The first 2 years were the hardest for her. During this time she made mistakes similar to many other White teachers and began imposing her own interests, needs, and agendas on her students. She took a great deal of time printing and posting quotes from those she believed were great thinkers around her classroom, mostly White. Her classroom library had very few non-White authors. Those Black and brown authors that were included were the direct result of a university level multicultural literature class. The cultural disability prevented Marcie from seeing past racial stereotypes thus causing her practices to emulate her own experiences and not those of her students.

Despite her good intentions, she had little positive contact with students or their families. When she attempted to reach out to the families of her students, she found it difficult to relate, and the interactions were wholly unsuccessful. Often she would notice how her families would interact differently with her than they would with her African American colleagues. Her confusion about the students' interactions was further amplified because she was not able to acknowledge the fundamental differences in social and cultural perspectives between herself and her students or their families.

Walking around Marcie's current classroom there is a drastic difference in what is seen. There are pictures and quotes from African Americans posted in the classroom and in the hallways near her classroom there is a display of showcasing the students efforts to contrast the works of Langston Hughes and Tupac. Although the ratio of books in her classroom library does not directly reflect the demographics of her students, it is predominantly filled with literature and poetry written by authors with black and brown faces. Marcie's relationships with families and students are also drastically different than they were when she began teaching. She has much more developed relationships with families and has gained their trust. Frequently students and families have chosen to share information with her that they traditionally would not share with individuals from outside of their community. These changes in instructional design and communication were predicated by an epiphany Marcie had during her third year of teaching. It was only then that she began to understand that the summation of her experiences was impacting how she interacted with her students and the relationships she built with her families. Up until that point, she was not even aware of the need to engage in her own identity construction.

Marcie's current school population is 100% African American and, consistent with the National Center for Education Information report, a large majority of the teaching staff are White. To accommodate for the cultural disability of whiteness, Marcie teaches toward a culturally relevant pedagogy (CRP). Ladson-Billings (1992, 1995) defines CRP as a theoretical framework that centers on three basic proposition: "a) Students must experience academic success, b) students must develop and/or maintain cultural competence, and c) students must develop a critical consciousness through which they challenge the status quo of the current social order" (1995, p. 160).

CRP can be implemented by each teacher differently, but is designed to meet the needs of the students the school serves. In teaching toward a culturally responsive pedagogy, Marcie is intentionally genuine with her students on a consistent basis. She works arduously to meet the needs of the students in a way that is meaningful to them. Her focus has changed from herself to that of her students. Her texts and assessments are carefully chosen with the specific needs of students in mind. At the beginning of the year when her students are in the getting-to-know-you phase, she starts with a unit that studies biographies of African Americans. During this time of building community in the classroom, she discusses the students' hopes and dreams and continues by helping the students set rigorous goals. She believes that the depth and activities in the biographies unit opens doors of possibilities for her students and sets the tone for the year ahead. Each subsequent unit infuses some aspect of cultural relevance for the students.

WRESTLING WITH CONTRADICTIONS

Marcie, has wrestled with contradictions stemming from the idea of "whiteness of good intentions" (Warren, 2015, p. 24) throughout her career, which represents the blind prerogative White female teachers take to teach students of color without fully understanding their experiences and points of view. The challenge of wrestling with these contradictions is synonymous with working to accommodate for the cultural disability of whiteness. Wrestling with contradictions seeks to provide suggestions to preservice teacher programs and teachers to consider as they seek to accommodate for the cultural disability of whiteness. We recommend that:

1. Prospective and practicing teachers critique their own beliefs about culturally diverse students, and how these affect their instructional behaviors
2. Teacher candidates embark upon the continuous journey of accommodating for the cultural disability of whiteness
3. Teachers are constantly reminded that it is important to have empathy over sympathy
4. Teachers cannot lower their expectations
5. Teachers must understand and acknowledge that their students' zip codes do not identify or limit their ability and must foster a mindset of growth and guidance toward the success of their non-White students
6. Teachers should recognize the humanness that exists and espouses students, teachers, and parents by looking past the socially constructed phenotypic identifiers that marginalize the students
7. Teachers should incessantly engage in personal development and exploration in order to continuously evolve as people, professionals, and teachers
8. Teachers should be prepared to interact with families and communities who are unlike their own
9. Teachers must apply the theoretical framework of culturally relevant pedagogy in practice not just in talk, hope, or aspiration

CONTRADICTION: WHITENESS BEGETS WHITENESS

Preservice teacher education programs must take the initial steps to develop their faculty before working to develop their students. They must recognize and acknowledge their own privilege and prejudices before influencing and educating White middle-class female teachers, or any teachers. They must ask the question, "What does it mean to me to be White?" As they answer this question, they can begin the diligent work of "diving into the contradictions" (Ayers, 2014) that have attached a stigma to working with non-White student populations. Teacher educators need to prepare their students to find comfort in the discomfort of engaging in the contradictions of racial mismatch in the classroom, thereby being fully integrated into living in an environment that is uncomfortable and intimidating. Often, these White middle-class female teachers will be thrust into situations that are uncommon and their views and beliefs will be challenged, altered, and hopefully reestablished.

Currently, a vast majority of college professors in teacher education programs are White; at the same time a similar majority of the students in teacher education programs are White. As we explored earlier, the majority of students being taught in K-12 schools are not White (Deruy, 2013; Feistritzer, Griffin, & Linnajarvi, 2011). Racial mismatch is problematic and hiring practices in the academy and in K-12 education continue to promulgate the problem. Current practices maintain the replication of whiteness as they back the "assumption: We—the respectable, the prosperous, the superior, and (especially in modern times) the professional—know what is best for *Them*" (Ayers, 1997, p. 41, original emphasis) where *Them* are Black and brown peoples. Ayers (2014) encourages us to reframe the hiring discussion realizing that if universities continue their current hiring practices, they will continue to produce the same results of disproportionate numbers of White professors and teachers. He continues to suggest that "we dive into the contradictions head-first in order to engage in that thorny contested space" (Ayers, 2014) of increasing teacher and professor diversity. We believe that hiring processes should be "driven by an intellectual desire to diversify [the academy] in terms of actual physical bodies, knowledge representation, and the politics of pursuing social and educational change" (Dei, 2001, p.1), where currently they are driven by a racial contract (Mills, 1997) that privileges Whites in positions of power to reify the status quo of the educational industrial complex (Fasching-Varner et al., 2014; Fasching-Varner & Mitchell, 2013). We challenge preservice teacher education programs to address the contradictions in hiring in order to open the door for students to become engaged with educators who are uniquely situated to deal with increasingly diverse student bodies or at a minimum help open up the idea of what a different identity landscape in education could look like (Deruy, 2013). The diversity does not stop with race or ethnicity, but progresses into diverse ideas, backgrounds, socioeconomic upbringing, religions, etc. Thus it providing future teachers with a faculty that has the ability and desire to continue to acquire cultural competencies for themselves and use cultural resources to facilitate better teaching and learning (Gay, 2013).

CONTRADICTION: ROADBLOCK IN THE MIRROR

Many educators, like Marcie, are ill-prepared to address issues of race or diversity (Fasching-Varner, 2012); they lack diverse cultural experiences or frames of reference (Gay, 2010b) with which to crafting meaningful instruction for their diverse student populations, and they are void in large measure of any understanding of their own racial identity (Fasching-Varner, 2012). We encourage current professors and teachers to attempt to accommodate for the cultural disability of whiteness through thought and collective self-reflection, a process described by Gay (2013) as "acquiring cultural competence and using cultural resources to facilitate better teaching and learning" (p. 51). Gay goes on to explain collective self-reflection as a way of teaching students through their cultural filters, not the filters of the teacher or professor. This type of culturally responsive teaching is contrary to teaching that is currently carried out in universities and K-12 schools across the country for the most part. As discussed earlier, the current expectation of public education is to proselytize whiteness under the auspice of saving children of color through an educational reform industrial complex that is violent and will sacrifice lives to protect the interests of making and retaining profit. Challenging the status quo in hiring and teaching practices is one way to change the focus from whiteness to humanness.

Gay (2013) recommends "that prospective and practicing teachers critique their own beliefs about culturally diverse students, and how these affect their instructional behaviors" (p. 55) as a way of challenging the status quo. Leonardo and Boas (2013) recommend that all teacher candidates embark upon the continuous journey of accommodating the disability of whiteness by: practicing critical reflection on how they are implicated in racialized and gendered histories, fighting to make race and race history a consistent part of the curriculum, teaching race as a systemic institutional structure that produces materially different outcomes; working toward the understanding of races as a sociohistorical construct not a biological one, and teaching that we are all produced through this system that has benefited some (White) people and left behind many (Black and brown) peoples. These recommendations are more easily written than they are placed into practice. They require teachers to embark on a journey that contradicts their formal training, and at times their epistemological understanding of their values. We suggest study abroad programs as one tool to begin this journey. Warren (2015) recommends empathy as another tool that should be used to provide high quality equitable educational experiences to non-White children. Warren (2015) suggests teachers use empathy to work out their own contradictions, stating, "empathy allows teachers the flexibility to see their instruction and student interactions through students' eyes" (Warren, 2015, p. 4).

Additionally, it is important to have empathy over sympathy (Warren, 2015; Warren & Hotchkins, 2015). Teachers must realize that by simply being sympathetic to their students, they are taking pity on their students and in turn becoming prejudicial toward the students they are charged to educate. To be successful, teachers cannot lower their expectations and take pity on their students (Fasching-Varner & Seriki, 2012; Irvine, 2010; Ladson-Billings, 1992, 1995, 2006). They must work to develop them and help them grow into intelligent and sociopolitically connected members of society (Fasching-Varner & Dodo Seriki, 2012; Irvine, 2010; Ladson-Billings, 1992, 1995, 2006). Teachers must understand and acknowledge that their students' zip codes do not identify or limit their ability and must foster a mindset of growth and guidance toward the success of their non-White students. White female middle class teachers must adopt a people first mentality. They must also recognize the humanness that exists and espouses students, teachers, and parents by looking past the socially constructed phenotypic identifiers that marginalize the students. In addition, teachers should incessantly engage in personal development and exploration in order to continuously evolve as people, professionals, and teachers. They must also be prepared to interact with families and communities who are unlike their own. Inevitably they will encounter complicated conversations (Pinar, 2004) because of the racial, ethnic, religious, gendered, and socioeconomic barriers that exist. Teachers must apply the theoretical framework of culturally relevant pedagogy in such a way that their cultural self-confidence does not become a roadblock in the mirror, but an avenue through which students are valued as human and not marginalized as non-White (Fasching-Varner & Seriki, 2012; Irvine, 2010; Ladson-Billings, 1992, 1995, 2006).

CONCLUSION

The challenge for White middle-class female teachers is that no matter what they do to relate, they will always be different from their non-White students. At the end of the day, the teacher's identity—White middle-class woman—is still the staunch reality that exists in the relationship dynamic. There is a fine line between acknowledging the differences that exist between teachers and students and having to accept those differences as fact. Regardless of how hard teachers work and try, they must recognize and accept that the process of building trusting relationships cannot eradicate the comfort found in knowing that at the end of the day they will return to a life of comfort, a life different from their non-White students.

Upon entering the teaching profession, White female middle-class teachers, and nearly all teachers, have much to contend with in regards to teaching in classrooms that exhibit racial mismatch. In situations of racial mismatch the task of preparing becomes more challenging, especially considering the propensity of teacher preparation programs to prepare teachers to proselytize for whiteness. Concurrently, teachers are battling with the cultural disability of whiteness that poses intrinsic obstacles to seeing past racial stereotypes, acknowledging and accommodating for differences in social and cultural perspectives between teachers and students (Warren, 2015), and actively engaging in self-identity construction (Fasching-Varner, 2012), which often results in both intentional and unintentional devaluations of non-White students (Kjolseth, 1983; McCollum, 1999). The cultural disability of whiteness, as with any disability, has no solutions to completely eradicate its effects, thus the characteristics of disconnects in identity will always be present when the identity of teachers and students is distanced.

Realizing that there is no cure, we offer several accommodations to assist preservice and veteran teachers to apply in an effort to minimize the effects of racial mismatch in their classrooms. We propose that White female teachers start the process by ceasing to proselytize the standard of whiteness. They can embark on this lifelong sojourn through thorough and collective reflection (Gay, 2013) applied with empathy (Warren, 2015). As they gain more understanding of their own racial identity (Fasching-Varner, 2012) and alter their own consciousness in order to contribute to an environment that is consciously promoting "social and cultural relevance" (Howard, 2003, p. 200), they will be better prepared to teach toward a culturally relevant pedagogy (Fasching-Varner & Seriki, 2012; Irvine, 2010; Ladson-Billings, 1992, 1995, 2006). Additionally, we encourage universities and K-12 institutions to challenge the status quo in hiring and teaching practices as one way to change the focus of education from whiteness to humanness. We are the roadblock in the mirror, and realizing that we are our greatest obstacle is the first step to accommodating for our shortcomings.

REFERENCES

Ayers, W. (1997). *A kind and just parent: The children of juvenile court.* Boston, MA: Beacon Press.

Ayers, W. (2014). *The myth of military might.* Retrieved from http://www.billayers.org

Bell, D. A. (1995). Who's afraid of critical race theory. *University of Illinois Law Review, 4,* 893.

Dei, G. J. S. (Ed.). (2001). *Indigenous philosophies and critical education: A reader.* New York, NY: Peter Lang.

Deruy, E. (2013). Student diversity is up but teachers are mostly White. *ABC News.* Retrieved from http://www.abcnews.go.com

Fasching-Varner, K. (2012). *Working through whiteness: Examining White racial identity and profession with pre-service teachers.* Lanham, MD: Lexington Books.

Fasching-Varner, K. J., & Mitchell, R.W. (2013). Capturing the moment to debunk the crisis. *Journal of Curriculum and Pedagogy, 10*(2), 124–127.

Fasching-Varner, K. J., Mitchell, R. W., Martin, L. L., & Bennett-Haron, K. P. (2014). Beyond school-to-prison pipeline and toward an educational and penal realism. *Equity & Excellence in Education*, *47*(4), 410–429.

Fasching-Varner, K. J., & Seriki, V. D. (2012). Moving beyond seeing with our eyes wide shut. A response to "There is no culturally responsive teaching spoken here." *Democracy & Education*, *20*(1).

Feistritzer, C. E., Griffin, S., & Linnajarvi, A. (2011). *Profile of teachers in the U.S., 2011*. Washington, DC: National Center for Education Information.

Ford, D. Y. (1998). The underrepresentation of minority students in gifted education problems and promises in recruitment and retention. *The Journal of Special Education*, *32*(1), 4–14.

Gay, G. (2010b). *Culturally responsive teaching: Theory, research, and practice* (2nd ed.). New York, NY: Teachers College Press.

Gay, G. (2013). Teaching to and through cultural diversity. *Curriculum Inquiry*, *43*(1), 43–70.

Gordon, B.M. (1990). The necessity of African American epistemology for educational theory and practice. *Journal of Education*, *172*(3), 88–106.

Hayes, C., & Fasching-Varner, K. J. (2015). Racism 2.0 and the death of social and cultural foundations: A critical conversation. *Educational Foundations*, *28*(1–4), 103–119

Howard, T. C. (2003). Culturally relevant pedagogy: Ingredients for critical teacher reflection. *Theory into practice*, *42*(3), 195–202.

Irizarry, J. G., & Raible, J. (2014). "A hidden part of me": Latino/a students, silencing, and the epidermalization of inferiority. *Equity & Excellence in Education*, *47*(4), 430–444.

Irvine, J. J. (2010). Culturally relevant pedagogy. *Education digest: Essential readings condensed for quick review*, *75*(8), 57–61.

Jay, G. (n.d.). *Teaching about whiteness*. Retrieved from https://pantherfile.uwm.edu

Kjolseth, R. (1983). Cultural politics of bilingualism. *Society*, *20*(4), 40–48.

Ladson-Billings, G. (1992). Culturally relevant teaching: The key to making multicultural education work. In C. Grant (Ed.), *Research and multicultural education: From the margins to the mainstream* (pp. 106–121). Bristol, PA: Taylor & Francis.

Ladson-Billings, G. (1995). But that's just good teaching! The case for culturally relevant pedagogy. *Theory Into Practice*, *34*(3), 159–165.

Ladson-Billings, G. (2006). Yes, but how do we do it? Practicing culturally relevant pedagogy. In *White teachers/diverse classrooms: A guide to building inclusive schools, promoting high expectations, and eliminating racism* (pp. 29–42). Sterling, VA: Stylus.

Leonardo, Z., & Boas, E. (2013). Other kids' teachers: What children of color learn from White women and what that says about race, whiteness, and gender. In M. Lynn & A. Dixson (Eds.), *Handbook of critical race theory in education* (pp. 313–324). New York, NY: Routledge.

Leonardo, Z. (2009). *Race, whiteness, and education*. New York, NY: Routledge.

McCollum, P. (1999). Learning to value English: Cultural capital in a two-way bilingual program. *Bilingual Research Journal*, *23*(2/3), 113–134.

McGrady, P. B., & Reynolds, J. R. (2013). Racial mismatch in the classroom beyond Black-White differences. *Sociology of Education, 86*(1), 3–17.

Mills, C. W. (1997). *The racial contract.* Ithaca, NY: Cornell University Press.

Milner IV, H. R., Pearman, F. A., III, & McGee, E. O. (2013). Critical race theory, interest convergence, and teacher education. In M. Lynn & A. Dixson (Eds.), *Handbook of critical race theory in education* (pp. 339–354). New York, NY: Routledge.

National Center for Education Statistics. (2014). *Racial/ethnic enrollment in public schools.* Retrieved from http://necs.ed.gov

Pinar, W. (2004). *What is curriculum theory?* Mahwah, NJ: Erlbaum.

Sue, D. W. (2006). The invisible whiteness of being: Whiteness, White supremacy, White privilege, and racism. In M. G. Constantin & D. W. Sue (Eds.), *Addressing racism: Facilitating cultural competence in mental health and educational settings* (pp. 15–30). Hoboken, NJ: Wiley.

Warren, C. A., & Hotchkins, B. K. (2015). Teacher education and the enduring significance of "false empathy." *The Urban Review, 47*(2), 266–292.

Warren, C. A. (2015). Conflicts and contradictions: Conceptions of empathy and the work of good-intentioned White female teachers. *Urban Education, 50*(5), 572–600.

CHAPTER 2

NAMING THE UNNAMED

White Culture in Relief

Ali Michael
University of Pennsylvania

Chonika Coleman-King
University of Tennessee, Knoxville

Sarah Lee
Friends Select School

Cecilia Ramirez
Partner, C-Luxe Axiom LLC and Producer, Hispanic Choice Awards

Keisha Bentley-Edwards
Duke University

This assumption that of all the hues of God whiteness alone is inherently and obviously better than brownness or tan leads to curious acts.

—W. E. B. Du Bois in *The Souls of White Folks* (1920)

White Women's Work: Examining the Intersectionality of Teaching, Identity, and Race
pp. 19–43

Is there such a thing as White culture? "Are you kidding me?" one South Asian American colleague replied when we posed this question,

> Culturally, White is summer camp. It's turkey on Thanksgiving. It's eating with a knife and fork. It's thinking your coworker's little brown Indian children are cute because they eat with their hands. It's hugging people you don't know well because they came to your house for dinner. I have spent my entire life trying to learn White culture. From the outside looking in, it's easy to describe what makes up a culture. For a cultural insider, however, it is almost impossible to see.

As the five coauthors of this paper (five women educators of different races), we set out to identify the cultural manifestations of whiteness in acknowledgment of the fact that there is no monolithic White culture, but many varied manifestations of whiteness and White cultural practices across the United States. We share stories of our lives as students—sitting in desks in the classrooms of White women[1] teachers—bumping up against cultural manifestations of whiteness and feeling confused, insufficient, unworthy, and judged for being who we were. It only became clear over time that the thing we were bumping up against was a whole set of cultural norms that were very different from our own. To the White women teachers in our classrooms, these norms seemed, frankly, normal. "Culture," as Gloria Ladson-Billings described it once in a talk, is nothing more than "how we do things around here." But for children who did not grow up in homes and communities shaped by White cultural norms, it felt alienating and oppressive. While not every point in this chapter addresses White women directly, the article as a whole aims to highlight a few of the myriad ways that the cultural manifestations of whiteness show up in schools so that White female teachers can begin to identify themselves as both cultured and raced—not culturally neutral and objective—and ask themselves to what extent the cultural manifestations of whiteness shape their behavior and expectations in school.

But first, a note: Though we write of whiteness, our work is rooted in the knowledge that race is not biologically real. As social anthropology has demonstrated, race is something that was created to divide, classify, and differentiate people (Frankenberg, 1993, 2001; Moses, 2004). Even though race is not biologically real, however, it has very real consequences for a society that has used it as an organizing principle for so long. For this reason, we persist in trying to describe the cultural manifestations of whiteness because its effects are real. We do this with the awareness that any semblance of a White culture is not the result of biological determinism, but the result of a group of people being classified, grouped, and treated as White in the present and in the past.

NARRATIVE ACCOUNTS

Sitting in the classrooms of White female teachers as children, we became experts on whiteness—and the ways that we did or did not fit into it. In this paper we use those interactions to begin to develop a framework for seeing whiteness in relief, in contrast with the lives of people who are not White. Because the cultural manifestations of whiteness shift by region and intersect with many other social identities, we decided to demonstrate what it looked like for us, in various different contexts, when we were growing up in American schools. As we share our reflections and experiences, we invite the reader to consider how your culture has shaped your expectations and behaviors, as well as your ideas of what is beautiful or normal.

The following accounts chronicle the experiences of individuals; they are not intended to be representative of particular racial categories. Our authorship team is comprised of women of different racial groups because the diversity of backgrounds brings into relief many different aspects of whiteness. But none of us intends to represent our whole racial group, or even our whole families; these are diverse, individual experiences of the cultural manifestations of whiteness.

SARAH LEE: CULTURAL (IN)VISIBILITY

Living in between as a Korean American has been a journey. I was born in the United States and grew up in California. My parents immigrated to America in the late 1970s after growing up in a country recovering from war. They brought with them the Korean culture and ways of thinking. In California, I lived with my family as well as my extended family—grandparents, and often uncles, aunts, and cousins. At a young age, I developed a positive attitude towards my ethnic origin. I associated being Korean with my family. My grandmother would often compliment me for my Asian eyes. "They are as beautiful as almonds," she would say (in Korean).

During my early elementary school years in California, about 30% to 40% of the children in my class were children of immigrant parents. Though most of my friends came from Spanish-speaking families, it was very normal that you had parents who spoke a language other than English. Even though our cultures were different, there was a common understanding that having a bicultural identity (though none of us knew that term or could name it) was a normal experience of life. It didn't feel "other" or "outside."

In the Korean culture, age is really important. Respect for your elders is deeply valued. I was raised to always bow to greet a Korean person older than me. When you speak Korean, there are many different levels of formality that indicate respect, closeness, and the type of relationship you have. I was taught to respect elders by using the proper honorific forms of speech. Depending on age and gender there are different terms that you use to address people.

Western culture emphasizes the individual and independence. Time is valued in a more linear sense (e.g. you are expected to be on time to appointments). Respect through equality. Eye contact is a way to show respect. By contrast in the Korean culture, people are more collective in their thinking. The group is emphasized over the individual. The concept of time is a bit more flexible, less linear. Respect through hierarchy. Eye contact to those older can be brazen and disrespectful. Deference is what's expected. One way of thinking about something isn't better or worse, but it's culturally different.

I was the first child. If you are male and you have an older sister, you must call her "Nuna" as a term of respect. My younger brother grew up calling me "Nuna." When I was in second grade, my brother saw me at recess and in a really happy voice said, "Hi Nuna!" I got really mad at him for using a Korean word at school. I was embarrassed and told him that he had to call me Sarah at school, but had to call me Nuna at home because I still wanted the respect of a younger sibling. As a Korean child growing up in America, there were moments when I tried to fit in by escaping my cultural heritage, although another part of me embraced my Korean heritage. There were times when I wanted to be what I thought was "American" in one setting and "Korean" only in certain settings. When I was 10, my family moved to Delaware. I lived in a neighborhood and went to a school that was much more homogeneous than my community in California. I was one of very few Asians at my middle school. There wasn't that common understanding that being of multiple cultures or growing up in an immigrant family could be another way to be American. Because of my Asian face, I was often asked if I spoke English. At school when my White women teachers would ask me where I was from, I told them that I was from California. They would respond by saying, "No, where are you really from?" My almond shaped eyes—features that were once cherished by my grandmother—were the means by which classmates would tease me.

More than overt, conscious forms of racism, it was those small daily interactions that I would experience regularly through my schooling that began to weigh me down. When classmates or teachers tried to get to "know" me, it was often in stereotypical ways (i.e. Where are you *really* from? or Are you Chinese?). Repeated comments and questions that implied that I didn't really belong in America began to create thoughts like "I wish I was White" or "I am less than." I had White women teachers who tried to compliment me based on my Asian features. Yet their comments were intertwined with implications that my "beauty" equated to being foreign. They didn't seem to realize that through their fascination and questioning I was being put on the outside almost as if they had the right to explore me out of their curiosity. At age 10, I didn't know how to name what I experienced at school from teachers and students. These experiences were not things I shared with my parents, as I did not know how to put into words what weighed me down and I knew that my parents were tired immigrants trying to figure out how to live within systems that were unfamiliar to them. Regarding my racial journey, I often felt invisible and alone because there was so much left unsaid during my years in school. There wasn't a category for multiple cultures and backgrounds in the way education was taught. I didn't see myself in books, history, or in the teachers who taught me. School could have been different if people had a deeper awareness of the nuances of multiple cultures. I felt like I was on the outside looking in. One culture isn't better or worse, but it's culturally different. Living in between two cultures—being Korean and American—is indeed another way to be American.

KEISHA BENTLEY-EDWARDS: CULTURE AS GATE KEEPER

I am an African American woman [who] grew up in Southern California, but had strong family roots in Alabama. Although my classmates were primarily Latino and Southeast Asian (Vietnamese and Cambodian), the institutional and cultural presence of whiteness—and particularly White women—was palpable in my educational experience. Despite the racial diversity of students in my overcrowded, inner-city schools, the vast majority of my teachers were White suburban women. As a matter of fact, in my entire K-12 experience, I can count the number of non-White teachers on both hands. The lack of cultural competence demonstrated by my White teachers placed me in precarious situations. I was seen simultaneously as both a shining representative of racial progress, and as a problem student destined to fall into some dire statistical category.

At my school, the tracking system occurred in the third grade, separating students into remedial, general, and gifted tracks based on 2nd-grade teacher recommendations (and parental social capital). Because each school, regardless of student enrollment, was granted only one gifted class, the selection process was competitive.

I was more fortunate than most of my peers because I benefited from my mother's experience navigating the school's tracking system with my older siblings. Prior encounters with the school let her know that she needed help from within the system. I was tested into the gifted program because my 1st-grade teacher, Mrs. Johnson, an African American veteran teacher, was able to override my 2nd-grade teacher who was a White woman and discounted my intelligence. In addition to my work in her class, she was able to advocate for me because she attended the church where I had been enrolled in the Head Start program, and knew that I was able to read even then. My 2nd-grade teacher was not aware of this context, and often mistook my boredom for a lack of comprehension. Despite her misgivings, I was given a provisional spot in the only gifted class in my elementary school—a 3rd through 5th-grade combined class of 30 students in a school of more than 300.

The gifted program was taught by one of the school's most highly regarded and awarded teachers. There were great things that occurred in the class: group projects, elaborate reenactments of the California gold rush, and conversations about domestic and global issues. The latter did not always go well. I remember being asked my specific opinion on the Martin Luther King, Jr. holiday—which was signed into law while I was in her class. Initially, I thought it was because my parents were from Alabama and grew up in the midst of the Civil Rights Era. However, this was the first of many spotlights I found myself in, being asked to provide my esteemed thoughts about race as an 8-year-old. In most of my classes, I was expected to be an expert on all things Black, despite my age. Throughout my schooling, it was clear that racial matters were not something that White teachers were expected and required to know.

Being in the gifted program, I created great dissonance for my White teachers. For them, I symbolized Black social and academic progress, yet to ensure my success I was encouraged to abandon my blackness ("Control your body! Don't dance or bob your head every time music comes on."), my Black friends ("I don't see what you have in common with those girls."), and community ("Get out of here and never look back!").

There were times in high school when I left my relatively safe environment in the gifted program and took general education courses that better fit my schedule. I quickly learned that my clever responses given in my gifted classes were seen as smart mouthed in the general education classes. Particularly with unfamiliar White teachers, it was not uncommon for me to be singled out and told that they were keeping an eye on me or to be randomly reminded of class decorum. Sometimes this occurred as I walked in the door on the first day of school. In an instant, I would go from being the *exception* to the rule of Black academic failure to *the rule*.

Despite these indignities, I worked hard to not be constrained by most of my White women teachers' zones of comfort and respectability. I had strong familial support and racial socialization to help me counter these stereotypes. My classmates understood and supported me. At my class reunion, several said they were not surprised I am a professor.

Interestingly, my first (and only) White racially aware K-12 teacher was my physics teacher, Mr. Calia. He was my first exposure to White allies and my introduction to White ethnic identity. He and one of my African American teachers, Ms. Anderson, were my resources for accurate historical information that was missing and unacknowledged from my school's curriculum. They also protected me when their colleagues' racial dissonance obscured their vision of my potential.

Like I said, I was more fortunate than most of my classmates. There were more times than I can mention where my life course could have easily been de-railed by the lack of cultural competence in my White teachers. The importance of cultural competence training cannot be underestimated; African American students should not have to be fortunate to achieve academic and social success.

CECILIA RAMIREZ: CULTURE AND BELONGING

I am Latina. My mother was Puerto Rican, born and raised in New York City, and my father was Ecuadorian—I think he was born there. My mom died when I was 11 and my father died in jail serving a life sentence when I was 24; I'd only met him once. My stepfather (who raised me from the time I was 3-months-old until I was 11) was Dominican, as was the neighborhood we lived in, Washington Heights. The fact is I didn't have parents for most of my life, so my identity was shaped, molded, and heavily influenced by my experiences in school, mostly by White women.

I went to grade and middle school with mostly Dominicans. My teachers were mostly White women and we never had any discussions surrounding race or ethnicity. That part of me was ignored at best. I was accepted into a magnet school for gifted students and the racial breakdown of the school was the same. I had no concept of power structures then, but I remember knowing, somehow, that rich people were White and lived in a neighborhood far from ours. I did not actually know any White people besides my teachers, and I didn't have a personal connection with my teachers.

When my mother died, my stepfather stepped out of the picture. I then decided to disconnect from [the] Dominican culture. I found solace in and gravitated toward the Black community in the neighboring housing projects. I felt closer to the Black community than I had ever felt to the Dominican one. The Black community was on the periphery of my neighborhood and was not known to intermix with our Latin community, and vice versa. I remember hearing stories of the dangerous projects filled with criminals; I was not allowed to be there. I ended up spending age 11 through 14 there. It was comforting. I felt accepted. We listened to the same music, spoke the same way and related to the world as outsiders. If you asked me then, I probably would have identified as Black even though I knew no one actually saw me that way.

My first direct exposure to whiteness and wealth was in high school. I was accepted into a specialized program for high-achieving students of color that placed me in a private boarding school in Massachusetts. My identity went from Latina and Black-identified to "other." My circle of friends was now comprised of anyone who was *not* White and we were known as the students of color or the poor kids. This was the start of when whiteness really began to shape my life because I could not be myself and fit into that school.

My school only had 300 students, three of whom were Latino. All of the teachers were White except for one Spanish teacher, and more than half of them were women. When I set foot on the 251-acre campus for the first time, I was immediately confronted by an unfathomable amount of wealth. I never knew that I was poor until then. I met teenagers with luxury cars, private homes, maids, and personal shoppers. My classmates' parents were owners of prominent technology, retail and banking companies. Our White female dorm parents asked where I was going over Christmas and spring breaks as if going home was not an option. The language everyone used was different. In English class, I remember wishing I could express myself as articulately and vividly as the others did when answering questions. I practiced learning new words at night and when I read aloud in classes, I made sure to pronounce words properly and without an accent, something I never previously knew I had. Mrs. Hudson, my White English teacher, often told me that my writing was so "real" and authentic. I did not understand what she meant.

White people were different. Their food was simple and bland. Their clothing came from stores I'd never heard of until then—J. Crew, L. L. Bean, Patagonia. Their vocabulary seemed so impressive, something out of a movie. Even the things they spoke about seemed foreign—politics, vacations, field hockey, skiing, boats, nannies, and the stock market. It felt as if I was studying abroad. Aside from multicultural student group meetings, comprised of all non-White students, my White teachers never had any discussions with me surrounding race. The two staff members who led that group were the only Black staff members in the school. I couldn't explain my struggles to my White teachers because they could not see the bigger picture of racial difference—their worldview was too narrow to comprehend my experience. I knew they would take my pain personally and react defensively, even though it wasn't necessarily about them.

A particularly big surprise in this new White world was the level of drug use among students. I grew up in a low-income community where I was used to seeing drug dealers on street corners daily. However, I had never seen as many drugs as I did in high school. They were everywhere and they were plentiful—cocaine, ecstasy, marijuana, mushrooms, and more. Alcohol was a casual pastime, but it was just as available. White kids took (parent-consented) weekends at their own homes to smoke, drink, and party. Prior to this, I had a naive image of White people as straight-edge goody two-shoes that lived in perfect homes with white picket fences. I was completely shocked by the reality.

The impacts of this new world were almost immediate. Like any teenager, I wanted desperately to fit in. Up against the whiteness of this private boarding school, this meant a drastic lifestyle change. I began to drink and smoke, I began to wear cardigans, play sports, exercise, listen to Sugar Ray and Jewel, and use words like "awesome" and "dude." I went to high school at a size 12 and graduated at a size 4, but I never quite felt thin enough. Actually, when I lost all of the weight, all of my friends and teachers complimented me and said how much better I looked.

By the time I was a senior, I was thin, in shape, academically strong and popular. Although I felt accepted, I never quite felt like a real member of my new community. I was that cool, sassy, (poor) girl from the tough part of New York, not to be confused with the other New Yorker students whose parents owned apartments on Park Avenue. When it was time to apply to college, I remember my White female college counselor telling me that I should make sure that I have some "safety" schools since so many of the 10 I selected were Ivies or highly-competitive. When I was accepted into nine and wait-listed at one, she half-heartedly congratulated me.

I was never treated badly, but by the time I graduated I felt scorned, jaded, bitter. The opportunities I was afforded by attending boarding school came with the price of disconnection from myself and my community. In a time of critical identity development, I had very few resources to support me in figuring out how to be academically successful while still being me. As an adult, once I was able to identify the ways in which whiteness had shaped my identity, I began to form an identity that encompassed every part of me. This included my Puerto Rican and Ecuadorian heritage, my Dominican upbringing, my experience with the Black community, my experiences in White education, and teaching in a Latino neighborhood. I am now able to see that I had no support and guidance during my identity development. There were so many layers of identity that I was trying to navigate alone. At my predominantly Dominican school, it would have been helpful to hear about different ethnicities so as to understand that my own was not insignificant. In high school, a conversation surrounding race would have been beneficial for both the White and non-White communities alike. It seems that for the majority of my schooling from grade school to grad school, the racial and power dynamics that were in place were simply not discussed. Educators just seemed to hope that problems wouldn't happen, and when they did, things like one-day diversity discussions or celebrations were thrown together to address them. While I cannot be sure that my journey would have been any different, I am certain that the journey through race would have felt easier if some of my teachers could have helped in guiding me, cheering me on, answering questions, and challenging me along the way.

CHONIKA COLEMAN-KING: CULTURAL RANKING

As an individual of African and Caribbean descent who was born in the United States, I choose to identify as Black. I prefer the term Black rather than African American because I believe it connotes a general connection to Africa, but also gives room for my nuanced, multinational, and multi-ethnic identities derived from my connections to the Caribbean and the United States.

From the moment my formal schooling began, I was charged with the task of deciphering cultures that were foreign to me. I was raised by a large extended family in a Caribbean enclave in New York City; everything from the food I ate, language I spoke, and expectations for decorum and household and familial responsibilities were uniquely Jamaican. Once I entered school, I often felt like an outsider. I had a hard time relating to my African American peers and White teachers. School is where I was forced to learn about and assimilate to African American and White American culture. Over time, I adapted to the culture of my peers. I had to, or I would have run the risk of social alienation. Although I looked like the other kids, I experienced school differently. I was teased at school for being an immigrant because my father, who would take me to school each day, had dreadlocks and my mom packed ethnic foods in my lunch box. These kinds of markers made it clear to my peers that I was different from them. However, my White teachers did not know the difference—to them, we were just Black, city kids.

Language

I had to navigate between my home (patois) and peer (African American English-AAE) languages and White American expectations that I speak "Standard" English. In my most meaningful relationships—those with family and close friends—my ethnic languages held the most currency, yet the very process of education I have undergone has taught me that those languages are inferior and their use should be avoided.

Through college courses and other interactions with mainstream society, I became more adept at speaking Standard English, but to do that, I had to unlearn the language rules of my home and community.

Family

Jamaican culture is generally organized around family. Close family ties usually include extended family and those adopted through formal and informal means. I often feared criticism from peers and teachers for living with my extended family. However, I benefited greatly from having a village of support whereby each person utilized his or her strengths for the betterment of the family unit.

I have found that White teachers regularly view children whose fathers are not in the home from a deficit perspective and assume children lack male role models, but growing up in an extended family and without my father in the home (after a certain point), I had the support of my father and uncles, my mother and aunts. I arguably had more support than children living in a nuclear family arrangement.

Social Norms

Between the media and experiences with White women teachers in schools, I grew to learn quite a bit about the cultural manifestations of whiteness. I perceived whiteness to be stoic and subdued, void of loud laughter and physical touch. Intimacy, whether emotional or otherwise, appeared to be something Whites avoided or reserved for private spaces. This lack of public intimacy also permeated the classroom; my teachers rarely went beyond teaching content to develop the kinds of relationships I was used to having with adults who were genuinely interested and invested in me.

Loud music, talking, laughter, and even arguments represented a type of liveliness that is often condemned in the White mainstream. This White mainstream adherence to stoicism also spilled over into perceptions of the body and movement. I remember choreographing and performing a Jamaican dance routine in high school. As is common in Jamaican dancing, there were lots of hip movements in our routine. I was later informed that the school principal found the routine inappropriate. How could a performance that made my family proud upset my principal? Having your culture misinterpreted and misunderstood at school creates a great deal of dissonance for students. These are the very tensions that often cause students of color to disengage.

To me, another cultural manifestation of whiteness is in the preference for conservative and casual style in comparison to the bold, elaborate styles of Africa and the diaspora where bright colors and excess embellishments are deemed fashionable. As students, my peers and I were often pressured to "tone down" our style and adhere to fashion norms my peers and I considered plain and shabby like visibly worn jeans, dirty tennis shoes, and mute colors.

In my culture, there is an emphasis on individual uniqueness even as members of a communal group. However, whiteness seemingly prefers plainness and uniformity over uniqueness and creativity. This is especially evident in the kinds of names Whites endorse or disparage. I remember White women teachers struggling to say my name (spelled Chonika, the Ch pronounced like the Ch in Cheryl), their disposition hinting at their displeasure. I once had a teacher call me Hanukah. As much as my name often seemed to be problematic to White teachers, I often wondered why White people all had the same names, spelled the same way. White teachers send a strong message to students when they do not make an effort to learn names that are unfamiliar to them.

Presumption of Superiority

I also experienced whiteness as a presumption of White superiority and Black inferiority, which often resulted in experiences with racism and racial microaggressions. I have always been a strong student. My dad had little formal schooling, but is one of the most exceptional thinkers I have ever encountered. My mother always excelled in school and was my first teacher, introducing and reinforcing academic skills at home. So, in fourth grade when my teacher chastised me in front of the entire class accusing me of plagiarizing an assignment, I cried. I explained that my mother helped me, but it was my work. She didn't believe me. It was not her expectation that a little Black girl had access to multiple sets of encyclopedias at home or that my parents were heavily invested in my academic development.

I continued to have similar experiences until college. My freshman year, I was encouraged to take a low-level math class required for my major although I had tested into one of the highest-level math classes on the freshman placement test. While working in a group to solve a math problem, my group refused to take my answer. I could see the surprise on the faces of my White peers when they realized I answered the question correctly and they had not. My White teachers never knew that I had these types of experiences regularly in their classes.

Consistently outperforming my White peers was evidence that their perceived superiority was a façade. Still, I knew I had to be well versed in the cultural manifestations of whiteness. I needed to know when to speak like them, straighten my hair, and dress like them in order to access benefits most often reserved for them. However, I always had outlets where I felt I could be myself and operate within my own cultural framework—one that evolved to include African American culture. I could escape to my home, community, or even to Jamaica. I always had a cultural home, engaging whiteness was temporary—it was a show for just a finite time. The relief I felt in home spaces was akin to getting home from a long day of work and taking off my high heels. I felt unbounded and free to take on my natural shape and size, free to be myself.

ALI MICHAEL: WHITE CULTURAL CAPITAL

I identify racially as White. Although if you asked me how I identified when I was growing up, I probably would not have understood the question. I grew up in the suburbs of Pittsburgh in a community where almost everyone we knew was White. I had one biracial peer in my 4th-grade class and another friend who had immigrated from Persia (now Iran) in third grade. Most of my friends, neighbors and parents' friends were White people. As a result of this homogeneity, we never really thought about or talked about race. This silence, I believe, is one of the cultural manifestations of whiteness.

I grew up Episcopalian in a family where all four of the children had blonde hair and blue eyes. When we studied the Punnett Square in biology, and I realized the rarity of having four children in one family with blue eyes, I can remember feeling special. I didn't think of it in terms race, but I did think about myself and my family as special. People have complimented my blue eyes throughout my life, just as they compliment my children's today. It wasn't until recently that I started to see these compliments as evaluations of how closely we align with standards of beauty based on whiteness.

I didn't have a teacher of color until college. My entire school career from pre-K to twelfth grade, I was taught by White teachers (almost all women) who looked like me and who talked like my mom—a middle-class White teacher herself. I loved almost all of my teachers and felt they helped me to be successful and comfortable in school, influencing both my self-esteem and my material success. My teachers gave me a lot of latitude to develop leadership skills, including letting me organize surprise parties for teachers' birthdays in elementary school, school dances in middle school, and overnight retreats in high school for student council.

After years of being a mediocre math student, to my surprise I was placed in honors algebra in seventh grade. It was this change of circumstance, along with an unexpected slate of straight A's that I received in my last semester of eighth grade that made me realize I might be smart and should continue to try to demonstrate that. The curriculum that I learned throughout school reflected me and a White worldview—teaching me that people who look like me were responsible for the important parts of history, and that scientists, mathematicians, and great writers were White. I did not learn about race in school until eleventh and twelfth grade, and only then when it was part of books that I chose for my summer reading. I can recall reading Toni Morrison's *The Bluest Eye* and Maya Angelou's *I Know Why the Caged Bird Sings*, and having my racial identity be awakened—and challenged—by this exposure to racism and resistance. We didn't, if I recall correctly, discuss these books in class.

Part of my family culture is that we know a lot about our ancestors. Multiple people in my family preoccupy themselves with researching our family tree. My ancestry is well documented and many of the names given to babies in my family come from those family trees. Even if we didn't have the documentation, I think that being White has meant that we are able to have a certain familial continuity that is not as readily available to non-White people. This showed up in school when we did family trees and I had multiple options for which lineage to trace. I have since learned how painful family tree projects are for many families of color, especially African Americans, who are reminded of the violent ways in which their family trees were cut down, and of how few records exist of who came before. My extended family has always been proud of having an ancestor on the Mayflower, and we have never discussed our connection to or culpability for the genocide of Native Americans or the slave trade.

How did whiteness manifest itself culturally in my house growing up? Again, everything we did. In my family, whiteness was tied to middle class culture and was related to financial stability and civic freedom that comes from feeling free and safe with regard to the state and other authorities. When I try to summarize the culture in my house, what stands out is fun. There was an overarching theme of fun in my life and the lives of my cousins and family friends. Block parties, weekends at a friend's lake house, drinking games (without the alcohol), Jello slurping contests, singing fraternity songs or cheers at the dinner table, going to summer camp, being a part of the "Indian Princesses," Girl Scouts, and camping trips were all critical aspects of my life growing up. My family and family friends had a certain sense of (what we considered "healthy") irreverence for the rules and for authority that feels very clearly related to privilege and to being White. Judging from the behaviors of my peer group, and on occasion my own behavior, I think whiteness promotes moderately reckless behavior; living with the certainty that if you break the rules, you can likely plead ignorance or youthfulness and the authorities (school administrators, teachers, police officers) will look out for your best interest and see the goodness that is in you—in spite of your negative behaviors.

Whiteness manifests culturally in so many different ways, but in my family and in my community, I have witnessed (and possessed) a commonly held belief that the way we do things is right. To that end, part of whiteness is othering and measuring to what extent others meet White Anglo Saxon standards—not only of beauty, but also of behavior, language, religion, naming, organization and customs. In my community, it was not uncommon to joke about African American names—seeing them as outlandish, tacky, and weird, rather than unique and creative. I can remember youth in my community (myself included at times) mocking Hindu bindis, foreign accents, and "smelly" ethnic food. I know from childhood photos that I mocked Asian eyes while eating in a Chinese restaurant when I was 9. I believe that I had very little understanding of what I was doing. But the fact that an adult at the table took a picture of me doing this makes me think that no one else did either. That suggests that this kind of racism and harassment was normalized in my community, that we didn't see it as incompatible with being good people. Two of the adults sitting at the table in that Chinese restaurant the day that picture was taken were White women teachers. And in a point that may seem like an extreme contradiction, those two White women are still two of the best people I know.

CULTURE AND WHITENESS

Scholars of whiteness have demonstrated how White Americans repeatedly assert that they do not have culture, that they are "normal" or "average" (Michael & Bartoli, 2014; Frankenberg, 1993; Perry, 2002). Whiteness informs cultural practices that do not even get recognized as cultural because whiteness itself is often not visible to White people.

When we think about "culture" in schools, we often think about how we dress, what we eat, what music we listen to, what language we speak; the main pillars of a multicultural curriculum are about these visible and tangible aspects of culture. Yet as our narratives reveal and recent scholarship bears out, culture includes much more nuanced and relatively invisible ways of being in the world, such as courtesy, contextual conversational patterns, concepts of time, personal space, rules of conduct, facial expressions, nonverbal communication, body language, patterns of handling emotion, tone of voice, attitudes toward elders and concepts of "self"

(Hall & Hall, 2001). These unseen aspects of culture are the very concepts that get taken up as "normal" and "objective" by people in the cultural mainstream, while they are very much culturally subjective for people who do not have the same background and assumptions.

Cultural manifestations of whiteness are not simply the product of individual White people, they are a product of whiteness. Whiteness, as defined by Robin DiAngelo, is "the specific dimensions of racism that serve to elevate White people over people of color" (DiAngelo, 2011, p. 56). Whiteness is a socially constructed phenomenon that includes, but is not limited to, the people themselves who identify as or are seen as "White." Historically whiteness was a construct closely aligned with the notion of being "American" (Lee, 2005) and was the template for American identity at the time when the Constitution was created (Haney López, 1996). Anthropologist Ruth Frankenberg's definition demonstrates how whiteness could be more than the people themselves.

> Whiteness is a location of structural advantage, of race privilege. Second, it is a "standpoint," a place from which White people look at ourselves, at others, and at society. Third, whiteness refers to a set of cultural practices that are unmarked and unnamed. (Frankenberg, 1993, p. 1)

In this paper, we write about the third aspect of Frankenberg's definition, the cultural practices of whiteness. Cultural manifestations of whiteness refer to the typically unmarked practices of White people that derive from and support a system of racism in which White people and White ways of being are framed as superior to people of other races.

Activists and scholars before us have tried to map out aspects of whiteness that shape broad cultural assumptions in the U.S. racial mainstream. These include: paternalism, either/or thinking, fear of conflict, valuing individualism over teamwork, not talking about race, interrupting or not seeing people of color, and assuming centrality in geographic and social spaces (Mattheus & Marino, 2014; Okun & Jones, 2001). Others see White culture as largely typified by Western culture and characterize it as focused on the individual; demanding self-reliance over interdependency; strongly preferring bland aesthetics; competitive; future oriented; avoidant of emotion, intimacy or conflict; action oriented and hierarchical in decision-making (Katz, 1978).

There is not one unitary White culture, but many cultures of whiteness, and they vary significantly depending on the other social identifiers involved, including religion, sexuality, ethnicity, geographic region and socioeconomic status. However, as anthropologist Stacey Lee writes in *Up Against Whiteness*, "(Al)though there are diverse White cultures, all Whites do share racial privilege" (Lee, 2005, p. 24). In other words, because all

White people are racialized as White, they share the status of having privilege, which in turn shapes their behaviors and expectations differently from groups lacking racial privilege. And yet, because this paper examines the cultural manifestations of whiteness found in schools and fostered by teachers, it is a particularly professional, middle-class and heternormative whiteness that we describe.

WHITENESS DEFINED IN RELIEF

"Whiteness is a relational concept, unintelligible without reference to non-Whites," writes sociologist Howard Winant (2001, p. 107). In other words, whiteness is one end of a racial spectrum; it only exists in relativity to other races along the spectrum. At the other end of the spectrum, according to Toni Morrison, is blackness. She writes that the majority of African Americans get erased from history, except for "their less than covert function of defining whites as the 'true' Americans" (Morrison, 1993). Whiteness is a relational identity: "Because "[i]dentity is ... continuously being constituted through social interactions," the assigned political, economic, and social inferiority of Blacks necessarily shaped White identity" (Harris, 1993, p. 1737). This talk of a racial spectrum suggests that it is hard to talk about the cultural manifestations of whiteness without seeing it up against the cultures of people whose racial designation is not White. For that reason, we chose to describe whiteness in relief—by demonstrating what whiteness is not—through the experiences of people of color who are impacted by the cultural manifestations of whiteness.

Teaching has historically been a profession that consisted primarily of middle-class White women. It is our assertion that this demographic fact reinscribes cultural practices in schools that reward students in possession of those cultural norms, and punish those who are not—largely students of color and students living in poverty. For individual teachers, recognizing one's role in establishing and maintaining such culturally particular learning environments is not easy. Many White Americans do not even see the cultural manifestations of whiteness as particularly cultural because their personal experience gets framed as "normal," "standard," and "right" while at the same time behaviors outside that standard are cast as "aberrant," "atypical," and "wrong." Psychologist Derald Wing Sue calls this "the invisibility of Ethnocentric Monoculturalism" (Sue, 2004, p. 764). Sue writes:

> On a personal level, people are conditioned and rewarded for remaining unaware and oblivious of how their beliefs and actions may unfairly oppress people of color, women and other groups in society. On an institutional level, people fail to recognize how standard operating procedures serve to

> deny equal access and opportunities for some while providing advantages and benefits for others. (Sue, 2004, p. 767)

METHODS

Drawing on critical race methodology,[2] we employed a methodological approach that privileges the experiences and narratives of individuals whose voices are marginalized in mainstream discourse. According to Solorzano and Yosso (2002),

> [C]ritical race methodology provides a tool to "counter" deficit storytelling. Specifically, a critical race methodology offers space to conduct and present research grounded in the experiences and knowledge of people of color. As they describe how they compose counter-stories, the authors discuss how the stories can be used as theoretical, methodological, and pedagogical tools to challenge racism, sexism, and classism and work toward social justice. (p. 23)

Many scholars have documented the long history of silencing that characterizes the experiences of racial (and other) minority groups. Narratives can be used to bridge the gap between various groups' conflicting understandings of the world and shed light on how members of certain groups experience it (Delgado & Stefancic, 2001). According to Delgado and Stefancic (2001), "Powerfully written stories and narratives may begin a process of adjustment in our system of beliefs and categories by calling attention to neglected evidence and reminding readers of our common humanity" (p. 43).

In this case, we have chosen to write personal narratives focused on naming and identifying the cultural manifestations of whiteness. The stories serve as counternarratives to hegemonic notions of whiteness that paint it not only as neutral, but desirable and superior to other cultural orientations. Writing these narratives was not easy. We had to excavate our analyses from our experiences and we found it most useful to do that together in community, rather than in isolation. Our team met by phone on a monthly basis (five times in nine months) to brainstorm how whiteness manifested in our lives. Each time we met we would establish prompts to respond to for the following call, and respond to them in an online forum to support ongoing exploration of our analysis between conversations. Throughout the process of writing this paper, our team compared notes and commented on one another's pieces. As we started to nail down what whiteness looked like for each of us, we also noticed themes and overlap. Our narratives are informed, not only by our experiences as students, but by our work as teachers, professors, and teacher educators.

ANALYSIS

As adults we know that just like the two women at the end of the final vignette, many of the White women who taught us were good people, committed parents, and valued community members. But being a good person does not mean that one is racially competent (Stevenson, 2014), and it is precisely this lack of racial competence that led to so much hurt, misunderstanding and mis-placements along our educational journeys. To that end, our analysis explores three themes that emerged from the narratives shared previously. After that, we have proposed strategies that White women teachers can use to counter the hegemony of whiteness in their classrooms and schools.

Theme 1: Superiority Complex

Chonika Coleman-King wrote about the presumption of inferiority that she faced as a Black student, her White teachers and her White college peers disbelieving in her capacity to produce excellent work or get the right answers in math class. This connects to Ali Michael's feeling that part of the culture of her White and upper-middle class community was a presumption of superiority or self-satisfaction. The stories from across the authors demonstrate how White teachers seemed to consider White names, habits, clothing, food, family structures and styles of communicating as "right." Any diversion from the "right" way of doing things was framed as rude, incompetent, ignorant, ugly, deviant, exotic, or strange. These judgments were not framed in terms of racial culture, but in terms of what is "right" or "American."

Theme 2: Value of Reconnecting to Racial/Ethnic Heritage

Each of the authors wrote about the value of connecting to their racial/ethnic heritage, to teachers who understood their racial/ethnic background, and to peers and teachers who looked like them. Those experiences affirmed racial identity, suggested "I'm not alone," and gave each writer the space to learn to identify themselves in all of their complexity. More importantly, for some authors it was teachers of color who saw them clearly and without bias that gave authors the motivation to continue to prove themselves to White teachers who, much more frequently, conveyed doubt in their abilities. It seems clear from these pieces that those spaces are critical for positive identity development because racism, and the demand for assimilation to whiteness as a means of professional and financial advancement in U.S. society, create a sense of alienation for students of color, which leads to a need for an affirming space. If whiteness didn't create this demand, if integration in the United States was truly integrative and not assimilative, this need may not exist.

Theme 3: The Demand for Assimilation

The most pervasive theme that emerged from all of the pieces was the extent to which the authors of color each spent some of their childhood wishing they were White, or that they had White names or features, to the detriment of their self-esteem, their own cultures, and connections with family. The absence of this kind of longing to be a different race in Ali's (the White author's) piece is also notable. The fact that the only author of five who didn't struggle with racial identity and belonging in school was White and middle class suggests that whiteness and middle classness may be a kind of de facto prerequisite—or at the very least a lubricant—for belonging in school. It also suggests that Ali, as a White student, was not taught many of the racial realities of our society. If White children were asked to learn the honest truth about the racial history of the United States, as well as the racial realities of their peers, they may have to grapple more with the meaning of their own whiteness, which could lead to greater empathy and awareness as members of multiracial communities.

Is this a problem with White women teachers themselves, or with a system in which success is so intimately linked to access to social capital, something that is much harder to access across racial and class difference? So much success in school is tied to being understood and valued by teachers, including, as the stories demonstrate, recommendations for gifted programs or special education, placement in honors classes or remedial classes, support with peer bullying, applications to elite magnet or private schools, navigating new school contexts, getting into college, etc., not to mention simply grading, evaluating, coaching, reprimanding, advising and counseling. Ironically the author on our team who least needed the social capital her teachers had to offer had the greatest access to it. This is clearly a systemic issue, but individual teachers within that very system have a lot of power to influence the experiences of individual students.

RESISTING THE STANDARDIZATION OF WHITENESS IN SCHOOL

If education is going to change so that alignment with whiteness and White cultural styles is not a requirement for academic success, and non-

White racial and ethnic cultures are accepted as part of a given school culture rather than something that should be assimilated out, White female teachers will need to develop the skills of going against White cultural norms and being willing to confront other White people who insist on White cultural standards of behavior. Going against the norm and engaging in conflict are notably not behaviors that are commonly part of White female socialization. For White female teachers to act as allies to students of color will require them to challenge their own racial and gender socialization.

We hope that after reading this paper, readers will have a better picture of what whiteness looks like to those who stand outside it. But we also want to leave readers with a list of practical applications for the classroom. These recommendations are designed to help educators support all students to build a positive racial identity in the context of a society that valorizes whiteness.

1. Start With Yourself

Your race and ethnicity play a role in the kind of teacher you are. Recognize it and verbalize it. Silence around race is one of the oppressive parts of whiteness. Create a joint exploration of racial identity development; model your own ignorance, questions and curiosity with your own identity. Share your racial story, be conscious of what you need to learn about with regard to race, ethnicity, or power. Encourage your students to do the same. Empower your students with tools on how to ask each other questions and handle topics that may not always feel "easy" to discuss. Welcome and cultivate an acceptance of tension, discomfort, and incompleteness. Start by talking about your own race and cultural identity before you try to talk about your students'. Ask your students questions from a place of curiosity and nonjudgment before you talk to them about race and ethnicity. Model for your students how to reflect on identity, culture, and difference. Be okay with difference. Remind students "difference is good—we should not be ashamed to talk about it."

2. Proactively Make Race and Culture a Part of Your Classroom

Create a safe environment on day one where students begin to explore what they want to learn about culture, identity, and race. Give them ownership of this difficult journey. Set ground rules together and establish norms and ways to handle inevitable disagreement. Support students to connect with their ethnic heritage. In all of our stories, this connection only happened in college. Why does K-12 education have to be so assimilative? Know that students of any age can "handle" discussions around race, ethnicity, and culture; start early. Start by practicing with your kids, your family members, your neighbors; it all impacts your teaching. Find and challenge the cultural manifestations of whiteness in all of your materials, grading, and lesson plans. Students need the freedom to learn about their history and their culture without fear of ostracism or exclusion. Studying one's history and culture is part of identity development.

Name whiteness as a racial category—even White kids in an all-White school are racialized. Help kids understand the way White people are historically and systematically advantaged by racism. Help kids learn to think in terms of systems that are bigger than themselves. Create spaces for kids to learn about racism and to learn to recognize it around them in their lives and in the media. Threats to student racial identities include questions such as, "Do you speak English?" or "Why does your mom talk funny?" These are threats because they imply nonbelonging and a bad kind of difference. Help preempt these types of questions by talking openly with students about difference. Create an understanding at Halloween that students are not allowed to use cultures as costumes.

3. Recognize That Healthy Racial Identity is Related to Academic Success, and That All Students Need Space to Develop Their Racial Identity

Help students (and yourself) understand that every "phase" of racial identity development is valid. Students of color should not be the only people in the room with a race or a culture; White people need to name and claim their race as well. When family culture is talked about, children should be encouraged to think about how they do things in their family culture—not harken back to five generations of past Danish culture. When it's a historical culture, and not a contemporary family culture, then it starts to seem irrelevant and anachronistic. Children who have a culture at home that is different from the mainstream culture will be made to feel more distant by this exercise. But if everybody is encouraged to be an anthropologist of their own lives, to examine what they eat, how they think of time, etc. in the current moment, then everybody has a culture. And in reality, everybody does. Physical features are off limits—no taunting, teasing or critiquing. They are part of who we are and they are all beautiful. Similarly, don't allow students to hurt one another by teasing one another about skin color, even when they're in the same racial group. Do not allow racial slurs in your classroom, even in jest.

4. Learn to Differentiate and Accommodate, Not Judge

Recognize the ways that whiteness operates in your life. See it and name it and learn to recognize when you diminish people from other cultural backgrounds by comparison. If a student talks about brothers and sisters or cousins that don't seem to fit into the family picture you thought they had, recognize that they may have a different definition of what family is than you do. If you find yourself remarking on the "loud Black students," reconsider whether cultural differences might be shaping your definition of "noise." (See Ali Michael's *Raising Race Questions* [2015] for a more extensive discussion of "noise" as culturally relevant.)

Do not assume you know everything about a child and their history just by looking at them. Commit to a practice of cultural humility (Tervalon & Murray-Garcia, 1998), which includes an acknowledgment that you don't know what you don't know, and a commitment to lifelong learning. Honor names. Do not participate in or allow the degradation of anyone's name. Learn names, remember them, use them and insist that your students do too. As you do these things, know that disrespect of names can break parents' hearts and sever their trust with an educator permanently.

CONCLUSION

Is it wrong to be White or to live by White cultural norms and styles? Definitely not. Culture is neither good nor bad; it simply is, and it is intensely personal. Having and participating in cultural manifestations of whiteness is not a bad thing. It becomes oppressive when we see it as superior to other cultures and demand assimilation to whiteness in order to be successful within U.S. schools. Whiteness can be particularly oppressive when we fail to see the cultural styles that derive from it as particular to a given group, and assume that it is actually representative of American culture or simply mainstream or normal culture. By not acknowledging its particularities as a culture that belongs to a racial subgroup, we allow the cultural manifestations of whiteness to define the norms and values in schools as if whiteness and the experience of White people was universal. In the interest of supporting all students' academic success, it is the work of all teachers to counter the oppressive aspects of whiteness in order to support a culture that includes all students.

NOTES

1. Because this book is about White women's work, we have adapted our chapter on White culture to address White women teachers specifically.

However, many of the things we have written here apply also to White men teachers and to White culture outside of schools as well.

2. Critical race theory (CRT), as a theoretical construct, focuses on several key elements: a) the intersectionality of marginalized statuses, b) challenges to dominant ideology, c) the centrality of narratives and experiential knowledge, d) the use of transdisciplinary approaches, and e) advancing a social justice agenda (Solorzano & Yosso 2002, 2010). Critical race theorists also critique liberalism and its focus on incremental change and ineffective civil rights legislation. According to Solorzano and Yosso (2002), "[C]ritical race theory in education is a framework or set of basic insights, perspectives, methods, and pedagogy that seeks to identify, analyze, and transform those structural and cultural aspects of education that maintain subordinate and dominant racial positions in and out of the classroom" (p. 25). In other words, CRT attempts to not only identify and theorize, but also dismantle racist policies and practices while simultaneously recognizing the extent to which racism is nearly inextricable from the very fabric of this nation. CRT scholars argue that even the research methodology traditionally used in the academy supports dominant master narratives of People of Color and is grounded in pervasive negative stereotypes and presumed cultural deficit. In fact, dominant narratives suggest that problematic cultural orientations are to blame for low educational achievement and socioeconomic status of racial minority groups.

REFERENCES

Delgado, R., & Stefancic, J. (2001). *Critical race theory: An introduction.* New York, NY: New York University Press.

DiAngelo, R. (2011). White fragility. *The International Journal of Critical Pedagogy, 3*(3).

Du Bois, W. E. B. (1920). The souls of white folk. In *Darkwater: Voices from within the veil.* North Chelmsford, MA: Courier Corporation.

Frankenberg, R. (1993). *White women, race matters.* Minneapolis, MN: University of Minnesota Press.

Frankenberg, R. (2001). The mirage of an unmarked whiteness. In B. Brander Rasmussen, E. Klinenberg, I. J. Nexica, & M. Wray (Eds.), *The making and unmaking of whiteness* (pp. 72–96). Durham, NC: Duke University Press.

Hall, E. T., & Hall, M. R. (2001). Key concepts: Underlying structures of culture. *International HRM: Managing Diversity in the Workplace*, 24–40.

Haney López, I. (1996). *White by law: The legal construction of race.* New York, NY: New York University Press.

Harris, C. (1993). Whiteness as property. *Harvard Law Review, 106*(8), 1707–1791.

Katz, J. (1978). *White awareness: A handbook for anti-racism training.* Norman, OK: University of Oklahoma Press.

Lee, S. (2005). *Up against whiteness.* New York, NY: Teachers College Press.

Mattheus, A., & Marino, L. (2012). *Whites confronting racism handbook.* Self-published.

Michael, A. (2015). *Raising race questions: Whiteness and inquiry in education.* New York, NY: Teachers College Press.

Michael, A., & Bartoli, E. (2014). What White children need to know about race. *Independent Schools Magazine.*

Morrison, T. (1993, December 2). On the backs of Blacks [Special Issue: The New Face of America]. *TIME Magazine.*

Moses, Y. T. (2004). The continuing power of the concept of "race." *Anthropology and Education Quarterly, 35*(1), 146–148.

Okun, T. (2006). From White racist to White anti-racist: The life long journey dismantling racism. Retrieved from www.dRworks.org

Okun, T., & Jones, K. (2001). White supremacy culture. From dismantling racism: A workbook for social change groups. Retrieved from http://www.cwsworkshop.org/PARC_site_B/dr-culture.html

Perry, P. (2002). *Shades of white: White kids and racial identities in high school.* Durham, NC: Duke University Press.

Solorzano, D. G., & Yosso, T. J. (2002). A critical race counterstory of race, racism, and affirmative action. *Equity & Excellence in Education, 35*(2), 155–168.

Sue, D. W. (2004). Whiteness and ethnocentric monoculturalism: Making the "invisible" visible. *American Psychologist, 59*(8), 761–770.

Stevenson, H. (2014). *Promoting racial literacy in schools: Differences that make a difference.* New York, NY: Teachers College Press.

Tervalon, M., & Murray-Garcia, J. (1998). Cultural humility versus cultural competence: A critical distinction in defining physician training outcomes in multicultural education. *Journal of Health Care for the Poor and Underserved, 9*(2), 117–125.

Winant, H. (2001). White racial projects. In B. Brander Rasmussen, E. Klinenberg, I. J. Nexica, & M. Wray (Eds.), *The making and unmaking of whiteness* (pp. 97–112). Durham, NC: Duke University Press.

CHAPTER 3

PRECARIOUS AND UNDENIABLE BODIES

Control, Waste, and Danger in the Lives of a White Teacher and Her Students of Color

Angela C. Coffee, Erin B. Stutelberg, Colleen H. Clements, and Timothy J. Lensmire
University of Minnesota

A MEMORY

Erin breathes in deeply, sharply. She leans her body on the edge of the teacher's desk for a moment, closes her eyes, and sees herself crumpling to the floor, curling up into a ball, letting everything go. Getting to the end of this 90-minute class feels impossible. She opens her eyes wide, looks out at the students sitting in rows in front of her working on their assignment, playing on their cell phone, doing nothing. She asked them to work quietly today. What a waste. She pushes herself up and off the edge of the desk, back on to solid ground. Maybe she needs to walk around, get her blood flowing, breathe and focus on something other than the pain of her cramps. Mind over matter. The doctors always said that her period cramps would get better as she got older. But they never

White Women's Work: Examining the Intersectionality of Teaching, Identity, and Race
pp. 45–67

really believed how bad it was. Her pain today is about as intense as it ever gets—and certainly as bad as it has ever been while she has been teaching. It feels like somehow it's her fault that it's still so bad, this invisible pain, that she's 23-years-old and she doesn't have control of her own pain and bleeding. She approaches a student sitting in the first row, "How's your reading going?" she asks. He keeps his gaze down on his book, "It's good, Miss." Maybe they don't notice. She wanders away from the student and across the front of the classroom; another wave of pain hits her. She clutches the waist-high stool in front of the chalkboard. Erin closes her eyes and drops into a crouch, clinging to the stool, then quickly pulls herself back up. When she turns around to sink onto the seat, she almost falls backwards. Then she sees them.

The two young men are suddenly there on either side of her. They are both tall and strong, one in his football jersey, the other in a baggy black t-shirt, hair shaved close to their scalps, smooth brown skin, a few little hairs jutting out from their chins. They are senior boys —full of confidence, with ear-to-ear grins, charming their way into class 10 minutes late. Now she notices how their deep brown eyes look at her. They are concerned. And afraid. "Are you okay, Miss?" one of them asks. She focuses on the floor now, breathing in and out, seeing only their tennis shoes, knowing who they are. Her students. Julio and Anthony. "I'm not feeling well. I'll be okay," she responds. "I just need a minute." The boys remain fixed by her side and their bodies block her view of the rest of the class. She closes her eyes again. She hears them: "Should we take her to the nurse?" "We can carry her there." Julio speaks louder now, "Miss, you don't look good. We can carry you to the nurse."

She freezes. She hears her heart beating in her ears: No. No. No. She sees herself in these young men's arms: through the hall, down a flight of stairs, past the front office, and through the commons to the nurse's office. She wonders, "What have I done?" That journey is too far away, too dangerous, too public. Already a class full of students has seen her; she is too ill to teach them. But she cannot let these boys pick her up and hold her in their arms. When she goes to the nurse— if she goes—she'll get there on her own. She opens her eyes and looks up. They would do this for her. "No...." she says loudly. "No one is carrying me anywhere. It's okay."

INTRODUCTION

In that memory, a young, White female teacher's authority was threatened when she became ill in her classroom. As she worked to perform her role through the pain, two of her male students of color recognized her need and offered to help. This offer exposed their collective vulnerability within a larger danger. In addition to the professionalism she was struggling to maintain, she also needed to protect her students from the potential threat her physical vulnerability presented to them, should they have been seen helping her and that act were misconstrued. Compounding and complicating the pain of this experience, Erin glimpsed the possibility for another way of being. "They would do this for her" became an aching hope for a different, more humanizing way of being together. While the students' offer invoked a deep and immediate fear, it also exposed an alternative. At the close of the story, Erin reasserted her White teacher authority and shut down discussion of her students' help.

We gathered around this memory, attempting to meaningfully and collectively examine, investigate, and grapple with our own experiences as White teachers in schools. This chapter will introduce collective memory work, contextualize Erin's story with a bit of theoretical and historical framing, and focus in on three important ideas from the story that help us think about the role of White women in education: the White gaze, waste, and danger.

COLLECTIVE MEMORY WORK

Collective memory work (CMW) is a methodological approach first developed by Frigga Haug's (1987) collective of feminist Marxist women in Germany during the 1980s. Its aim is to capture the "richness, subtlety, and complexity of ... embodied thinking and being in the world" through an analysis of memory and language (Davies & Gannon, 2006, p. 3). Bronwyn Davies and Susan Gannon (2006) write that memories are always already part of qualitative research (i.e., in the form of interview responses and observational field notes); CMW simply makes those remembered lived experiences the central focus of the method. CMW does not position memory as "the truth," but rather uses the literacies of writing, telling, listening, and analyzing our own and others' memories to produce truths in relation to what cannot actually be recovered—the moment as it was lived (p. 3). These particular, local, and situated truths help us to understand how we are socially constructed and discursively constituted through the moments we remember and the ways we retell our stories. Through this methodology we bring theory into collision with our everyday lived experience (p. 3).

The memory that starts this chapter was written as data within the process of CMW by Angela, Colleen, and Erin, who for several years have been working together, under Tim's mentorship, around their shared interest in the methodology and what it offers research in teaching and learning. In previous workshops we have conducted with CMW, we have explored prompts with our participants like "write about a time when gender mattered (in the context of school)" in order to use lived experiences as a catalyst for deep theorizing about the construction of gender and schooling. The memory in this chapter was produced from the writing prompt: "Write about a moment related to teaching when you became aware of your precarious, vulnerable, and undeniable White body." This prompt triggered specific, embodied memories that we each wrote in the third person, detailing the thoughts, feelings, and experiences of that moment in time as thoroughly as possible.

When we met again, we shared our memories, and then conducted a close, collaborative analysis of each one. This part of the process is akin to critical discourse analysis, where language construction, grammatical structures, and linguistic features are considered, and multiple, even contradictory meanings are entertained. Our ongoing work with our memories evolved into theorizing sessions with Tim, whose critical work on White racial identity challenged and strengthened our readings. While this chapter will work particularly with Erin's memory, our collective engagement with all three of our memories intricately influenced the process, attuning our analyses to particular things.[1]

THEORETICAL AND HISTORICAL FRAMING

Gloria Ladson-Billings and William Tate (1995) call for a theoretical foregrounding of race in school, stating that "class- and gender-based explanations are not powerful enough to explain all of the difference (or variance) in school experience and performance" (p. 51). Class- and gender- based explanations are also not powerful enough to meaningfully theorize the incredible prevalence of White women teachers in the U.S. teaching population (Sato & Lensmire, 2009). Critical engagement with the histories positioning and naturalizing White women in schools is necessary in the dismantling of colonial patterns of power in educational spaces.

NATION BUILDING

The overrepresentation of White women teachers in schools today has emerged from a complicated and dangerous history in education, one that has harnessed White femininity (constructed as caring, innocent, and inherently good) to the colonial project of nation-building. Erica Meiners (2007) asserts the particular role that whiteness plays in the presentation of control as mediating civility: "Empire building had always required control of institutional education, and White women, historically, have functioned to mask the Racial Contract in education" (p. 46). The racial contract Meiners alludes to here, building upon the work of Charles Mills, is maintained through a particular kind of silence, the cloaking of White supremacy beneath a veil of "commonsense" or taken for granted assumptions about structures of power (p. 44). White women serve to legitimize and promote this silence. Indeed, the overrepresentation of White women within the field of education is the "result of an expressed logic of a system," as White women have played a crucial role in the civilizing enterprise of nation building (Meiners, 2007, p. 45).

During the early part of the 20th century, the United States' structures of power were shifting. Reconstruction, the wake of the Industrial Revolution, and the massive influx of immigrant communities into urban centers required profoundly new systems of infrastructure and support. It was during this pivotal period in American history that White women teachers began flooding into classrooms, making up 86% of the U.S. teaching force by 1920 (Tyack, 1974, p. 61). These teachers served an economic purpose. Growing populations required more teachers, and women (who were paid significantly less than their male counterparts) met this need.

FAMILY OF THE STATE

Furthermore, women's positioning within schools enabled the discourse or notion of the state as family to circulate and gain power, de-legitimizing the power and autonomy of individual families in sacrifice to that of the state. In her book *Bitter Milk: Women and Teaching*, Madeleine Grumet (1988) weaves feminist theory and educational philosophy together around the topic of women and teaching. School was imagined as a kind of new domestic space that might employ the feminine "self-sacrifice, purity, and domesticity into moral superiority that could be dispensed in schools" (Grumet, 1988, p. 40). This familial conceptualization of national morality enabled a pathologizing and controlling of particular groups of people. "Working-class, farming, and immigrant children became, by definition, unfit to participate in the national ethos of self-discipline and productivity without the ministrations of the school" (p. 39). Rather than questioning the shifting of class structures and the radical transformation of the nation, the structure of education transferred "the onus of poverty and disorganization onto the character of the poor" (Grumet, 1988, p. 39). The moral character of students became linked to their economic and racialized locations that were taken up as the responsibility of the state, oftentimes through the bodies of White women. We recognize these multiple historical narratives influencing Erin's story.

DISCIPLINING FEMININITY

In addition to the economic role White women teachers played, their presence shifted and aligned with the restructuring of a national ethos. Through strategically harnessing the notion of White women's assumed inherent morality while exploiting them as a cheap labor source, education deepened the complex and contradictory image of White women: "The ideal teacher was one who could control the children and be controlled by her superiors" (Grumet, 1988, p. 43). This contradiction became naturalized within the profession of teaching, positioning female teachers as malleable by their male superiors, while simultaneously able to control students. David B. Tyack (1974), in his historical work on the U.S. education system, writes that:

> Hierarchical organization of schools and the male chauvinism of the larger society fit as hand to glove. The system required subordination; women were generally subordinate to men; the employment of women as teachers thus augmented the authority of the largely male administrative leaderships. (p. 60)

Women's positioning within the structures of education heightened the power and legitimacy of those organizations, while reifying the gender dynamics of power within the culture.

In addition to the hierarchical structuring of women within schools, women also served as crucial tools within a structure of surveillance, maintaining adherence to the status quo. Meiners (2007) writes:

> The role of teaching (and social work) was to execute class-based surveillance and monitoring. Female social workers and teachers were not trusted to create the template for this surveillance, but they were viewed as cheap, malleable, and relatively unthreatening mechanisms to execute this work.... These professions are intimately linked to the economy and to the political needs of the nation-state. (p. 47)

Situated as the eyes of the state, women's bodies were harnessed to meet its controlling and capitalist needs. While they clearly exerted power over their students and represented the power of the state, they did not play a significant role in the development or administration of that power.

CONTROL

Erin's disciplining of her body in an attempt to maintain authority and control in the classroom can be further understood through the notion of the panopticon, or "all-seeing eye." Michel Foucault's (1977) reference to the panopticon is based on the construction of actual prisons (as opposed to prison-like schools), in which there is a centrally located sentry who allows visual access to all parts of the prison and its inhabitants at once and at all times. The effectiveness of the panopticon in terms of discipline lies in the fact that one can never be certain that actions go unseen. This threat of punitive observation acts as a means for individuals to be coerced into self-discipline and self-control, in order to avoid punishment by the authority of the state.

It is from within this Foucaultian framework of surveillance that we are taking up the notion of the White gaze for the purposes of this work.[2] In this conceptualization, we consider that the White gaze operates in constructing both non-White and White bodies in particular ways. As opposed to the "double vision of the 'white eye'" to which Stuart Hall (1995) refers, which highlights the good/bad sides of *primitivism* in media representations of non-White bodies, our use of the concept of the White gaze is more in keeping with Frantz Fanon's (1986) description of his own identity construction in a White-dominated world. In *Black Skin, White Masks,* Fanon describes the bodily consciousness of a Black man within a White world. He writes: "Consciousness of the body is solely a negating activity. It is a third-person consciousness" (p. 110). This experience is shaped by the White gaze, which has provided the elements of identity construction, "who has woven me out of a thousand details, anecdotes, stories."

The White gaze, according to Ruth Frankenberg (1993), acts as a social construction "in examining the formation and contestation of White women's race consciousness" (p.18), and is akin to Foucault's understanding of the assumed authority that lies in the self-disciplining power of the imagined panopticon. As such, the normalizing and controlling authority of White, patriarchal, heteronormative and capitalist structures constitute the White gaze. In reading Erin's story, we considered the ways in which the White gaze operated both through and on Erin, as a White female teacher, and the ways in which it functioned to enforce the separation of White female bodies and brown male bodies.

THE WHITE GAZE

One theme that is present in Erin's story is the question of what was seen and by whom. Erin's story described her closing and opening her eyes as a way of negotiating the space between her inner reality, in which her young, female body was wracked with pain, and her outer reality with her students, in which she felt the need to discipline her body by denying the presence of pain caused by her female sexual organs, lest she lose her authority as "the teacher." We read this example as a repetition of a significant historical notion that is present in narratives of education in the United States, wherein the authority of the state is enacted by and through the disciplined body of a White, female teacher (Grumet, 1988: Meiners, 2007).

One way of reading Erin's story is in relation to her worry about her students' potential reactions to her bodily precarity, and any loss of authority and control that may result from her inability to discipline her female body. Inherent in this worry is what may be seen and by whom: by her students, for one, but there is another worry about being "seen" that is manifest in her concern over the loss of her authority. This worry is not only related to any other witnesses who are bodily present in the room, but to the larger sense of the controlling White gaze.

In Erin's story, she was both being disciplined by the White gaze as well as turning the White gaze on her students and their reactions to her physical pain in the classroom. Within this gaze lies the power and authority related to normalization and control regarding patriarchal capitalism, knowledge, and sexuality—all key components of the historical construction of race in the United States. Initially in the story, Erin felt the White gaze on her undisciplined body, as the pain of her menstrual cramps and the implicit threat of the presence of her blood in the classroom caused her to deny the physical reality she was experiencing. She did this to maintain her authority and control over her classroom.

Initially, Erin "closes her eyes, and sees herself crumpling to the floor, curling up into a ball, letting everything go," implying that to acknowledge her pain would require the relinquishing of her authority over her body and her students, and her ability to maintain the controlling gaze. This vision is quickly dispersed, however, and Erin reasserted her authority by directing her gaze back to her students. In this sense, the White gaze was simultaneously constructing her as she maintained the controlling gaze directed at her students.

The next part of Erin's story depicted her embodiment of the White gaze being trained on her students, as she moved around the room to monitor their progress in their reading. We see her seeing her students through and in this White gaze. She acknowledged the pressure this placed on her students in her description of an interaction with a student: "She approaches a student sitting in the first row, 'How's your reading going?' she asks. He kept his gaze down on his book, 'It's good, Miss.'" By averting his own gaze, Erin's student attempted to avoid, and perhaps resist, the White gaze embodied in his teacher's visual monitoring of her classroom. In that moment, however, Erin's concern about her student's reading progress was perhaps not as important to her as her fight to maintain control over her pain-wracked body, again, as an example of the power of the White gaze to act both on and through the body of the White, female teacher.

Erin once again lost momentary control of her body, this time in a way that the students could not help but notice. At least two of them got out of their desks to physically assist her, and she noted this by making yet another reference to seeing:

> Then she sees them. The two young men are suddenly there on either side of her. They are both tall and strong, one in his football jersey, the other in a baggy black t-shirt, hair shaved close to their scalps, smooth brown skin, a few little hairs jutting out from their chins. They are senior boys—full of confidence, with ear-to-ear grins, charming their way into class 10 minutes late. Now she notices how their deep brown eyes look at her.

This was an important moment, when Erin and her students seemed to truly see each other. For an instant, the White gaze seems to be dropped.

This experience seemed significant in that it forced Erin to turn her gaze to the floor, until she closed her eyes once again:

> She focuses on the floor now, breathing in and out, seeing only their tennis shoes, knowing who they are. Her students. Julio and Anthony. 'I'm not feeling well. I'll be okay,' she responds. 'I just need a minute.' The boys remained fixed by her side and their bodies blocked her view of the rest of the class. She closed her eyes again.

Erin breaks her gaze with her students when she "notices" how her students are looking at her. The concern she reads in her students' eyes threatened the fragile authority she was fighting to maintain in her classroom. Erin described what might be seen in potentially dangerous terms: "That journey is too far away, too dangerous, too public."

It seems that Erin is constrained by the White gaze in that she is all too aware of the risk to herself and to her students if this young, White-bodied, female teacher is seen being carried aloft by her brown-bodied, male students—an act that subverts all the authority inherent in the structure of the school. To subvert this authority poses a danger to Erin; it is also dangerous for her students, whose proposed actions may be misconstrued by others in the school (we return, later in the chapter, to explore these dangers in more detail). In this way, the White gaze works to maintain power and authority even when the fragility of the teacher's body puts her at risk, causing her to deny the pain she feels and deflect the care offered by her students in order to avoid the commingling of white and brown bodies, which could potentially subvert her all-important role as teacher and instrument of the normalizing White gaze.

WASTE

While the control and authority maintained by the White gaze is primarily a means to perpetuate the White supremacist project of nation building, it also serves the interest of scientific management and efficiency. The teacher's gaze works to preserve control and "manage" the students in her classroom while the institutional eye on the teacher monitors her labor, time, and energy. We now turn to the students to examine how they are positioned in Erin's memory, reading them through two different theories of waste. Ultimately, control works in service of the elimination of waste in a system that both negates its value and relies on it as a necessary byproduct of production. In an industrial system, waste is a subject position constructed in opposition to what is good, desired, whole, and usable. It is unwanted excess. It is mistakes and missed opportunities. It needs to be managed and dealt with, controlled and isolated. It is what we are when we aren't enough: wasting time, wasting potential, wasting energy, wasting away. It is in this system that Erin must confront the inevitable presence of waste.

In the beginning of her painful episode, as her discomfort intensified, Erin surveyed her students, "working on their assignment, playing on their cell phone, doing nothing. She asked them to work quietly today. What a waste. But she should go check on those who aren't doing their work." With this description of her students, Erin recalls narratives of efficiency, production, teaching, and learning, and race that permeate her classroom. The line, "What a waste" is also a linguistic peculiarity in Erin's memory; the article "a" points to nothing in particular and thus relies on the reader to decipher what "waste" might refer to. Therefore, in order to understand the contradiction and tension embedded in Erin's work as a White woman teacher, we need to historically read and reread waste in educational discourse, searching for multiple interpretations of how and why Erin constructs something in her classroom as waste.

READING WASTE

The preoccupation with waste is most palpably a part of American discourse during the Era of Industrialization, when the country moved from an agriculture-based economy to a market economy based on industry.

During this "age of efficiency," scientific management experts captured the imaginations of Americans, insisting that their system could cure society's ills and be applied by anyone with "common sense" (Callahan, 1962). The doctrine of scientific management purports that progress is made through the elimination of waste. While even efficiency experts admit that waste cannot be completely eradicated (in fact, it is a necessary byproduct of industry and capitalism), working toward the elimination of waste will bring immediate rewards. Soon, these experts were conducting "investigations" of school districts and reporting waste of various kinds: labor, time, facilities, resources and materials, and ultimately profits. In 1912, Franklin Bobbitt, of the University of Chicago, published a well-known piece entitled, "The Elimination of Waste in Education," examining a school in Gary, Indiana, which had taken up the principles of scientific management. Bobbitt argues that waste exists not only in school schedules and facility use, but also in the labor of teachers and the "retardation" of students—those "laggards" and "backward" pupils who don't learn material at the same rate or quantity as their peers (Bobbitt, 1912, p. 266). In this way, the scientific management movement mapped waste onto the bodies of students and teachers who were deemed "inefficient" by this system.

When we move almost a century forward in time, we find Erin teaching in a system still entrenched in these narratives of scientific management and efficiency, now compounded by neoliberal, market-based reforms, competition, high-stakes testing, and accountability policies. These new narratives continued to function in the service of colonial nation building as they placed impossible expectations on Erin as teacher that include the management, control, and ultimately the elimination of "waste" in her classroom. Erin and her mostly White, middle class, women colleagues were waste managers. They were given scripted curricula to teach that mimicked the industrial model of production: the same input (lessons) will produce the same output (student learning). She was expected to manage her classroom and her students so that not a moment of instructional time was wasted.

Despite the extreme pain that almost caused her to lose consciousness, Erin felt compelled to "check on those who aren't doing their work," echoing and responding to Bobbitt's (1912) description of students who create waste by "falling behind." For efficiency's sake, she needed to pedagogically embrace the "banking model" of education in which she, the expert, held and distributed knowledge to her students (Freire, 2011). However, Erin also resisted this model in her memory by grammatically equating "working on their assignment" to "doing nothing," as if she believed that the individualized, traditional, seatwork lesson she'd provided them with on this day was ultimately meaningless. But the pressure

Erin felt to follow the banking model and conceptualize learning as a linear, discrete, measurable entity was real and came with serious consequences. The stakes of waste are high. Because Erin taught students who were perceived as deficient based on their racial, linguistic, and socioeconomic backgrounds, there was even greater scrutiny on her work from the state. It was simply assumed that waste already resided in her classroom—that her students, as Bobbitt characterized them, were "laggards," that she was also not working hard enough, (i.e., her Value Added Measure (VAM) score would never be good enough). As a White woman, Erin's role in working for the state was to be the moral authority and family for her students, to mother and manage her students' morality as she reinforced White supremacy and controlled classroom waste.

Grumet (1988) argues that "dominated by kits and dittos, increasingly mechanized and impersonal, most of our classrooms cannot sustain human relationships of sufficient intimacy to support the risks, the trust, and the expression that learning requires" (p. 56). Erin's undeniable menstrual pain made evident the repercussions of our obsession with waste. In a moment when her physical safety depended on trust, vulnerability, and her ability to openly express her emotions and needs to her students, Erin instead took stock of the classroom and saw waste because her students were not doing what she asked them to do and in some cases were doing, as she writes, absolutely "nothing."

In order to participate in the compliance and standardization of the banking model, a kind of emptiness is demanded of women teachers. When reading waste within the narrow view of knowledge and learning constructed by the efficiency narrative, the day was essentially wasted for Erin and her students. This waste existed as a direct result of her inability to maintain the authority of teacher; the pain of her menstrual cramps became a waste of her labor in the classroom. Erin's menstruation itself was also a form of waste—it was unnecessary blood and mucus her body was working to expel that needed to be efficiently and discretely collected and thrown away. Erin sought to control this bodily waste and was frustrated by her inability to "have control of her own pain and bleeding." As is required of efficiency, in the classroom Erin needed to avoid intimacy, vulnerability, or an expression of her needs and emotions around her monthly bleeding. But as her pain caused Erin to lose control of her body and its waste, she could also no longer manage the waste of her classroom. Reading waste this way helps us to understand how the narratives of efficiency and standardization have shaped White women teachers in their role as colonial nation builders and how they worked to prevent Erin from fully developing human relationships with her students.

REREADING WASTE

John Dewey's (1915) third chapter in *The School and Society* is titled "Waste in Education." Unlike the efficiency experts' conceptualization of waste, Dewey characterized waste as the byproduct of a discontinuity between what happens in the schoolhouse and "out there"—in the homes and the communities of children and their families. For Dewey, waste was the result of a lack of coherence; schools operated to isolate students from the world, subjects from one another, and minds from bodies, thus producing waste. Thoughtful organization, however, could unify these entities, bringing a sense of connectedness to students' lives and their academic studies. Dewey thought that the

> question is not one of the waste of money or the waste of things. These matters count; but the primary waste is that of human life, the life of the children while they are at school, and afterward because of inadequate and perverted preparation. (Dewey, 1915, p. 64)

For Dewey, standardization, compartmentalization, and efficiency in schools produced waste, a waste of human life. Both students and teachers generated this waste in the form of short-circuited growth, disconnected experiences in the world, and the reproduction of inequity and injustice.

Dewey's discussion of waste triggers for us the depressing conclusion that schools are doing exactly what they were designed to do. If the waste of school is that students are not able to utilize their outside experiences in the classroom nor take their school learning with them back into their communities and apply it, then school will function to reproduce and privilege a very narrow way of being. Grumet (1988) points to the waste that is produced through the separation of public and private spheres and the creation of school as a place to be liberated from one's familial context. It is for "other people's children" that standardized curricula and the principles of efficiency are developed in order to make up for the "deficits" of their family and culture (Grumet, 1988, p. 171). And it is the teacher's role to maintain that system of inequity to preserve White, middle-class, and hetero-patriarchal values. In this system, the curriculum seeks to exclude the influence of the family from the classroom and the teacher takes on the role of proprietor of a "common culture" (p. 171). That White women teachers are still the majority of practitioners in the field despite ever-changing racial demographics in America points to the power of the system to reproduce itself—through "school's capacity to sort, stratify, categorize, and identify the children of the nation" and teachers acting as benevolent mothers who do this work in the name of democracy, equality, and nation building (p. 172).

A rereading of Erin's declaration, "What a waste," therefore, allows us to see the waste in Erin's classroom as a product of systemic racism and oppression. Erin's Black and brown-bodied students who lived in or near poverty and brought diverse linguistic and cultural funds of knowledge into her classroom were constructed as human waste when confronted with the "common curriculum" that feigned neutrality while advancing White, middle-class, and hetero-patriarchal values. Ultimately, her students' lives, cultures, and communities were disconnected from school, not accidentally but purposefully as the public school system served to reinforce White supremacy. As a White woman teacher, Erin was charged with the reproduction of a system that, in producing this waste, was doing exactly what it was designed to do. Meiners (2007) writes that White women teachers play a role that is contradictory: they "mask racist and sexist exclusionary educational practices" in schools by adamantly opposing such injustices, while also participating in a system that reaffirms them (p. 43). Erin became what Meiners calls, drawing on the work of Helen Harper and Honor Ford Smith, a patriotic "Lady Bountiful" who reproduced patriarchal values and colonial epistemologies (p. 46).

However, Erin also rejected the charge of the White Lady Bountiful—sought to resist and subvert it—as evidenced by her acknowledgment of the waste she was complicit in producing. The White Lady Bountiful must perpetuate a facade of justice through the narrative of education as a meritocracy. Her obedient, caring, and "good" White woman body serves as the mediating agent between her Black and brown-bodied students and the powerful colonial state. When Erin admitted (albeit, via internal monologue in her memory) that there was human waste in her classroom, she cracked open that facade, calling into question the Lady and her participation in a system of inequality. Thus, "What a waste" was both surrender and battle cry. It is in Erin's state of corporeal vulnerability that she was able to see and expose the wasting human lives sitting before her in neat rows.

DANGER

Preceding her forceful refusal of help, in the wake of an imagined journey through the school, carried in the arms of her students, Erin asked the question: "What have I done?" The question remains: What had she done? What was the action she was naming here and how was she entangled in its complicity?

There is a simple clarity underlying this story: a woman was in pain; her body demanded to be felt and cared for; she nearly fell, crouched, closed her eyes, and focused on her breathing. There was simplicity to these actions, a vivid need and appropriate response. Likewise, her students' actions followed a simple and clear progression. Their teacher, who they cared for, was hurting. She needed help and they wanted to help her. They wanted to pick her up and carry her to the nurse. This seemed, for them, the best way to aid her. So, why did these sensible and caring responses inspire such panic in the teacher? Why did her body in pain appear to threaten her role as a teacher? Why did self-care appear to be a last option? And why was her students' offer met with such dismay and denial?

This story doesn't make sense until one considers the multiple and contradictory currents of power influencing the spaces that White women inhabit in schools. Schools—particularly schools in which White women work with students of color—become places where the contradictions tied up in the production and maintenance of race, gender, and class are exorbitant. Within patriarchal culture, a woman should be desirable, subservient, and need help. However, within a White supremacist society, a White woman should be desirable only to White men. As a teacher, a woman must be in control of her body, of the bodies of her students, and of their minds. Put another way, as a woman, one must be carried; as a teacher, she cannot be. In our memories, our bodies consistently illuminated the contradictions and anxieties tied up inside our roles as teachers. Our physical bodies—and moments of distress or struggles within them—helped to illuminate the illogical and violent contradictions that teachers and students are required to live out on a daily basis.

So, what had Erin done? In that moment, threatened by her body's failure to perform its duty, she had violated multiple expectations for her position. Erin's extreme physical pain in the classroom led to threats to teacher authority, White femininity, and rules against interracial intimacy. Her need to suppress her physical pain, in the service of maintaining White patriarchal authority in the classroom, results in another kind of pain, for herself and her students, in this moment and beyond.

TEACHER AUTHORITY

Within Freire's (2011) banking model of education, teachers deposit knowledge into the (ideally) passive vessels of their students. "The more completely she fills the receptacles, the better a teacher she is. The more meekly the receptacles permit themselves to be filled, the better students they are" (Freire, 2011, p. 72). For this model to be enacted, an enormous division between teacher and student must be sustained. Erin's physical struggle opened up a space for her students by dissolving the distance between them and her. Her students' strengths, desires, vision, and agency were vividly operating as they approached her with an offer of help.

Erin experienced this possibility, envisioned their journey down the hall, one in which her control and authority was beyond redemption. For a moment, she imagined closeness, a relief from the demands of maintaining her role, the dissolution of positions into a more equitable and humanizing sharing of responsibility. And then, as if awakening from a dream, she snapped back into the reality of where and who she was. She was a young, new teacher, only a few years older than the students who were offering her help. The precarity of her role within this space could not sustain this proximity and relief. It was with wonder and regret that she considered the possibility for closeness that her students had opened: "They would do this for her."

WHITE FEMININITY

In addition to her authority as teacher, Erin's precarity in her classroom also violated—thereby exposing—expectations for White femininity. In her book, *Ain't I a Woman,* bell hooks (1981) explored cultural and historical shifts in the 19th century, in the United States, in relationships between race and gender: shifts that produced/constructed White women as the carriers of morality. Prior to this—and in the context of readings of the Christian bible that privileged White men—White women, like all women, were assumed to be carriers of sin and corruption. However, what hooks traces is how sin and corruption was extracted from White women and projected onto Black women. That is, during a period when enslaved Black women were being brutally and sexually exploited, these Black women also started being used, symbolically, as a contrast to a new image of White women. Now, Black women were the carriers of sin and corruption, while White women became "extolled as the 'nobler half of humanity' whose duty was to elevate men's sentiments and inspire their higher impulses.... She was depicted as goddess rather than sinner; she was virtuous, pure, innocent, not sexual and worldly" (hooks, 1981, p. 31).

hooks reads the sentimentality of White men toward White women as a veiled expression of contempt: "Forcing white women to deny their physical beings was as much expression of male hatred of woman as was regarding them as sex objects" (p. 32). This mythological turn demanded the sacrifice of a body; the possession of virtue meant a denial of sexual desire. White women's bodies were taken away from them. Disembodiment became the cost of virtue for White women within White supremacist patriarchy.

Racialized notions of femininity further complicate the roles White women are expected to take up in schools. Katerina Deliovsky (2010) writes:

> In the context of a society founded on European imperialism and colonialism, normative femininity is never signified outside a process of racial domination ... historically, 'white' women's whiteness and femaleness have been interwoven and conflated in such a way as to constitute hegemonic femininity. (p. 103)

Normative femininity then, within the context of racial domination, becomes rendered into control of one's body. "When women do not engage, or appear not to be engaged, in this constant self-surveillance ... it can be interpreted by society, family/friends and even themselves as a moral failure on their part as *women*" (Deliovsky, 2010, p. 106). A lack of self-scrutiny and bodily control threatens gendered and racialized expectations for White women.

What had Erin done? First, she had a body, an undeniable and vulnerable body. Second, her body was not being controlled or policed according to the expectations of the space she inhabited and was tasked to produce. Third, Erin's bodily vulnerability was particularly salient because the offer of help was coming from brown male bodies, bodies of which she was extremely aware.

FEAR OF INTIMACY

Decoteau Irby (2014) contends that the desire for White racial purity is an important factor to consider in more fully understanding race and gender in school spaces. Historically, segregation imposed distance between Black and White bodies. Desegregation exposed deeply embedded anxieties around racial purity, and—while rarely named or acknowledged—Irby asserts that these anxieties are still very much at work within educational spaces. He writes, "I suggest that in predominantly White desegregated schools, disciplining heterosexual Black boys represents a new campaign of institutionalized violence and intimidation that reflects a subtle, but nonetheless pernicious, White male segregationist agenda" (p. 785). White female bodies are implicated in this violence, as they are positioned as endangered by Black male bodies, thus providing a justification for violence toward Black boys and youth.

Both Black males and White females are disciplined by this White male desire for racial purity, but they are disciplined differently. Irby notes that "young White female bodies are disciplined through surveillance and coerced into compliance, conformity, and docility. Young Black masculine bodies are disciplined through spectacles of harsh punishment and removal" (p. 786). The removal of heteronormative Black male bodies is often justified as a way to protect "the bodily safety and academic achievement of heteronormative White girls" (p. 783). While Irby's work focuses on Black boys and white girls, it opens up another way to consider Erin's story, and what she fears she has done.

What had Erin done? She had imagined herself in these young men's arms. She had imagined herself being *seen* by other White teachers and administrators in these young men's arms. In this moment, what she stood to lose by being carried by her students went beyond the loss of her teacher authority and included danger for the very students who wanted to help her. "Already a class full of students has seen her; she is too ill to teach them. But she cannot let these boys pick her up and hold her in their arms." As a White woman whose body had been harnessed to the production of White supremacist patriarchy, she knew the danger that close proximity to her body presented to her male students of color.

This story could be read as an account of Erin's sexual desire toward her students. Erin's description of her students' bodies was detailed and attuned. In her account of the imagined journey down the hall, she no longer referred to her students as boys; at that moment, she described them as young men. Her description of the act they are proposing is intimate and sensual: "She sees herself in these young men's arms ... she cannot let these boys pick her up and hold her in their arms." The image of bodies holding each other prompts her forceful response. "'No,' she says loudly. 'No one is carrying me anywhere. It's okay.'"

This story could also be read as a desire for intimacy of another kind, and Erin's genuine fearfulness for her students' safety if others were to perceive it. As a White woman within a context of White supremacy that has constructed White women's bodies as threatened through their proximity to non-White male bodies, she knew the harsh disciplinary measures that could be directed toward her students. She knew the unspoken and unacknowledged racial anxieties leading to disciplinary actions cloaked in school policy. She knew the risk her students were offering to take. And while we can't know what Anthony and Julio were thinking, as students of color within the education system, we believe they knew the risk they were taking if they were to be seen carrying their White teacher's female body through the school, that they were not naïve to the ways that school positioned them as waste. "They would do this for her," in our reading, becomes a radical and dangerous challenge to the White supremacist patriarchal pursuit of racial purity that demands distance between bodies.

CONCLUSION

It is difficult to think about what further actions to "recommend," given that as White teachers, we (the authors) cannot escape our implicatedness in the problem of the reproduction of White supremacy. But even as we face our implicatedness, we still believe we have a profound responsibility to offer a set of recommendations to our readers based on this work. First, we would recommend the process of collective memory work as a way for teachers to theorize moments of significance with regard to their own racialized identities and bodies. Affordances of this methodology include the ability to move toward and live in moments of precarity and discomfort, as the collective examines and explores these tensions alongside and through their relationship to historical and social narratives of power and oppression. We have found that the methodology is best taken up over time and in the context of ongoing, caring relationships. Communities of people are necessary for doing this work because together we can be smarter and more courageous as we hear one another's difficult stories and have the opportunity to speak our own aloud and feel that they are heard.

In discussing these recommendations, we all centered on the moment in Erin's story when she realized the lengths to which her students were prepared to go to care for her, and the resulting shift in their relationships that took place in that moment. Erin's corporeal vulnerability created a space for her students' care to enter into their relationship, and for a moment they saw each other without the interference of the White gaze. As we thought more about the significance of this moment for Erin and her students, we realized that there always already exist multiple possibilities for these humanizing interactions between teachers and students in any given moment, and it is both simple and hard to choose to respond to them. Our second recommendation, then, is for teachers to welcome and live in moments of vulnerability in the classroom, as they can offer us new and more humanizing ways to be in relationship with our students.

Eventually, Erin made a journey down the hall without her students' assistance to get the medical help she needed. But these moments in her memory—of seeing her students more clearly for a split second, of internally acknowledging the waste, and of understanding that "they would do this for her"—these cracks and fissures are glimpses of possibility for what could be in a system deeply entrenched in *what is*. Erin doesn't need to be carried down the hall by her brown-bodied male students in order for a new story to be written; she needs to open up and live in the possibility that "they would do this for her."

We recommend that teachers and teacher educators—in their own practice—not only move toward discomforting memories and new readings of familiar stories, but that they take up serious theorizing about White women teachers. We suggest in particular an engagement with the work of Reverend Thandeka (2000), Katerina Deliovsky (2010), and Decoteau Irby (2014) in order to begin a critical exploration of the precarious construction of White teacher bodies. We believe that this work offers a place of critical resistance grounded in the lived experience of those doing the work, as an alternative to racial diversity trainings and practices in schools that can often involve outside entities and canned curriculum, and may oversimplify and reify issues of race and difference in education.

After this moment of disorientation, vulnerability, and precarity in her classroom, things shifted for Erin in her role as a teacher. And things continue to shift every day as, through her memory, she sees differently now. Here we run the risk of valorizing the White lady teacher as the hero of the story. So we aim, as much as possible, to tend to Erin's students who, through their attempts to take action with their bodies, opened up the possibility for an alternative story to be told. Because of Julio and Anthony, Erin began to cultivate more radical and loving relationships with her students. Student and teacher were no longer static roles to be enacted in particular ways: Erin began to see them as more fluid and open, with the potential for intimacy and learning. This possibility felt dangerous because she still feared, for herself and her students, the ways that closeness between her White female body and the brown and Black bodies of her students would be punished. But for a moment she saw the care those bodies could have for her and give to one another and how that radical care might begin to peel away at the layers of authority, surveillance, hierarchy, and control embedded in her classroom. In this moment, the gaze was softened, waste was vibrant and alive, and Erin's body and thought and feeling became less constrained.

NOTES

1. A brief summary of the other memories is included here.

   Angela's story narrates a complex time in a young, White teacher's life when, in her first teaching job, she encounters the historical and cultural heaviness of the role of White, female teacher to students of Indigenous backgrounds. The teacher in this story feels a deep responsibility toward her students and a need to use her "authority" as a teacher to put them at ease; she simultaneously recognizes the danger of embodying the colonial violence associated with the kind of authority she feels her role as teacher is embedded within. This tension coalesces in her uneasy "teacher" smile: a smile she constructs and interprets as being welcoming and encouraging, as well as rigid and dangerous.

Colleen's story begins inside of a conversation about racism in a teacher education classroom. In response to an itch, the teacher (Colleen) begins contemplating the ways that her students and colleagues perceive her. Her "mom" body is filtered through assumptions accompanying it, and juxtaposed alongside of more radical markers of difference. Glimpses into her past clash with her current presentation of self. Her body appears to invalidate the struggle she is calling for, and her habitation of this body—her careful and conflicted creation of it—threatens to conceal the truest parts of herself.

2. According to Foucault, starting in the 17th century, the power over life evolved into two main forms. One centered on the body as machine and was concerned with the anatomo-politics of the human body, which came to characterize the disciplines of the body, the optimization of its capabilities, its usefulness and docility, and its integration into economic systems. The other form of this power over life centered on the body as species and served as the basis for biological processes related to life, managed through regulatory controls: a bio-politics of the population. Hence, sovereign power over death is replaced with the careful and calculated management of life.

This resulted in "an explosion of numerous and diverse techniques for achieving the subjugation of bodies" ushering in "the era of 'biopower'" (Rabinow, 1991, p. 262). New disciplines were embodied in places such as universities, schools and the army; and concurrent new techniques for population control came into existence, such as demography, the evaluation of the relationship between resources and citizens, the construction of tables to analyze wealth, the establishment of school-based norms, and standardized testing, to name just a few. In addition, the emergence of biopower is recognized as being instrumental in the development of capitalism, given the need for "the controlled insertion of bodies into the machinery of production" (p. 263). The techniques of biopower created in the 18th century infiltrated every level of the social body and institutions, particularly the family, army, schools, police, individual medicine, and the administration of the population. They also acted as forces for segregation and the creation of hierarchies, which resulted in "guaranteeing relations of domination and effects of hegemony" (p. 263).

Another major development in the rise of biopower is the new significance of "the norm" in disciplining subjects. Danaher, Schirato, and Webb (2002) argue that one of the primary technologies of biopower is schools. As a result, schools and teachers become a crucial element of biopower, both in their regulation of educational functioning, as well as in the policing of their own behavior relative to the discourses of normalization. Ladelle McWhorter (2005) argues that biopower is useful in understanding the normalizing power of whiteness in U.S. culture. Applying this logic to the notion of whiteness as normalization in U.S. schools would mean that all students who attend school in the United States are, to some extent, influenced by the normalizing power of whiteness. In addition, while White, female teachers are agents of White normalization in schools, the normalizing forces of whiteness, most often conceived as a male experience, are simultaneously acting on them.

REFERENCES

Bobbitt, J. F. (1912). The elimination of waste in education. *The Elementary School Teacher, 12*(6), 259–271.

Callahan, R. (1962). *Education and the cult of efficiency.* Chicago, IL: University of Chicago Press.

Danaher, G., Schirato, T., & Webb, J. (2000). *Understanding Foucault.* Thousand Oaks, CA: Sage.

Davies, B., & Gannon, S. (Eds.). (2006). *Doing collective biography.* Maidenhead, England: Open University Press.

Deliovsky, K. (2010). *White femininity: Race, gender & power.* Halifax, Nova Scotia, Canada: Fernwood.

Dewey, J. (1915). *The school and society.* Chicago, IL: The University of Chicago Press.

Fanon, F. (1986). *Black skin, white masks.* London, England: Pluto.

Frankenberg, R. (1993). *White women, race matters: The social construction of whiteness.* Minneapolis, MN: University of Minnesota Press.

Freire, P. (2011). *Pedagogy of the oppressed.* New York, NY: Continuum.

Foucault, M. (1977). *Discipline and punish: The birth of the prison.* New York, NY: Random House.

Grumet, M. R. (1988). *Bitter milk: Women and teaching.* Amherst, MA: The University of Massachusetts Press.

Hall, S. (1995). The whites of their eyes: Racist ideologies and the media. In G. Dines & J. M. Humez (Eds.), *Gender, race and class in the media: A text-reader* (pp. 18–22). Thousand Oaks, CA: Sage.

Haug, F. (1987). *Female sexualization: A collective work of memory.* London, England: Verso.

hooks, b. (1981). *Ain't I a woman: Black women and feminism.* Boston, MA: South End Press.

Irby, D. J. (2014). Revealing racial purity ideology: Fear of black–white intimacy as a framework for understanding school discipline in post-Brown schools. *Educational Administration Quarterly, 50*(5), 783–795.

Ladson-Billings, G., & Tate, W. F. (1995). Toward a critical race theory of education. *Teachers College Record, 97*, 47–68.

McWhorter, L. (2005). Where do white people come from? A Foucaultian critique of whiteness studies. *Philosophy & Social Criticism, 31*(5/6), 533–556.

Meiners, E. R. (2007). *Right to be hostile: Schools, prisons, and the making of public enemies.* New York, NY: Routledge.

Rabinow, P. (1991). *The Foucault reader.* London, England: Penguin.

Sato, M., & Lensmire, T. (2009). Supporting teachers to work with children of poverty. The *Phi Delta Kappan, 90*(5), 365–370.

Thandeka. (2000). *Learning to be white: Money, race, and God in America.* New York, NY: Continuum.

Tyack, D. B. (1974). *The one best system: A history of American urban education.* Cambridge, MA: Harvard University Press.

PART II

INVESTIGATING WHITE TEACHER IMAGE AND IDENTITY

CHAPTER 4

DOUBLE IMAGE, SINGLE IDENTITY

Constructive Academic Relationships in Multiethnic Classrooms

Stephen D. Hancock
University of North Carolina, Charlotte

In multiethnic classrooms throughout the United States of America, cultural knowledge is a necessary and beneficial commodity for effective instruction. Gordon (2014) described culture as a multidimensional construct that supports the judgmental or normative, cognitive, affective, skills or psychomotor, and technological dimensions. While each dimension is salient in the development of double image consciousness and academic relationships, the judgmental/normative dimension is the focus of this chapter. The judgmental/normative dimension of cultural identity encompasses values, social experiences, and epistemological assumptions (Gordon, 2014). The normative dimension of cultural identity should not be underestimated. It provides a framework for cognitive function and it conceives what is right, good, and normal. Hence, if teachers are to provide quality learning experiences it is important that they reflect on the judgmental/normative dimension of their identity in an effort to teach in

White Women's Work: Examining the Intersectionality of Teaching, Identity, and Race
pp. 71–86

nonbiased ways. In addition, the normative dimension also influences perceptions on equity and social justice. I submit that the values and experiences that teachers bring to the classroom hold the essence of their knowledge of equity, social justice, and quality instruction.

Quality educational experiences coupled with equitable practices are essential for student mobility and global competitiveness. Though there has been marginal success in closing the opportunity gap, many racially marginalized students continue to attend schools that provide neither quality teaching nor equitable student-teacher relationships. In an effort to provide productive experiences for all students, attention to the relationship between White women teachers, racially marginalized students, parents, and the curriculum must be addressed. If pre-K–12 schools are going to increase access to quality learning, equitable policies, and competitive outcomes, then the education community must attend to a blueprint that supports constructive academic relationships. However, before these constructive academic relationships are realized, teachers, and in particular White women, must develop a healthy and realistic image of themselves as it relates to the community of their students and families. In this chapter, I first discuss the concept of double image and its impact on identity. Then I grapple with the concept and impact of whiteness in multiethnic classrooms, particularly how White women teachers develop their identities in the context of academic relationships with students of color. Finally, I wrestle through a nascent framework for the development of constructive academic relationships. Throughout the chapter, narratives are used to highlight White women teacher's experiences with double image and constructive academic relationships in multiethnic classrooms. The chapter weaves together the connection between critical reflective practice and how it supports double image consciousness, which in turn has the capacity to dismantle prejudicial attitudes in an effort to create constructive academic relationships.

DOUBLE IMAGE: SINGLE IDENTITY

Double image is understood to be a consciousness, one that strengthens the capacity for White teachers to critically reflect on self, specifically as it relates to negotiating genuine interaction with diverse others in multiethnic contexts. Double image sensibilities provide a deeper understanding of how Whites see themselves and are seen through the socioracial lens of others. It is not necessarily a permanent consciousness that moves across varying situations and time, rather double image can be customized and temporal to fit the context (Seidl & Hancock, 2011). The culture of power that permeates whiteness enables Whites to control the narrative about their image and more likely to isolate themselves from the gaze of socioracial perspectives. White people, and particularly White women teachers, tend to have fewer opportunities to consider issues of race and racism, in part because they participate in segregated living patterns. As a result, when racial issues and incidents arise, they have little experience, language, and desire to effectively navigate situations of race (Seidl & Hancock, 2011). Hence, the intent of developing double image sensibilities is to support the growth of White teachers through a continuum that can start at a naive understanding of their racialized image, to an awareness of diverse perspectives of whiteness, and then to a critically mature image of how cultural others might perceive their actions and intent.

Double image requires that deliberate and consistent attention to critical self-reflection is practiced. Working in multiethnic classrooms will always require a thoughtful consideration of the socio-racial history that continues to perpetuate the racial perfidiousness between White women teachers and diverse students. Historically, Whites possess a higher degree of ignorance about race relations in the classroom and they may cradle ingenuous perceptions on the socioracial reality of diverse students and how these students perceive them. Supporting teachers' self-perception "through the history of racism and race relations allows us to speak explicitly to the emotional, relational, and intellectual needs inherent in this work and provides explicit teaching and deliberate and sustained support, or socialization, toward such a consciousness" (Seidl & Hancock, p. 696). In their seminal work on double image, Seidl and Hancock (2011) stated that, "a double image is a sensibility or consciousness that gives White people a deeper understanding of how they are seen and raced by others, particularly People of Color" (p. 687).

Double image consciousness has the capacity to support the growth of White women teachers in their knowledge of how stereotypes and racism are perpetuated and sustained through a master narrative that is partly driven by their presence in urban schools. However, the development of such consciousness is hard work that creates friction and personal discomfort as White women teachers awaken to the multiple and often unflattering images that whiteness carries in the socioracial context of the classroom. When these teachers begin to perceive and accept themselves as racial beings through the socioracial eyes of their students, they start the process of embracing double image consciousness (Seidl & Hancock, 2011). Unfortunately, many White women teachers occupy racially privileged dispositions that make it difficult for them to discuss, accept, and counter racial injustices and stereotypes. Seidl and Hancock (2011) warn that the resistance that White teachers display toward race may reflect a genuine confusion in the role of whiteness in the perpetuation of stereotypes and racial injustices. Because the classrooms of White women teachers are constructed in their socioracial beliefs and attitudes, it is important to support their growth beyond an ethnocentric perspective. The development of double image consciousness, though it will cause friction and discomfort, supports White teachers as they transition from naïve to a place of socioracial awareness. Seidl and Hancock (2011), suggest that White teachers must "grapple with and successfully challenge a variety of insecurities, fears, beliefs, and tensions as they deal with the sometimes less-than-positive images they see reflected back to them" (p. 697). These less-than-positive images are often couched in racism. However, the label racist is an identity that many White women teachers resist with the same power and fear that invoked the racist image. Though the role of unconscious whiteness perpetuates stereotypes and racial injustice, it is imperative that White women teachers consciously operate in antibias ways in order to project a more favorable image.

WHITENESS AS RACISM

Race is a nebulous construct designed to support a sociopolitical hierarchy. Race was constructed for the purpose of oppressing an "unvalued other" through power, manipulation, and fear (Hancock & Allen, 2015). As the dominant race in the teaching force, White women teachers unwittingly and passively maintain the dominance and hierarchy of racism through classroom practices and methods. Unless these teachers are moving through the continuum of double image consciousness, the negative impact of whiteness in the classroom will be difficult to dismantle. Carroll (2014) suggests that the difficulty or resistance to antiracist ideology may rest in fact that White teachers do not want to relinquish or share the benefits and power of whiteness with racially conscious students. In many classrooms whiteness depicts goodness and normalcy. Conversely, diverse students and multiethnic epistemologies are considered less than good and abnormal. This duplicitous rationale that whiteness is normal and right strengthens the resistance to deconstruct White identity, power, and inequity in the classroom. In fact, resistance to antiracist ideology is sustained by a White identity that purports racelessness in an effort to passively hold on to privilege and power. White women teachers who claim the common phrase "I don't see color," only strengthen their invisible dominance while further marginalizing non-White students. Unless whiteness is examined in racial contexts, White women teachers will not be able to acquire a double image of themselves. Examining socioracial realities and prejudicial attitudes in the classroom will illuminate oppressive schools that place teachers and principals as messengers of oppression toward diverse students (Carroll, 2014). In addition, an investigative approach to prejudicial attitudes may also highlight issues of equity and social justice in the classroom.

Van den Berg, Denessen, Honstra, Voeten, and Holland (2010) conducted a study on prejudicial attitudes and their impact on teacher expectation of diverse students. The conclusions purported that prejudicial attitudes of White teachers were negatively impactful and different toward diverse students (van den Berg, et al., 2010). The prejudicial attitudes were based on the fact that White identity is normal and fair in the classroom context, and though the study was conducted in the Netherlands, its implications are generalizable across borders. The examination of socio-racial realities and prejudicial attitudes as it related to expectations revealed three major premises. First, White teachers generally held different or lower expectations for students with different ethnic origins and higher expectations for White students (van den Berg, et al., 2010). While this was consistent in every class in the study, it shows the pervasiveness of the resistance to antiracist ideology and development of a double image. The evidential actuality of prejudicial attitudes found in this study should motivate White teachers to support a more balance and antiracist identity. The second premise, found a direct correlation between implicit prejudicial attitudes and the low expectation and size of the non-White achievement gap (van den Berg, et al., 2010). Unfortunately, diverse students' identity are negatively impacted by this reality (Brown, Kanny, & Johnson, 2014), while White teacher identity maintained its power and place. Finally and most disturbing, but not surprising, van den Berg, et al. (2010) found that White teachers that believed diverse students were less intelligent and had a less promising future displayed negative prejudicial attitudes and had larger achievement gaps in their classrooms. It is important that the pervasiveness of prejudicial attitudes is curbed through the development of double image sensibilities that will perhaps support healthy White teacher identities and constructive academic relationships. Consequently, until the impact of whiteness on prejudicial attitudes are examined, issues of equity and justice in teaching and interactions will persist.

DOUBLE IMAGE: WHITE WOMEN TEACHER IDENTITIES

White teacher identities, as all identities, are complicated, multifaceted, and contextual. In particular White women teacher identity is couched in a culture that supports the "what and how" of behavior (Gordon, 2014). It is important to distinguish that since identities are contextual, the context of school culture produces a particular identity for White women teachers.

In the school context, many teachers take on the identity of *in loco parentis*, which dictates that the relationship of students and teachers is common to parents and children. However, identities like cultures are constantly shifting and evolving to meet the demands or quality of the context (Gordon, 2014) and the in loco parentis ideology has waned due to the multiethnic context of many schools. To support White teachers' development of double image sensibilities, it is important to understand whiteness as a culture and a nuanced identity. Understanding how White women teachers construct, negotiate, and project their identities is often known by diverse students in ways that are seemingly contrary to what White women want to display. Consequently, White women are surprised when their students direct an unflattering image of their teacher identity. While many White women teachers are "nice" and "well intentioned," they are not aware of the double image concepts where there is a culturally contrary perspective on their behavior and intentions.

In the initial work on this subject, I discuss two pervasive identities that White women teachers embody as teachers of diverse students. Many of their initial motives were to teach in inner city schools as a choice or last resort to "save" or "help" poor, disenfranchised minority children work toward a "better" life (Hancock, 2011). Without a critical examination of their disposition, many White women teachers enter diverse classrooms with good intentions to support a better life for their students. Unaware that many diverse students don't see them as a "savior" or "helper," rather after only a few months, many diverse students understand their nice teachers to be oppressive and demeaning toward their culture (i.e. language, epistemology, activities, etc.). In fact, students and conscious teachers readily see the microaggressions and microinequities wrought by "nice" teachers who lack a deeper understanding of how they are perceived by others (Seidl & Hancock, 2011).

TROPE NARRATIVES: THE WHITE WOMAN TEACHER

In urban and multiethnic schools across the United States of America, White women are leading classrooms and influencing the minds of young people. It is imperative that their teacher identities are grounded in academic rigor, equity, and social justice. Trope narratives are based on two tropes that were common realities in my experience as an elementary teacher and are pervasive in the ideology of many preservice teachers who sit in my multicultural course.

Trope 1: Mrs. Jones

Raised in a home where her mom was a professor of psychology and her dad a superintendent of the school district, Mrs. Alie Jones always knew she wanted to work in the field of education. She taught fourth grade at Bandy Elementary School, which was located in the inner city. Bandy Elementary was a pre-K-5 school with a student population of 570 students. Fifty percent of the students were Hispanic, and of that population 30% were English language learners. Thirty percent of the students were African American, 15% were Asian Indian, and 5% were White. Ninety-two percent of the students were on the free and reduced lunch program, and the school was performing in the bottom quarter of the district. Yet, Bandy Elementary was a conscious choice for Mrs. Jones and she believed that it was her calling to shield her students from impoverished perspectives and led them to a better emotional state. It was the middle of her third year at Bandy and seventh year as a teacher. Though her two previous years were met with student resistance and low achievement, Mrs. Jones felt it was due to growing pains or what she called "knowing pains." She felt that there was a period of knowing pains where she had to become familiar with the school culture and students in order to effectively teach and garner high performance.

The fourth graders in Mrs. Jones class were well taken care of. There were snacks for hungry students, she often took children home in her car to protect them from the elements and dangers in the street, and she fed them a constant diet of her empathy and purpose to save them from poverty by providing an education that will help them rise above their present circumstances. However, for some students Mrs. Jones empathy was not perceived in ways she thought she projected. Her words and attitude made Jasmine and several other students feel uncomfortable and ashamed. On a December afternoon a week before winter break, Mr. Rogers an African American father came to pick up his daughter, Jasmine. Having heard his daughters concern about feeling emotionally and culturally unsupported, he waited until all the children were dismissed to talk with Mrs. Jones. As he explained his daughter's feelings of being marginalized, slighted, and tolerated, Mrs. Jones listened intently and waited for Mr. Rogers to finish. She proceeded by telling and showing Mr. Rogers what she does to support every student in both academic and social ways. She commented about the poor neighborhoods, the fatherlessness many of her students' experience, and how she is the only bright spot in the day for many of her poor students. Finally, she expressed that if his daughter needed special attention she would work at providing it, but she was vehement against the idea that she marginalized any of her students. Out of frustration, Mr. Rogers retorted, "You're not the savior of these children! Your intentions to help only confuse and isolate my daughter because you look at her as a poor, helpless, loveless, creature that needs you to provide, protect and love them. That's not your job." At this Mrs. Jones was visually shaken and perplexed. She had good intentions and just wanted to provide a safe, academically rigorous, and nurturing environment. The image that Mr. Rogers and his daughter had was not the image Mrs. Jones had of herself or her purpose for teaching at Bandy.

Analysis

Mrs. Jones embodied the savior/rescuer identity that many White women teachers unwittingly bring into low wealth, urban schools. It is an identity that says, "I am here to provide you with protection, opportunities, and provisions in order to save you from your current environment." Endemic in this identity is a deficit perspective that says to the students, "You need me to save you from your culture and lifestyle because mine is better and more sophisticated." Though Mrs. Jones went in with good intentions to help students, the absence of double image consciousness catered to the lack of —and desire to develop—socioracial knowledge of her students and school community. In addition, Mrs. Jones used as her teaching motivation the basic plot of overcoming, where she was the protagonist "called" to overcome the antagonist of poverty and low culture through the injection of her cultural ways of knowing and behaving. This major plot is often undergirded by the theme of good over evil where Mrs. Jones was casted as the good overcoming the bad in the students. While Mrs. Jones undoubtedly saw herself as a rescuer and good person, Jasmine saw her as a misguided teacher that hurt more than she helped. Mrs. Jones could not accept the image of a hurtful teacher because it wasn't her intention to marginalize non-White students. However it is important, to note that since a constructive academic relationship was not formed between Mrs. Jones and her diverse students, the image of misguided and hurtful was not only a relevant description, it was true in the eyes of the diverse students in the classroom.

Trope 2: Ms. Scott

Abigail Scott taught 7th- and 8th-grade language arts at Centrum Middle School. After completing her student teaching at Centrum, she realized it wasn't where she wanted to work. However, she was offered the language arts job before she graduated and accepted. Ten years later, and after winning many district awards as a language arts teacher, Abigail felt that teaching at Centrum was a good decision. Though she lived 45 minutes away, she knew that the distance, trek through traffic, and navigation through low income and dilapidated neighborhoods was her mission. She believed that she carried the keys to successful promotion, high school matriculation, and eventually a good career. Abigail often repeated to her diverse students that if they were able to master the English language in both verbal and written context, they could rise above their present conditions. She felt that it was her destination to share her knowledge and skills with her students. She taught both the low and high performing seventh and eighth graders. Though Centrum was a school of 1,000 students from eight different countries (mostly Central America and Somalia), it had a predominately White population of 52% and a sizable African American population of 28%. Many of the White students lived in low-income homes on the fringe of the school community and were on the free or reduced lunch program. Though the students shared similar socioeconomic characteristics and community situations, Abigail's high performing seventh and eighth graders were all White. She orchestrated the class makeup because it was her vocation and belief that diverse students needed differentiated lessons.

Two days after a snow break, Abigail arrived to school 55 minutes late and missed her first period 7th-grade class. Her class was covered by Trisha, a Hispanic women who had taught 6^{th-}grade language arts for 8 years. There were 26 students in the class and they were African American, Hispanic, and Somalian Americans. It was clear to Trisha that the students were not performing at the level she knew they could and she was surprise to see some of the students in Language Arts 1 because she recommended that they be admitted to Language Arts 3. As she went about the room helping students understand the writing assignment, she made a note to ask Abigail for a rationale about her recommendations. After school, Abigail came to thank Trisha for covering her class. Trisha took the opportunity to ask Abigail why several students in her first period language arts class were not in the advanced class despite her recommendation. Without hesitation Abigail responded that it was her calling to help diverse students understand the mechanics and operations of the English language, and in her experience teaching all her diverse students in the same class was the most effective way to provide them with the differentiated lesson they required. Trisha was astonished to hear those words and she challenged Abigail's presumption. The challenge was met with great resistance, and since Abigail was the chair of the department she brushed off Trisha's concerns. For 10 years Abigail worked at Centrum by choice and she was sure that her mission and methods helped many diverse students pass and do well in high school.

Analysis

Ms. Scott perpetuated the missionary/helper identity with a strong and well-intentioned personality that was driven by a moral assignment. It is an identity that says, "My mission is to leave my familiar, to trek the distance, drive through the blight, try to understand the unfamiliar, and arrive at my destination to deliver my experiences, resources, and hope." Without a mature double image conscious, Abigail's disposition can be construed as normal, supportive, and in some ways as a sacrifice. However, a more critical analysis of her behavior reveals self-fulfilling bias that is an attribution based on an elitist and oppressive disposition. Abigail framed her position as a teacher in the quest plot where she was the protagonist setting out on an important mission while facing objects, trials, and tribulations. This is a common narrative for White women teachers who presume that they can bring a sense of hope to a community they do not know, are fearful of, and have no interactions with. The culture of power that permeates whiteness enabled Abigail to control the narrative about her image and to retreat from the gaze of Trisha's socioracial perspectives. In this sense, Abigail actively resisted the development of double image sensibilities to reinforce the trope as "helper of" and "missionary to" diverse students.

CRITICAL REFLECTIVE PRACTICE

The tropes played by both Mrs. Jones and Ms. Scott may be common in multiethnic classrooms. The savior/rescuer and missionary/helper tropes are different sides of the same coin. Both tropes are linked to the notion of superiority and support the ideals of self-sacrifice. In addition, the savior/rescuer and missionary/helper tropes paint the picture of nobility and goodness that afford many White women teachers' a social and moral rationale for working in diverse low-wealth schools. Unfortunately, the narrative of White nobility and goodness for teaching in "these schools" is couched in the prejudicial attitudes of whiteness that perpetuate the dominance and hierarchy of racism. Therefore, it is imperative to support the development of double image consciousness so that White women teachers can combat the lure of detrimental and racist tropes.

Prior to developing double image sensibilities, however, it is important that Mrs. Jones and Ms. Scott participate in critical reflective practice. Critical reflective practice will enable White women teachers the capacity to "navigate racism, fears, prejudice, and ignorance" in an effort to "critically assess personal motives and beliefs (Hancock, 2011, p.108)." Reflective practice as a tool requires teachers to scrutinize their epistemologies, deep-seeded beliefs, and self-perceptions. It has the capacity to expose unconscious motives and hidden agendas as teachers investigate questions like:

- Why do you believe what you do about "diverse" others?
- What supports your beliefs?
- Who do you believe yourself to be?
- What do you believe others think about you?
- Why do you teach in multiethnic environments?

Critically reflecting on self in multiethnic context can usher teachers into an understanding of the educational benefits of double image consciousness. In addition, deep self-examination helps develop cultural competence toward personal epistemologies. A critical awareness of self also imbues White women teachers' with a capacity to reflect on how diverse students perceive them, which in turn may have a great influence on their ability to form constructive academic relationships.

Critical reflective practice undergirds the development of double image consciousness, which acts to dismantle prejudicial attitudes that support whiteness as superior. When White women teachers possess double image consciousness they are able to form constructive academic relationships with all students.

CONSTRUCTIVE ACADEMIC RELATIONSHIPS

Before constructive academic relationships are realized, White women teachers must participate in critical reflections in order to develop a healthy and realistic double image of themselves as it relates to the community of their students and families. Double image consciousness as a conceptual framework has as a core function to dismantle aspects of deficit ideology. For example, White women teachers who are unaware of how they are viewed by diverse students lack a critical perspective of themselves that will enable them to promote equity in their classroom. Contrarily, White women teachers who possess double image sensibilities understand how deficit ideology frames perspective of others and work toward building genuine relationships with students to influence constructive and personally congruent perspectives of themselves. Although building genuine relationships should start with double image sensibilities, there must also be an understanding of the dynamics of the teaching and learning relationship.

Pianta (1999) contends that relationships between teachers and students are essential for relevant learning and adapting in schools. In my experience teaching in diverse public schools, I found that the primary issue in the classroom was the interaction between students, teachers, parents, and the curriculum. While these interactions are commonly overlooked or taken for granted, the implications these interactions have on learning are far-reaching. School relationships are established through consistent and continuous interactions that center on behavior, communications, and boundary codes (Pianta, 1999). As a result, teachers must combat deficit ideology and be cognizant of prejudicial behavior and communication patterns as they relate to forming constructive academic relationships. For me the term constructive academic relationships is based on interactions between students, teachers, parents, and the curriculum. Though the concept of relationships in schools has been comprehensively researched, the framework for academic relationships is couched in antideficit ideology or equity consciousness that encompasses concepts of language, values, and experiences.

Language in this framework is multifaceted in quality and comprehensive in scope. Meaning the multifaceted quality of language is seen as a tool for communicating, a conduit of power, and a method for empowerment. Comprehensively, language as a tool for communicating encompasses the micro and macro conversations within the academic relationship as well as nonverbal expressions and communicative patterns and styles that are consistent and continuous. As a conduit of power, language can either perpetuate hierarchy through deficit perspectives or it can empower students and teachers through validation. For example, at the core of the academic relationship is the curriculum. When the curriculum is written in ways that disenfranchise language patterns and structures through the perpetuation of one "right" language pattern, the curriculum writers have used the power of language to support deficit ideologies. Conversely, when the curriculum is inclusive of language patterns and structures of varying cultures, students, teachers, and parents are empowered and validated in their cultural epistemologies. Practically, the use of books, poems, storytelling, lyrics, and stories that support a variety of language patterns can offer an inclusive and affirming view of language in the academic relationship. In essence language represents the cognitive component in the constructive academic relationship framework (CARF).

Important to the constructive academic relationship framework (CARF) is also the concept of values. Values in CARF refer to the beliefs and moral imperatives that support quality and mutually beneficial interactions. First, moral imperatives in this framework include trust and respect. Trust between teacher, student, parents, and the curriculum is only developed when there is a confidence all entities are striving for the same outcome. For example, when teachers genuinely work to align the curriculum to sustain the identity of students and families, students and parents are more apt to trust and participate in the academic relationship. The basic idea behind respect in academic relations rests in the act of appreciating what students, parents, teachers, and the curriculum brings to the interaction. It is important, however, to note that respect doesn't always mean agreement. Second, the beliefs that are perpetuated by the curriculum and that of parents, students, and teacher must be known. Oftentimes in classroom settings the beliefs of the teacher trump student, parents, and even curricular convictions about teaching and learning. Since beliefs are a catalyst for classroom culture, it is tantamount that multiple convictions are accepted and validated.

Experience in CARF involves the complex, cultured, and varying escapades that are seminal in the lives of teachers, students and parents. Many schools are governed by a White middle classed notion of important experiences. Tests are created, assignments of developed, books are written, and curricular are developed based on the seminal experiences of White middle-class lore. For example, students are often prompted to write about their summer vacation at the beginning of the school year, or to write about skiing, and horseback riding; some activities and objectives require students to have background knowledge in summer camp activities or passes to amusement parks; however the most problematic experiences are perpetuated when students are tested on material that wasn't covered in the curriculum, at home, or by the teacher. Hence, it is imperative that seminal experiences that are common for all students and families in the classroom must be established. CARF suggests that when the experiences of students, parents, and teachers are aligned with the curriculum, strong academic relationships can be formed.

NARRATIVE: ACADEMIC RELATIONSHIP

Katie was a newlywed and she was getting use to her new last name, identity as a wife, and position as a 5th-grade teacher in an inner city school. At 24-years-old, Katie was experiencing many new identities, and though she was prepared to be called by a new last name and readily accepted her identity as an elementary school teacher, she was not prepared, however, to be identified as a racist. But on an unseasonable warm day in December when she'd believed that there was a strong and nurturing culture in her classroom, she overheard a couple of her Latino students say, "She don't care about us cause we don't speak good English, that's racism." Katie was devastated to hear the candidness and certainty in the voices of her 8- and 9-year-old students. She believed that her actions toward all her students were equal and fair. She couldn't imagine how students could make such inaccurate accusations about her character. Katie pondered how to address the students in an effort to clear up their confusion about her identity and image. During free play later that afternoon, she called the two students to her desk and asked if she treated them badly. Michael bluntly stated, "Every time you correct us, you tell us that our language is bad and improper and you mock my family when you act like our culture is unimportant and un-American. You don't know us!" Katie was even more shocked at Michael's analysis and accusations.

As the dismissal bell rang, she thought about Michael's proclamation, "You don't know us!" She thought deeply and realized that she didn't know her Hispanic students as well as she knew her White students. Even though the Hispanic students represented one-third of her class, she had not developed strong relationships with them. As she thought about her interactions with her Hispanic students, it became clear that they were unconsciously marginalized. While she provided them with dual language activities, she spent little time in face-to-face discussions and support. They were visibly invisible in her class. Katie used language as a form of hierarchy and she promoted experiences that were common in middle-class ideology. Unfortunately, Katie did not develop constructive relationships with her Hispanic students and consequently experienced what happens as a result.

Analysis

Examining Katie's class provides insight into her ability and desire to develop academic relationships. As a teacher, she had not critically reflected on her attitudes toward her Hispanic students, nor had she thought about how they viewed her. Both reflective practice and double image consciousness were unknown to Katie. As a result, there was no genuine academic relationship developed. The development of constructive academic relationship involves participating or being aware of school and home experiences that are seminal in the lives of teachers, students, and parents. In addition, critical self-examination helps develop understanding of personal epistemologies in an effort to form meaningful interactions with students.

CONCLUSION

It is evident that American schools are based on a White, middle-class ideology, and consequently schools value the knowledge base, beliefs, and perspectives of such a culture. Students who live outside of the White culture, like all children, come to school desiring affirmative academic relationships. It is because schools are based on a White, middle-class ideology that diverse students are marginalized, and in some instances pitied or blamed for not being literate of the White middle-class language, values and experiences. The development of double image sensibilities that support the development of constructive academic relationships are imperative if White women are to be successful at navigating oppressive and segregationist ideals that are endemic of the White, middle-class ideology in American education. Double image consciousness strengthens the capacity for White teachers to critically reflect on self as it relates to developing constructive academic relationships with diverse others in multiethnic classrooms.

White women teachers must clearly and vehemently oppose the attributional biases that support the savior/rescuer or missionary/helper trope, while suggesting that diverse students and families are somehow less studious than White students. To subliminally harbor such ethnocentric thoughts, or to not oppose it consciously, perpetuates a meritocratic, classist, and racist ideology that fosters deficit thinking toward culturally diverse students. The duplicitous rationale that purports Whiteness as normal and right, strengthens racist identities. In fact, resistance to the antiracist ideology is sustained by dysfunctional academic relationships that allow White women teachers the capacity to hold on to privilege and power. It is the work of double image consciousness that dismantles deficit orientations and racist ideals toward non-White students in an effort to establish constructive academic relationships. In instances where teachers, students, parents, and the curriculum participate in genuine and beneficial interaction, the issues of missionary or savior trope can be mitigated. However, in the absence of double image awareness White women teachers will only form superficial and tolerant relationships with their diverse students. Consequently, due to the absence of a constructive academic relationship, no matter how hard some students try to learn they will never become fully invested in the classroom culture. Not because they can't, but because the teacher has not reached the student to create a bridge to the culture of academics. It is imperative that White women teachers, and indeed the education community, understand that diverse students must not only learn to navigate a new language pattern, they must also become acclimated to a new system of values and experiences all while also trying to learn the complexities of the curriculum.

REFERENCES

Brown, E. L., Kanny, M. A., & Johnson, B. (2014). "I am who I am because of here!": School settings as a mechanism of change in establishing high-risk adolescents' academic identities. *The Journal of Early Adolescence, 34*(2), 178–205.

Carroll, S. (2014). The construction and perpetuation of whiteness. *Journal of Unschooling and Alternative Learning 8*(15), 92–116.

Gordon, E. W. (2014). *Pedagogical imagination a conceptual memoir: Using the master's tools to change the subject of the debate.* Chicago, IL: Third World Press.

Hancock, S. D. (2011). White women's work: On the front lines of urban education. In J. Landsman & C. Lewis (Eds.), *White teachers diverse classrooms: Creating inclusive schools, building on student diversity, and providing true educational equity,* (pp. 93–109). Sterling VA: Stylus.

Hancock, S. D., & Allen, A. (2015). Common threads: Culturalized patterns and conceptual understandings of race, research, and the politics of schooling. In S. D. Hancock, A. Allen, and C. Lewis (EDS), *Autoethnography as a lighthouse: Illuminating race, research, and the politics of schooling,* (pp. 3–9). Charlotte, NC: Information Age.

Pianta, R. C. (1999). *Enhancing relationships between children and teach*ers. Washington, DC: American Psychological Association.

Seidl, B., & Hancock, S. D. (2011). Acquiring double images: White preservice teachers locating themselves in a raced world. *Harvard Educational Review 81*(4), 687–709.

Van den Berg, L., Denessen, E., Honstra, L., Voeten, M., & Holland, R. (2010). The implicit prejudiced attitudes of teachers: Relations to teacher expectations and the ethnic achievement gap. *American Educational Research Journal 47*(2), 497–527.

CHAPTER 5

DOING WHITENESS IN THE CLASSROOM

White Liberal Pedagogy and the Impossibility of Antiracist Subjectivity

Amy Brown
University of Pennsylvania

Naomi Reed
University of California, Los Angeles

Tears welled up in Ms. Carr's eyes, as she said:

> I have been thinking of nothing other than this conversation for the past week. I feel extremely misrepresented, and I feel like this is a witch hunt. Maybe I'll look like a White savior when I [tell you] all the things I've done to connect with students in my 5 years, and honestly, I bled out for those kids because I love them. You don't become a New York City public school teacher for the money. You don't do it for the prestige. You don't do it for the hours. You do it for the kids!

She continued, crying:

White Women's Work: Examining the Intersectionality of Teaching, Identity, and Race
pp. 87–106

> The fact that you sort of end these case studies, you know, in your own words, saying, essentially, teachers like Lisa and I dehumanize our students! Amy, I was like, the genocides that happen in our world dehumanize, prison camps dehumanize … I mean, God forbid, are you saying I treated the students like animals? I find Barbara to be like insanely, inspiringly in touch with her White privilege … and I find Martina's work with young women to be absolutely really inspiring, so … I don't want to diminish any of that, so, but I say, like, we all grapple with it, we all grapple with it!

This follow-up conversation with Marie Carr, one of the teachers whom Amy focused on, was the most painful, but also the most eye opening interview of Amy's 2-year ethnographic study of the College Preparatory Academy (College Prep), a traditional public high school in New York City where she was also a teacher.

In this chapter, we examine data on the racialization of Black students that can occur when a White female teacher uncritically attempts to employ liberal or "emancipatory" curricula. We use the classroom observations of a White teacher that were collected by another White teacher and ethnographer to show a need for a methodological response to this often racist classroom phenomenon. This exchange between a White teacher and Black student can be understood through notions of neoliberal multiculturalism (Hale, 2005, 2006). More specifically, we demonstrate how an ethnographer's skill in dealing with issues of critical reflexivity can inform and train White teachers in urban classrooms to question their own subjectivities and be open to other worldviews, namely their students'. In collecting and analyzing this data, Amy, a White female teacher/ethnographer, grapples with her own whiteness through a lens of neoliberal multiculturalism. She recognizes that there are limitations on how she can move beyond the privilege that she embodies, but does not use this recognition to fuel political paralysis. Instead she occupies the role available to her and is simultaneously critical of it as she acts. This becomes an ongoing response to what Robyn Weigman calls the "impossibility of antiracist White subjectivity" (1999).

For this chapter, we analyze data gathered from one participant, Ms. Carr, one of the White teachers whom Amy focused on for her original study, and then conducted a follow up interview with in 2013. Based on a case study of Ms. Carr we explore the possibilities for methodologies that inspire White women to grapple with privileged subjectivities, and to become comfortable with the discomfort of White positionality in and beyond the classroom. When we employ the term White positionality, we are referring to a racially and/or ethnically White individual's lived experiences specifically with race and racism and engagement (in this case) in the classroom with non-White students.

Rather than merely criticizing the ways in which neoliberalism manifests on a macrolevel scale, this chapter not only interrogates the ways in which whiteness and neoliberal subjectivity work together to shape the local politics and actions of a White female teacher, but also demonstrates how neoliberal subjectivity, if occupied and critiqued, can serve as a space for resistance and critical emancipatory pedagogy. These data demonstrate the ways in which White teachers' good intentions and comfort with liberal politics can problematically exceptionalize them from their own complicity in White supremacy. In other words, their acceptance of the superficial diversity of neoliberal multiculturalism can lead them to occupy a subject position that furthers, rather than undermines, racial hegemony, often under the guise of liberal social justice.

KEY QUESTIONS

The question we ask here, and the question that the liberal White women at the head of many classrooms must ask, is "how"? How can liberal White women reconcile themselves with the impossibility of the antiracist White subject (Wiegman, 1999), and get to the point where they are comfortable fully engaging and embodying the discomfort of White subjectivity? With full awareness of anthropology's past as a colonizing discipline, and of anthropologists' reticence at taking a position on the politics and practices of the communities we study, when "studying up" (Nader, 1969), what responsibility do anthropologists have to take on subjects who are in positions of privilege and power as "pupils" who might become practiced at self critique and at "speaking truth to power?" What potential does the qualitative researcher have to be both an observer and a teacher, in the interest of working toward a more humanizing, equitable and just world? These questions formed the crux of Amy's approach to using her ethnographic data to interrogate, with Ms. Carr, the relationship between privilege and authority for White women in a neoliberal educational context, and represent one possibility for the use of collaborative qualitative methods as a tool to critique whiteness.

AN INTRODUCTION TO MS. CARR

Originally from a small, predominantly White town in the northwest, Ms. Carr was in her fourth year of teaching history at College Prep when Amy interviewed her. She gives colleagues the impression of being well-organized, businesslike, and efficient at work: unlike other teachers, she seems, even at moments when she is not in front of College Prep students, to be utterly focused on her job. She avoids bringing her work home, grading and writing lesson plans in one of the teacher's offices in the building, or working in her classroom. She spends long hours at the school as a result, and she told Amy that she is usually there at least until 5:30 P.M., and sometimes as late as 9:00 P.M. This, she explained in a follow up interview in 2013, was because at the time that Amy interviewed her and sat in on her classes, Ms. Carr was the school's testing coordinator, and was also finishing her master's degree. She frequently woke up at 4 A.M. to study, was at school from 8 A.M. to 7 P.M., and then studied again from 7 to 9 P.M. Additionally, she, explained, she graded 3,000 papers a marking period (she taught 100 students, and each student turned in 30 papers). Explaining this schedule to Amy, she mentioned that she knew that she was not the only person at College Prep who experienced these kinds of demands on their time.

In a move to further separate her work and home life, Ms. Carr is invested in being an effective and engaging pedagogue, but purposefully maintains some emotional distance from students. She spoke about this in the follow-up interview, and she explained her reasoning. When she started teaching, she started as a long-term substitute teacher:

> All the kids that nobody wanted to deal with from other classes got pushed into my class … I was green, like I was brand new … [the kids needed nothing more than a] seasoned teacher, and so I spent a lot of time just talking with [them], and there was this one kid that I'll never forget, James Gilbert, and every time I would go out for a coffee, this kid would beg me to get him a coffee. Anyway, this kid opened up to me about his life. Within a three-month time span, his brother was shot outside of a Kennedy Chicken and killed and his mother was killed in a collision with a taxicab. All I could do for days was go home from work and then sob my eyes out. And like, my father called me one time while I was in the middle of this crying … and he said "Look, you either need to toughen up or you need to find a new job" … I know that not all of our students are gonna have situations like this, but the fact that this kid was coming to school every day, I was like, oh my God, I feel like I have something to offer, like I am very sensitive but I am very strong. Very stable, very consistent. I am not going anywhere, I have a big heart, and I am bright, so I feel like I have a lot that I can offer and so that was why I felt like, you know what, I want to do this work, but I have to figure out a way to manage my time and also like manage these relationships in a way that I don't burn out because if I burn out then I am not gonna be a teacher who is in that school for 20, 30 years, and that was my goal.

Ms. Carr sees teaching as a lifelong career, but knows that the system is not necessarily conducive to that, for her, both in terms of time management and managing her personal connections to students. While one might read her regimented schedule and her somewhat purposeful distance from students as embodying a corporate or neoliberal ethic, Ms. Carr reveals that she does not see teaching as a step to some other career path, and therefore does her best to ensure her own longevity for the sake of students whom she cares a great deal about, and who deserve a seasoned teacher.

Ms. Carr tries to maintain a balance of being encouraging with students and making sure that they are following her expectations of discipline. When students accidentally mispronounce words in the textbook, Ms. Carr encourages them for trying, using phrases like "you're doing great," or "you have a sense of it ..." She expects students to be physically and intellectually engaged in her class at all times, and she corrects students explicitly if she sees them slouching or if they put their heads down (e.g., "Natalia, can I see you sitting up? It's an expectation."). Ms. Carr also quickly corrects students who are having side conversations (e.g., "The more you talk the less chance you have of sharing." "Ladies, if you are going to continue this conversation, it's not going to be in my room, it's going to be somewhere else." "If you are going to give me an attitude, you're going to do it in the dean's office.") Most times, students concede to her expectations.

CONTEXT: COLLEGE PREP AND RESEARCH METHODS

College Prep opened as part of former New York City Mayor Michael Bloomberg's New Century Schools Initiative (NCSI), in which he and former schools' Chancellor Joel Klein (with the support of philanthropic finding from the Gates, Carnegie, and Soros foundations) opened hundreds of small, themed schools of choice, many of them in New York City's poorest neighborhoods (Shiller, 2011). College Prep opened its doors to its first 9th-grade class in 2004, and added a new 9th-grade class each year. When Amy began to conduct research there in 2008, there were 458 students enrolled at the school. Eighty-one percent of the school's students identified as Black, 17% identified as Hispanic, 1% as Asian/ Pacific Islander and less than 1% as White or American Indian (NYSED, 2008, 2009). Approximately 78% of students qualified for free or reduced price lunches. Out of 35 teachers, 23 identified as White, seven as Black, two as Hispanic or Latino and three as "biracial" or "mixed race." Of 23 White teachers, 13 identified as female.

The school's high student graduation rate (93%) and college matriculation rate for seniors (97%) stand out as compared to New York City's average graduation rate of 62.7% (New York City Department of Education, 2010). This is largely due to the school's acquisition of resources, including a well-staffed college office; classroom supplies (LCD projectors, interactive whiteboards, mobile and standing computer labs); and support for extracurricular and summer activities for students. College Prep was able to acquire these extra resources and support due to an in-house nonprofit organization created in 2008 (The Foundation) in order to solicit donations from the private sector. Contributors to the school included the Gates Foundation, the Robin Hood Foundation, and a Manhattan corporate firm (The Firm) that also acted as a partner in founding the school. Especially because of its entrenchment in marketing itself as both needy and deserving of corporate and philanthropic funds (Brown, 2012, 2015a, 2015b), College Prep was an especially interesting location to explore the implications of White liberal politics and social justice ideologies in education; the school's theme statement integrated ideas about social justice, and many of the school's teachers and funders saw themselves as contributing to social justice. However, as Amy has asserted elsewhere (Brown, 2012, 2015a, 2015b), it seemed that the school's dependence on corporate philanthropy actually furthered and reified social inequalities: in other words, rather than working toward social equity, the school's existence depended on a hierarchy of elite, White corporate donor, savior teacher, and needy but deserving, Black or brown college-bound students in order to exist. This dynamic strongly influenced the pedagogical choices and politics of teachers at the school.

Amy's data, part of a larger ethnographic study, come from 2 years of ethnographic research, including participant observation of the school's students, staff, parents, and alumni; informal and formal ethnographic interviews; focus groups; Freirean cultural circles; a school-wide student questionnaire; and documents and materials related to the school's curriculum, pedagogy, and fundraising events. As Amy focused closely on White female teachers, she conducted, recorded, and transcribed interviews with each of the 13 White women at the school. Each of these interviews lasted between 1 and 2 hours. She also observed each of their classes at least once. She focused more closely, and conducted more regular (weekly) classroom observations of, four of the teachers for a semester. Parents, colleagues, and students saw each of the four women that she focused more closely on as effective teachers: students demonstrated evidence of learning in each of their classes and each saw herself as a social justice educator. In addition to conducting classroom observations of these teachers, she observed these teachers at staff events and faculty meetings, and paid close attention to what colleagues, students, and parents said about them. Importantly, as mentioned above, Amy conducted follow-up interviews between 2011 and 2014 with three out of four of the White women whom she originally focused closely on. Inspired by the engaged, activist research of Sherry Marx (2006), Amy wondered what the possibilities activist and antiracist qualitative work held for White female teachers who struggled with the politics of their positionality in urban classrooms.

RESEARCHERS' POSITIONALITY

Amy began teaching in Brooklyn in 2003, but taught English and conducted research at College Prep from 2008–2010. She identifies as a White, middle-class woman, and she grew up in a small, college town in central Pennsylvania. Her own positionality and experience formed the foundation of her interest in White female teachers. Growing up, her classmates and teachers were predominantly White. Race, never mind whiteness, was never a topic of conversation, and it wasn't until she was an undergraduate that she had a teacher who was not White, and took classes that specifically engaged race. As we know, this experience was not unique to Amy; in fact, White teachers, mostly women, are at the head of most classrooms in the United States (Picower, 2009), and we still struggle to develop a way to have conversations that explicitly and productively problematize structures of both U.S. and global White supremacy. As a former New York City Teaching Fellow (she entered the program in 2003), Amy became interested in the race and gender dynamics of White women at the head of urban, predominantly Black and brown classrooms, especially in the wake of alternative teaching certification programs and the trend of hiring younger, inexperienced often White teachers in charter schools as a "reform" measure in urban education. What were White women doing as teachers and as race-makers—both intentionally and unintentionally as agents of a failing state, and/or agents of increasing privatization or marketization in education? Despite what may be the best of intentions, what kinds of visible and hidden curricula were present in White women's classrooms that worked to perpetuate already present inequities and hierarchies? Amy's race and gender positionality as well as her training as a race scholar and anthropologist seemed to aid her during qualitative observations and interviews with White women, who oftentimes discussed their discomfort in talking about race in racially mixed company. Especially in the context of College Prep, where White women by and large had good intentions, but found comfort and escape in an ostensible kind of "neutrality" or objectivity in the "colorblind" classroom as they taught students to be "professional" (Brown, 2012) and upwardly mobile in the context of neoliberalism, Amy's positionality served to tease out sometimes uncomfortable conversations about race—always the elephant in the room (Jackson, 2008; Pollock, 2008).

Not so similarly, Naomi has always been aware of race. Coming from an interracial home and moving through life as a Black biracial woman who sought to understand race more critically, she was relieved to find that through anthropology one not only gains the tools to deconstruct major social and political categories like race, but also learns to apply these tools to others' subjectivities as well as one's own. Naomi's work has long dealt with White elite students in Houston, Texas, and their epistemologies of race and privilege that inform perceptions of blackness (Reed, 2013). Throughout this research there has been a desire to extend critical racial knowledge to the White elite teachers whom she was working with. As mentioned before, however, there did not seem to be a method that was "ethically" accepted in traditional ethnographic studies that aided in this type of knowledge transfer. The critical turn in cultural studies in fact discouraged this linear exchange of knowledge that was so common during modernization (Van Loon, 2001). Naomi immediately recognized that studying up creates a very different power dynamic between researcher and informant and pushed her research participants on this issue. For example, she asked one of the teachers why he was so relaxed about her presence in his classroom. He responded, "I am a White male teacher that the parents love and there is nothing you can do to threaten my job." Although there is much to unpack from this statement, and the gender privilege that he asserts and possesses does not apply to White female teachers, his recognition of the fact that he is in a position of authority and Naomi's subjectivity (which is of course exacerbated by Naomi's blackness, and perhaps the fact that she was in her late 20s) as an ethnographer does not threaten or overpower that in any way is important to note. It was this moment that allowed for perhaps a new turn in ethnography. Naomi consequently at the end of the year gave a small lecture and had a meeting with him and revealed her findings about his own racial epistemology, much like Amy did with Ms. Carr.

We feel it is time within studying up projects to use this shift in power that has, in some sense, leveled the exchange between researcher and participant, to demonstrate to White female teachers that critical thinking about one's own subjectivity, privileges, cultural blind spots, and epistemologies of race is something ethnographers are trained to do, regardless of our backgrounds. It is also a skill that ethnographers can offer to those whom we study, especially in the context of neoliberal multiculturalism (Hale, 2005, 2006), which we explain in greater depth in what follows.

CASE STUDY: MS. CARR

When Amy asked Ms. Carr to describe the school culture, she said that it is

> Pretty positive. We try to maintain cordial relationships with the students, that we say hello and how are you, and, you know, we follow up with each other, we try to interact with the kids on, you know, on a personal level in terms of like, oh, did you get new glasses, they look really nice, or like, great job at the game, but maintaining a nice professional distance in order to show them what that looks like and what that feels like to have a professional relationship with someone. Kids understand that there's the importance of getting into college and everyone is college motivated and they look to us as models for what that could mean for them.

This description is backed up by how she interacts with students: In her initial interview with Amy in 2009, she described her interactions with students as cordial while maintaining a "nice professional distance." She expects students to rise to her academic expectations, and to see her as a model for how to be a "professional." As Amy has documented elsewhere (Brown, 2012), professional behavior and language were part of the overt curriculum for students at College Prep; teachers, including Ms. Carr, gave students a daily "professionalism" grade for students' conduct. Usually, teachers at College Prep carried a clipboard with them in class to deduct "professionalism points" from students when teachers interpreted students' behavior as "unprofessional." Students could lose professionalism points, negatively affecting their marking period grades, but could not earn professionalism points. Although there was a rubric for professionalism in the ninth grade in 2010, Ms. Humphries, an administrator at College Prep, called professionalism "nebulous" and "hard to define." Often, points were taken away from students for language, speaking volume, or dress that teachers viewed as inappropriate. Sometimes, one student wrote on a school-wide student questionnaire administered in 2010, professionalism points were taken from students for "not directly looking at a teacher during a lesson." Professionalism points at College Prep functioned to further a narrative of color- and class-blind, neoliberal meritocracy; that is, if Black and brown students could perform professionally enough in the eyes of the (predominantly White) institutional authorities, then they would be recognized in the "real world," by the eyes of the state, as legitimate subjects, transcending their race and class positions without a critique of ongoing racial hegemony and inequity. Through adopting the language of professionalism, Ms. Carr sees it as her job to "give students the cultural capital to belong" [in the middle class]. This ties into the class culture that Ms. Carr, with the best of intentions, sees as vital for students to learn in order to be successful in college or careers after they graduate from College Prep, but at the same time represents a tension between the school's ideology of neoliberal saviorism and the importance of valorizing and affirming the (non-dominant) cultural capital that students may bring (Carter, 2003). In the end, it rearticulates the same ostensibly diverse, but fundamentally inequitable and uncritical power dynamic of neoliberal multiculturalism, and further insulates Ms. Carr's subject position therein.

An urban school such as College Prep can be said to be a multicultural neoliberal institution in that this school's overall agenda is purportedly to maximize the urban student's individual opportunities in a global and professional future workforce. The focus on individual success is of course neoliberal, and not very different from the ways in which public school education has shaped American students for years (Foley, 2010; MacLeod, 2009), but as teachers like Ms. Carr prepare Black and brown students at College Prep through manipulation of students' dress, vernacular, values, and other cultural aspects of their developing identities, we see the ways in which neoliberalism injects itself not only into the cultural realities of urban students and progressive White teachers, but also the ways in which Ms. Carr must situate her progressive ideals within the neoliberal agenda. More specifically, if Ms. Carr wants the state to recognize her as a progressive teacher and maintain her position as an educator in this system, she must embody progressivism in a particular (racially ambivalent) way. Ms. Carr's eager acceptance of College Prep's goals is not only evidence of her uncritical "dehumanizing" of her students and their realities, but it is also a necessary step in her own process in becoming a recognizable individual in the neoliberal American school system. For Ms. Carr to criticize College Prep for blindness towards the racial injustice that is perpetuated within many urban schools would be to commit a form of suicide as a multicultural neoliberal subject; the state would no longer recognize her, and her progressivism would no longer be valid. On the surface, her acceptance of College Prep's agenda is, in fact, progressive; we don't immediately recognize that individual freedom and social justice do not always go hand and hand (Harvey, 2005).

MS. CARR AND PARENTS

Ms. Carr told Amy that although she thought that she and the school do a satisfactory job of connecting with parents, that sometimes she had a hard time getting in touch with parents and that when she did, it could occasionally be "unproductive." When Amy asked her to elaborate on this, she shared an anecdote about one student who she sent out of class for being disruptive during a quiz. When she called the student's home, the student's mother "screamed" at Ms. Carr and said that her daughter hadn't done anything wrong. She elaborated on this, however, in the follow up interview, stating that this was not at all the case with most parents. In fact, she took several students on an international trip and was in frequent contact with each student's parent or guardian over a period of months. She said that these interactions were overwhelmingly positive.

Ms. Carr sees her mission as a history teacher at College Prep as "peace through education, and preparing my students for global citizenship and leadership in the 21st century [to be people who can] can transform and not just react." She told Amy that she will help students to gain the tools to break down stereotypes that others might form about them; although, she said that many people will see College Prep students and will "type" them as "at-risk" or as not ready to be competitive in the 21st century, she felt that the rigor of her class at College Prep, and others like it, would help students to be able to ascend class and status hierarchies. The school's ideals, she said, contributed to her opinion that this school is, in itself, an act of social justice, and is a place with the highest aims for both teachers and students. Ms. Carr does not come by this mindset as a result of coming from a privileged background; rather, she told Amy in their 2013 follow-up interview that her upbringing was very challenging. She grew up in a working class family. Ms. Carr described her mother as unstable, and as someone who alienated her from her father. She elaborated: "I mean, I had White privilege, that's for sure ... and there was definitely a college going expectation even though I paid every penny myself. The opportunities that I saw the students were able to have at College Prep were the things that I never even dreamed of." She sees College Prep as representing possibility for students because it offers opportunities she didn't have. She is aware of a world beyond College Prep where opportunities often come to those who have already had them. She believes in the neoliberal mission of College Prep because it represents an unfair and challenging reality.

While Ms. Carr acknowledges her White privilege and names her experience of oppression as forming the foundation for teaching students how to properly function in the context of neoliberal multiculturalism, her response to inequity is ambivalent and partial. She does not see it as her duty to challenge her own, or her students', or their parents', subject positions within the context of the neoliberal state. Rather, her duty is to teach students to embody acceptable subject positions within this context. In doing this, she also embodies an acceptable, liberal White subject position, which is especially gendered because she does this through a particular mode of pedagogical "caring" (Toshalis, 2011). If caring White teachers like Ms. Carr can teach students to be professional enough, in other words, they may gain the opportunity to become recognizable as marketable subjects in the context of neoliberal hegemony (Demerath, Lynch, & Davidson, 2008). The narrative that College Prep sells to its funders emphasizes the fact that the school (not students' parents or communities) is responsible for professionalizing and teaching its students to embody acceptable neoliberal subject positions. Thus, while it is standard and, in fact, expected for College Prep teachers to communicate regularly with parents, the school (and thus, many of its teachers) does not see it as a priority to include and actively collaborate with parents, especially in undermining a fundamentally unjust and unequal system.

CONCLUSIONS: MS. CARR

Ms. Carr places great faith in the school's curriculum and extracurriculum as libratory for the students who are willing to take it in. While this may be true for some students, it is important to remember that a minority of students are chosen by staff members to enjoy the privileges of the school's extracurriculum (after-school programs, internships, mentoring activities, trips). Amy's interviews with Ms. Carr inspire important questions about the mechanisms by which structural privileges and oppressions work in the United States, and about the role of agency in those structured oppressions. Ms. Carr both embodies and complicates the trope of the White neoliberal subject in urban schools. Precisely because College Prep's students are Black and brown and come from a public school in New York City (although not all are poor or working class), the ways that they must move throughout the world as young people, and someday as professionals, will be different from the ways that Ms. Carr will ever have to move. In her follow up interview, Ms. Carr brought up a point that many White liberals, especially in the context of segregated Black and brown schools wrestle with:

> How do we talk about race in a way that takes teachers who have a lot to bring to the table but who are still in conversation with themselves and with society about what White privilege means, about who they are as White women, how do you construct courageous conversations about race that actually are courageous and honest? I can say that the fear of feeling like there's a witch hunt that if you, as a seeker, as someone who is trying to learn more, that if you say the wrong thing, that a scarlet letter is gonna be put on your back and people are gonna chase you out of the school for, like, saying the wrong thing, like, it's terrifying!

Ms. Carr represents teachers who are, as Ms. Carr puts it, "not perfect" but are "always trying to do better." This represents an important aspect of Ms. Carr's ideology, and of our analysis. On one level, Ms. Carr wants to explore the difficulty of the ways in which whiteness impacts her students, her colleagues and her teaching, but also expresses fear and awkwardness around raising the issue.

Ms. Carr engaged with and cared a great deal about her students, and continually wrestled with finding productive ways to work toward becoming an excellent and humanizing practitioner in the context of White supremacy and neoliberalism. Ms. Carr stated a self-reflexive desire to push herself to get to the point where, in relation to racial politics, she is more "evolved," "open," "present," and "plugged-in." She expressed that she felt maligned by the first version of Amy's manuscript, and expressed fear that she would be seen by colleagues, especially Black colleagues, as uncritical and dehumanizing of students. "How can I," she asked, "as a White woman, fully understand the Black experience in this country? And I don't want to offend anybody, but through my own lack of understanding I just want to grow." She spoke in our follow-up interview about reading and learning from Caribbean women's literature in graduate school:

> These women, even though they were conversant in Creole, they chose to write in French because it was the language of the controlling class and by subverting that way and by using that language against their oppressor they were able to be heard by writing, so I mean if I can, like, essentially, I am not giving them a voice, but if I can help them find their voice ... figuratively just as an educator, like I don't know another way to do it like just as an educator, with the tools that I've been taught, to help them find those tools, they can use them, and when they themselves can access the halls of power then they can write new rules.

Here Ms. Carr expresses a nascent critique of the inequities that are produced and furthered in a neoliberal context, yet also expresses reluctance and fear of taking on the system herself. This manifests through her belief in the impossibility of radical social change. She wrestles with, in her words, how "deeply" to get into social problems of racism and inequity with students because,

> When you are 17, you are supposed to be young, motivated, hardworking, idealistic, goal setting, dreaming, living into an as yet unwritten future. You are the author of your own life, you've got all this creative potential, I mean, obviously you don't want to push them off a cliff into this complete shock of a reality, but I don't think the students are unaware of the fact that life isn't fair.

Ms. Carr's fundamental belief in the power of the individual to be the "author" of his or her own life and ambivalence about addressing social inequality represents a kind of buy-in to color- and class-blind neoliberal subjectivity that both allows Ms. Carr to preserve herself, and does not lead her to take responsibility for social change, or to delve more deeply into her White liberal discomfort. The conversations she had with Amy about the manuscript led her to begin the discomfiting process of analyzing her own disposition toward her students and herself in the context of neoliberal multiculturalism.

WHAT IS A NEOLIBERAL MULTICULTURAL SUBJECT?

Ms. Carr struggles to make sense of Amy's read of her liberal pedagogic approach to urban classrooms. Her instinct is to claim that her hands are tied or that the only other option available to her is political paralysis. She feels that the claim of antiracism being impossible for her as a White woman is unfair, but we are asking that she consider her positionality in the classroom in tandem with this statement. We are asking that she and other White women teachers "occupy" and hold in tension the liberal tendencies that are more legible to the multicultural neoliberal state with a more critical understanding of race and whiteness as she moves forward. We are not asking Ms. Carr to dismantle White supremacy, but we are asking that she be critically aware of the White supremacy that she and any other White teacher embody. Cultural identity in a multicultural state is no longer a singular phenomenon that all citizens embody, rather there are many "cultural" ways to be. Neoliberalism over time begins to absorb and incorporate these cultural varieties into its ideological pull on agents of the state such as indigenous populations or in this case teachers and urban students (Povinelli, 2002). Neoliberalism, in this sense, begins to shape the cultural material of the individual, so that an indigenous group or a student who is to be interpolated by the state must embody the state's imagined form of their cultural identity (Althusser, 1971; Hall & Du Gay, 1996) without a shift in racial hegemony (Hale, 2006).

In fact, in his discussion of the Ladino/Maya divide in Guatemala, Hale (2006) writes of a divide that is characterized by Ladinos both positioning themselves as culturally superior and harboring deep anxieties about Maya ascendancy, but at the same time being cautious advocates of multiculturalism. Reluctant to forego their social position, Ladinos endorse diversity, but do not support any overall shift in power. Hale categorizes this as *racial ambivalence*, that is, "[embodying] desires for two incompatible social outcomes: [Ladinos] want to shake free of their racist past, to live according to a more egalitarian ideal; yet they also believe, and continue to benefit from the structured belief that Ladinos are *más que un Indio*" (Hale, 2006, p. 11). In other words, Mayas are "allowed" by Ladinos in Guatemala to have their own "culture," but "paradoxically, these egalitarian sensibilities do not require Ladinos fully to acknowledge ongoing relations of racial dominance, much less to dismantle them" (Hale, 2006, p. 19). Like racial ambivalence, Hale argues, neoliberal multiculturalism embodies a key paradox, an ostensibly "progressive" response to societal ills serves to perpetuate the problem in a new guise (Hale, 2006, p. 12). We see a similar kind of racial ambivalence embodied in U.S. White liberal subjectivity.

Neoliberalism wedded with multicultural identity politics, according to Hale, reimagines the "individual" as a part of "cultural groups." Hale contends that neoliberal multiculturalism is then the political logic of rugged individualism applied to political groups, usually racialized or ethnically specific groups whose cultural identities are determined by the state (2005). Once a multicultural individual is recognizable by the state, he or she must also then adopt the goals that the state has for its citizens in order to participate in economic or social (educational) competition (Hale, 2005). Neoliberal multicultural subjects are then given a choice to either "occupy" the neoliberal subject position that the progressive state offers or go unrecognized and perhaps develop grassroots avenues of success.

PROGRESSIVE WHITE TEACHERS: URBAN ACTIVISTS OR MULTICULTURAL NEOLIBERAL SUBJECTS?

When a teacher's actions are reduced to accountability to the state and not to the vulnerable Black and brown student population (that some teachers, such as Ms. Carr, claim to be serving), then the teacher's actions begin to manifest in a manner recognizable by the state. At the point in which a teacher's activist intentions become co-opted by the state, she is no longer acting on behalf of the students' individual freedoms. Instead, she strengthens her own multicultural neoliberal subjectivity as a progressive White teacher, reifying the state's interpolation of the student as well as herself, perpetuating race and class inequity and the unjust agenda of individual "freedom" in education.

In the context of neoliberal multiculturalism, people are forced to act politically within the confines of the state's notions of valid cultural identity discourse (Hale, 2005; Loperena, 2012). Progressive White teachers like Ms. Carr fall into a neoliberal trap: there is no recognizable way to both be a White antiracist and a neoliberal multiculturalist. Ms. Carr is an example of this as she embodies an identity that is recognizable by the state. For Ms. Carr to truly account for the structural limitations of whiteness with respect to antiracist or racially emancipatory activism, Wiegman (1999) would argue that she would need to be aware of the inevitability of reproducing White supremacy due to the fact that she is a White body operating in a White supremacist space. Ms. Carr, as we saw previously, expressed to Amy on a number of occasions that she feared that her reputation as a progressive teacher would be tarnished if she truly began to publicly explore the contradictions and limitations of her emancipatory impact on the students due to her whiteness. Perhaps this reputation is another name for the state's perception of her? She cannot account for White privilege and racism and at the same time be valuable to the school and to the state. Ms. Carr then must perform progressive White teacher activism in a manner that supports White teachers uncritically offering students training to become "professional" multicultural neoliberal individuals, as well as members of state-approved cultural groups.

Our understanding of White liberal teachers as both activists and also agents of the multicultural neoliberal state puts a new spin on the notion of activists and provides a different type of critique of the "nice" White teacher. We are not invested in making Ms. Carr see herself as an oppressive force representing the state, because she is not that. In fact, she recognizes racism and the problematic ways in which a myth of meritocracy manifests at College Prep, yet feels paralyzed in terms of her options for taking on the system herself. She seems to feel deeply the conundrum of, on the one hand, working through her own racial politics and positionality and becoming an antiracist and also effectively meeting the school's—and the state's—expectations. Rather, we are invested in showing how the state manipulates teachers like Ms. Carr and injects them into a neoliberal manifestation of social justice, perhaps a form of social justice that does not disturb the status quo of the elites, but superficially presents itself as a new avenue for the oppressed to occupy and employ.

RECOMMENDATIONS: FINDING POSSIBILITY IN IMPOSSIBILITY, COMFORT IN DISCOMFORT

In order to understand progressive White women teachers beyond the hegemonic grip of neoliberal self-preservation, we often critique ideology or the state while failing to bridge the "on-the-ground" gap between the agency of the teacher and the powerful ideological pressure placed on the teacher in educational institutions. More specifically, we ignore the very real restrictions that teachers (especially White women teachers) face when trying to make a difference in the urban classroom. We often uncritically leave progressive White instructors' beliefs, specifically about their own subjectivities and their raced limitations in activism, unquestioned. We are then left at an impasse when we see that those teachers' actions and roles within the school and in relation to the students do not truly emancipate, but instead somehow reify dominant oppressions of urban students. It is more difficult to look at the teachers' beliefs and actions, the repercussions of their actions, and the complexity of their actions as a mix of self-preservation and sincere concern for their students under the structural and ideological constraints of the multicultural, neoliberal state.

Ms. Carr, like many educators, wants to be a "good" progressive White teacher at College Prep, but also does not want to throw her neoliberal self/subjectivity under the proverbial (school?) bus (Applebaum, 2005). She wants to "help" students not only for the sake of their own subjective freedom, but also to strengthen her own occupation of her identity as a progressive White teacher within the neoliberal agenda of the school. Neoliberalism requires that teachers within an institution make choices and be accountable for those choices, as those choices will make the teacher recognizable to the state.

Despite expressing a nascent critique, teachers like Ms. Carr also voice frustrations and perhaps even resentment when asked to hold their unyielding subjectivities in tension with their liberal goals and intentions in the urban classroom, because they feel they are doing the best that they can. Even when teachers absorb critical evaluations of their reification of certain power relations and pathologic ideologies in the classroom, they often revert back to the self-preserving perspective that makes their version of (un)critical consciousness acceptable (Marx, 2006), because they and many scholars and activists as well have resigned to the impasse or aporia (Fassin, 2011) of politics. Acceptance of this impasse or inability to go beyond one's subjectivity is especially appealing when dealing with state institutions such as public and chartered schools. In order to begin to cope with this impasse, we recommend that ethnographers help White female teachers to understand and deconstruct their subjectivities in the same way that critical and reflective ethnographers do. More specifically, the training the ethnographers bring to the field can be applied to the classroom, and then used to inform teachers' praxis, including their interactions with students and students' parents or guardians. Critical reflexive ethnographic methods could potentially map out a tangible manner in which White teachers might hold their subjectivity in tension with their liberal goals.

As ethnographers, we see ourselves as dealing with contradictions between our own subjectivities and our goals in the field, in the academy, and in the world. We feel that the push in anthropology to critically reflect on our own privileges and structural identities has enabled us to produce research that at the very least is overtly aware and expressive of the potential reification of structural oppression. We believe that ethnographers can "give" this knowledge to teachers.

Clearly anthropology (and more specifically, ethnography) has a long, arduous and often harmful past with notions of "giving" or paternalism in the field (Clifford, 1988). Subsequently, there has been a long maintained shift in anthropology to be more critical and understand one's informants to be "epistemically privileged" (Alcoff & Potter, 2013) rather than unconscious premodern vessels that need to be "taught" civility. Of course this critical turn, coupled with cultural relativism and notions of "alternative modernities" (Comaroff & Comaroff, 2001) has its place and has done much to push back against the colonial past of ethnography, but this new paradigm, we venture, is not always appropriate when studying up (Nader, 1969).

Studying up can occur in different ways, whether the structural subjectivity of the ethnographer is hierarchically "inferior" to the informants, or whether or not the informants are agents of authority in the world more generally. All teachers, we feel, fit this latter criteria. For this reason, we feel critical ethnographers can perhaps "give" teachers the appropriate tools to employ a more critical self in the classroom if they see themselves as ethnographers, their students as informants, and their classroom as the field. Why exactly do we feel that studying up enables this shift away from the critical turn in ethnography? We observe that if, in fact, epistemic privilege is something gained from below, then the ethnographer, being potentially "below" the informants, in this case, has knowledge that perhaps the elite or authoritarian figure is blind to, due to the unyielding nature of her privileged and empowered subjectivity.

Wiegman (1999) discusses the necessity of all White liberals (conservatives, supremacists, etc.) to recognize the "impossibility" of an ongoing state of antiracism for themselves. We believe that teachers who aim to truly be progressive should recognize the possibility of this impossibility and keep this reality in tension with their political goals (Wiegman, 1999). As we unravel the web of state expectations on teachers, teachers' natural self-preservation, and the truly emancipatory efforts that all teachers continue to employ, we hope to reveal some space within the neoliberal multicultural institution that we as researchers and teachers can occupy and use to actually transform the state and emancipate the urban student. As we see with Ms. Carr, who stated in her follow-up interview that reading Amy's manuscript, although a painful process for her, "definitely raised some points of view that [she] just hadn't considered before," that she "grappled" with what to tell students as they entered what she knew to be an unfair and nonmeritocratic world, and that she struggled with figuring out "what kind of change [she] could effect," engaging with the nuance and complexity of qualitative research provided an opening within which she could consider other uncomfortable possibilities for subjectivity in the context of College Prep. In other words, reading and discussing a qualitative critique helped Ms. Carr to painfully confront, head on, the tension between White liberal interpolation and self-making in the context of state-sanctioned multiculturalism (Althusser, 1971; Hall & Du Gay, 1996). Perhaps, then, qualitative research and whiteness scholarship might move toward taking on the project of encouraging White liberals to go further in vigilantly maintaining their comfort with the discomfort of an inevitably oppressive subjectivity. Moving through and beyond the critical turn represents the possibility for anthropologists who study up to have a powerful and important impact on those whom we study. Whether through one-on-one follow-up interviews, focus groups, book clubs, graduate level classes, or professional development, White women teachers can learn from anthropologists the practice of thinking ethnographically, critically and self-reflexively, thus beginning the struggle to undermine their complaisance in inequity and injustice.

REFERENCES

Alcoff, L., & Potter, E. (Eds.). (2013). *Feminist epistemologies*. New York, NY: Routledge.

Althusser, L. (1971). Ideology and ideological state apparatuses: Notes towards an information. In *Lenin and philosophy and other essays*. New York, NY: Monthly Review Press.

Applebaum, B. (2005). In the name of morality: Moral responsibility, whiteness and social justice education. *Journal of Moral Education, 34*(3), 277–290.

Brown, A. (2012). A good investment? Race, philanthrocapitalism and professionalism in a New York City small school of choice. *International Journal of Qualitative Studies in Education, 25*(4), 375–396.

Brown, A. (2015a). Philanthrocapitalism: Race, political spectacle, and the marketplace of beneficence in a New York City school. In B. Picower & E. Mayorga (Eds.) *What's race got to do with it? How current school reform policy maintains racial and socioeconomic inequality* (pp. 147–166). New York, NY: Peter Lang.

Brown, A. (2015b). *A good investment? Philanthropy and the marketing of race in an urban public school*. Minneapolis, MN: University of Minnesota Press.

Carter, P. (2003). "Black" cultural capital, status positioning, and schooling conflicts for low-income African American youth. *Social Problems, 50*(1), 136–155.

Clifford, J. (1988) *The predicament of culture*. Cambridge, MA: Harvard University Press.

Comaroff, J., & Comaroff, J. L. (Eds.). (2001). *Millennial capitalism and the culture of neoliberalism*. Durham, NC: Duke University Press.

Demerath, P., Lynch, J., & Davidson, M. (2008). Dimensions of psychological capital in a U.S. suburb and high school: Identities for neoliberal times. *Anthropology and Education Quarterly, 39*(3), 270–292.

Fassin, D. (2011) Noli me tangere: The moral untouchability of humanitarianism. In E. Bornstein & P. Redfield (Eds.), *Forces of compassion: Humanitarianism between ethics and politics* (pp. 35–52). Santa Fe, NM: School for Advanced Research Press.

Foley, D. (2010). *Learning capitalist culture: Deep in the heart of Tejas* (2nd ed.). Philadelphia, PA: University of Pennsylvania Press.

Hale, C. R. (2005). Neoliberal multiculturalism: The remaking of cultural rights and racial dominance in Central America. *PoLAR: Political and Legal Anthropology Review, 28*(1), 10–19.

Hale, C. R. (2006). *Más que un Indio: Racial ambivalence and neoliberal multiculturalism in Guatemala.* Santa Fe, NM: School of American Research Press.

Hall, S., & Du Gay, P. (Eds.). (1996). *Questions of cultural identity.* London, England: Sage.

Harvey, D. (2005). *A brief history of neoliberalism.* Oxford, England: Oxford University Press.

Jackson, J. (2008). *Racial paranoia: The unintended consequences of political correctness.* New York, NY: Basic Civitas.

Loperena, C. (2012). *A fragmented paradise: The politics of development and land use on the Caribbean coast of Honduras.* (Doctoral dissertation). University of Texas, Austin, TX.

MacLeod, J. (2009). *Ain't no makin' it: Aspirations and attainment in a low-income neighborhood* (3rd ed.). Boulder, CO: Westview Press.

Marx, S. (2006). *Revealing the invisible: Confronting passive racism in teacher education.* New York, NY: Routledge.

Nader, L. (1969). Up the anthropologist—Perspectives gained from studying up. In D. Himes (Ed.) *Reinventing anthropology.* New York, NY: Pantheon.

New York State Education Department (NYSED). (2008–2009). *New York State school report card: 2010.* Retrieved from https://data.nysed.gov/archive.php?instid=800000081568

Picower, B. (2009). The unexamined whiteness of teaching: How White teachers maintain and enact dominant racial ideologies. *Race Ethnicity and Education, 12*(2), 197–215.

Pollock, M. (Ed.). (2008). *Everyday antiracism: Getting real about race in school.* New York, NY: The New Press.

Povinelli, E. (2002). *The cunning of recognition: Indigenous alterities and the making of Australian multiculturalism.* Durham, NC: Duke University Press.

Reed, N. (2013). *White lies: The White epistemology of race and blackness in a White upper class school.* (Doctoral dissertation). University of Texas, Austin, TX.

New York City Department of Education. (2010). [Home page]. Retrieved from schools.nyc.gov

Shiller, J. (2011). Marketing new schools for a new century: An examination of neoliberal school reform in New York City. In P. Kovacs (Ed.), *The Gates Foundation and the future of U.S. "public" schools.* New York, NY: Taylor & Francis.

Toshalis, E. (2011). The rhetoric of care: Preservice teacher discourse that depoliticize, deficit, and deceive. *Urban Review, 44*(1), 1–35.

Van Loon, J. (2001) *Ethnography: A critical turn in cultural studies.* In P. Atkinson, A. Coffey, S. Delamont, J. Lofland, & L. Lofland (Eds.), *Handbook of ethnography.* Thousand Oaks, CA: Sage.

Wiegman, R. (1999). Whiteness studies and the paradox of particularity. *Boundary 2, 26*(3), 115–150.

CHAPTER 6

"BECKY PLEASE!"

White Teachers and *Their* Issues With Whiteness

Cheryl Matias and Naomi Nishi
University of Colorado, Denver

The new cohort for the Urban Teacher Education program filed into the lecture hall for their first convocation. Malina, a dark-skinned mestiza Filipina Colombian teacher candidate, peered around the room, fidgeting nervously in her seat. As she expected, she was the only person of color in the cohort, including the faculty teaching them. The convocation began with a White female professor asking the teacher candidates to get into small groups and discuss the reasons as to why they want to become a school teacher, specific to urban communities. Malina turned around, hoping to join a group nearby. Instead, she was met with the backs of other White females who have already began excitedly introducing themselves to each other. Without a group, Malina panics. She looks up and catches the eye of the White female professor who was conducting the convocation. The professor moves to the middle of the lecture hall, stops the activity, and announces, "Is there a group open? We need a group for ... what is your name?"

"Malina Lopez," Malina answers.

White Women's Work: Examining the Intersectionality of Teaching, Identity, and Race
pp. 107–122

"What a beautiful exotic name. Does it mean anything?" questions the professor.

"Umm, no. Just a name," Malina responds.

The professor seems pleased with Malina's response and turns to the whole group again and continues her announcement, "Yes, we need Mah / lean/ /uh/—did I pronounce that right? [Malina nods]—to be placed in a group to participate in the activity." After a momentary delay and another prompting from the professor, one group reluctantly raises their hands. As Malina treks to that group under the scrutinizing gaze of her classmates, the professor whispers, "We are so glad you are here and really appreciate the expertise you will bring." Though a bit patronizing, the professor pats Malina on the back and moves off to another group. The chattering picks up and Malina listens in as each of her group mates begin to talk about why they want to become an urban school teacher.

"I want to become an urban teacher because I want to help those who are less fortunate than I was. I totally find myself to be a cultural person and welcome diversity. I used to date a Hispanic man and learned a lot about Hispanic culture so I really know a lot about it," Haley, a White female, professes. Others nod in agreement while Malina takes a deep breath, trying to calm herself down. Back in her mind, Malina cannot help but feel disgruntled when people equate their cultural competency to dating "ethnic" people. "What if I said I knew about White culture because I've dated a White man," Malina thinks to herself.

Another White female teacher candidate named Allison chimed in. "Well, I grew up in a good community in Vermont and I know all about White privilege." [Upon saying "White privilege" the other group mates physically cringe]. "I just thought I need to give back to the disadvantaged. I just hope 'they' don't discriminate against me because I am White." Upon saying this the others chimed in on how fearful they are that the urban students will be prejudice against them because they too are White. Malina closes her eyes, rolls her neck trying to control her discontent, and loosens her shoulders.

In response to Allison's comment about White privilege, Kate, a White female from the suburbs of Chicago that has very few people of color clarifies, "Well, I don't think it's because I'm White, because I grew up in Chicago and it's super diverse there, but some students don't have access to things. Like, supportive parents, or they can't even speak English, so I want to be able to provide those things for students." After saying this, the group starts talking about how urban communities are replete with violence, drugs, and failing schools. Malina, having graduated from an urban high school could not help but avoid eye contact with her peers. To assuage her frustration she starts to physically clasp her hands and rubs them together furiously. She hated how White folks would strategically engage urban cities like Los Angeles, Chicago, or New York as a symbolic marker of their experience with racial diversity. Yet upon further investigation, these students later reveal how they lived in very White communities away from "the City" and its racial diversity.

The fourth teacher candidate adds her answer to the group. "I was in the Peace Corps and worked in Africa for six months. I learned a lot and am ready now to advocate for urban students," professed Rebecca, a White teacher who later divulged she does missionary work throughout what she calls "third world countries." Impressed with her travels abroad, Haley responds, "Wow, Becky, that's amazing. Good for you. Urban students really need people like you. Bless your heart."

It was all too much for Malina. The intoxication of well-intentioned teachers drenched in their do-good whiteness makes Malina snap. She stands up, stares them straight in the eyes, and finally screams out, "Becky please!"

INTRODUCTION

The title of this chapter employs a fictionalized name, Becky, because it has been popularized by the introductory dialogue in the rap song "Baby Got Back" by Sir Mix-a-Lot. In this introduction, two White girls talk derogatorily about the size of a Black woman's rear end, which speaks to their ontological disgust of blackness (Matias & Zembylas, 2014). In fact, at the end of this monologue one White girl says (with great disgust) "She's just so Black." In application, the sardonic, "Becky, please!" then refers to the inner dialogue faculty or students of color may have in direct response to the ludicrous and dehumanizing nature of whiteness exerted. With respect to the previous story, Malina, having survived in a White world, already expects whiteness upon entering the graduate teaching preparation program, and through her interactions with professors and classmates learns that in order to succeed she must navigate it. From her professor's racially microaggressive remarks that both shift the White gaze onto her obviously darker complexion and Spanish sounding name, to her peers' savior-like mentality about helping disadvantaged communities and being apt to do so by virtue of their proclaimed access to "good" education and/or experiences with people of color, Malina is surrounded by White teachers and *their* issues with whiteness.

We the authors, specifically and deliberately shift the theoretical gaze on race away from it being a "people of color problem" to a problem of White folks who invest in their whiteness strictly because focusing solely on the former keeps the permanence of whiteness and White supremacy intact through its silence (Matias & DiAngelo, 2013). That is, although exploring the impacts of racism on people of color helps us understand the dynamics of how race operates and is felt, it is but one side of the racial coin. In order to understand how whiteness and White supremacy are maintained through enactments of racism, we must first examine whiteness and White supremacy itself. As Perez Huber, Benavides, Malagon, Velez, and Solórzano (2011) suggest, racism is just a symptom of the larger disease of White supremacy, we thus begin with the disease itself.

By employing storytelling and poetry this chapter illustrates the commonplace phrases, ideologies, behaviors, and situations that are rooted in whiteness in order to expose how whiteness operates in White teachers and a White educational system. The purpose here is not to demonize White teachers, but to purposefully demonstrate the following:

1. How whiteness is exerted and felt by people of color
2. How White teachers can participate in antiracist teaching practices by critically self-investigating their own investment in whiteness

Simply put, teachers, many of whom are straight White, middle-class females, must, as Helms (1990) argues, take the racial realization journey themselves before they can expect to successfully lead urban students of color. And this journey is imperative for us, the authors, both professionally and personally, because we are educators in higher education responsible for preparing antiracist teachers and are both critical race mother-scholars whose children are or will be enrolled in public schools. The first author of this chapter is brown-skinned Pinay who grew up attending and teaching in public schools in Los Angeles. She is now a professor who teaches classes in an urban-focused, teacher preparation program in Denver and is thus responsible for the next generation of antiracist educators. Since her own children attend the public school system, she is personally invested in ensuring that local teachers have the proper training to positively impact the racial identities of their urban students of color. The second author is considered a White ally who has been working in higher education both as an instructor for aspiring intercultural trainers and a Critical Whiteness Studies scholar. Having taught numerous courses on intercultural training in higher education, she realized how many of her graduate students (many of whom are White), though committed to diversity, refused to talk about their whiteness. Through her experiences, she realizes how problematic it is for intercultural trainers to be equipped with the knowledge of race and diversity if they cannot even engage in a topic about how their whiteness impacts intercultural training itself. As a result, we both are personally and professionally committed to better preparing White teachers/trainers with a deeper understanding of whiteness and how such investment in whiteness ultimately impacts their attempt at culturally responsive, racially just, or antiracist teaching (Matias, 2013a).

THE DISCLAIMER THAT DEBUNKS READING UNDER THE INFLUENCE OF WHITENESS

Before we delve further in understanding whiteness inside White teachers, we are aware that directly positioning this phenomena as a problem causes great discomfort to readers, many of whom are White teachers themselves. First, we acknowledge that whiteness can be embodied in internalized ideologies, behaviors, and emotions within people of color, albeit through a means of survival. Yet, that is not the focus of this chapter. The focus of this paper is how whiteness is embodied in White teachers/educators and how overlooking one's investment in whiteness negatively impacts students of color, and moreover maintains a White supremacist educational system.

Second, the terms whiteness, White supremacy, and White people will be employed in this chapter to illustrate larger racial dynamics. As such, when the term White teachers/educators is engaged, we understand there are various ways that some Whites resist whiteness. However, despite personal and/or individual intentions and actions, White people, in general, still benefit from a White supremacist society. As Allen (2004) suggests, Whites then can be *antiracist white racists* at best because as some Whites defy whiteness in their daily lives they nonetheless continue to reap the benefits of White privilege. Additionally, terminologies like whiteness and White supremacy are often used synonymously. Notwithstanding, we define whiteness as follows:

> If blackness is a social construction that embraces Black culture, language, experiences, identities, and epistemologies, then whiteness is a social construction that embraces white culture, ideology, racialization, expressions, and experiences, epistemology, emotions, and behaviors. Unlike blackness, whiteness is normalized because White supremacy elevates Whites and whiteness to the apex of the racial hierarchy. (Matias, Viesca, Garrison-Wade, Tandon, & Galindo, 2014, p. 290)

One's individual subscription or application of whiteness then, in turn, supports the institutionalization of White supremacy through educational policies (e.g., English only), practices (e.g., standardization, scripted curriculum), and systemization (e.g. tracking, school funding, etc.). For instance, if a White teacher exerts her whiteness ideology by forcibly stopping the use of Spanish in the classroom because he/she believes English is the "proper" language, he/she is more likely to support policies that institutionally ban Spanish altogether. And, since whiteness is the politically dominating culture, it will enact White supremacist policy like English only in classrooms (Shannon, 1995; Shannon & Escamilla, 1999).

Third, as critical race and whiteness scholars, we, the authors, often experience the disgruntledness of readers and audience members, most of whom are White, when we deeply engage whiteness from a person of color perspective, or as Zeus Leonardo once personally told us "from a Black Whiteness Studies." According to the emotionality of whiteness, this is commonplace (Thandeka, 1999). Often invoked from naysayers is how research on whiteness defies methodology or is presumed too theoretical. We find this to be another enactment of whiteness. For when John Dewey, Paulo Freire, and/or Horace Mann investigated the dynamics of education and offered educational remedies in the forms of pragmatic education, socially just education, and/or curricular innovations, they were not challenged on the lack of methodological prowess and/or its overly theoretical disposition. With this in mind, we ask that White teachers who are truly committed to antiracist education remain open to engage the theoretical postulations of this chapter instead of disregarding it because it causes emotional discomfort. In fact, we argue that it is through one's discomfort where one finally learns. As such, feel it; for if one is to feel comfortable, they are simply placating to one's already understood knowledge and ego (see "racial fetish" in Matias, 2015).

"BUT I WAS MARRIED TO A HISPANIC..."

"Don't go there!" retorted Becka, a middle-aged, White female, 5th-grade teacher enrolled in a doctoral class on urban educational justice. Her doctoral classmate, Mirabel, one of the only Latina teachers present in the course, had just dared to suggest that the presence of teachers of color was important, especially for students of color in urban schools.

Becka continued on her reasoning as to why teachers of color are not that important. "Why, just last week a Brazilian teacher asked me to take an Ethiopian kid off her hands because he couldn't speak the language. It was I who told her that of course he could speak Ethiopian. She was the one who said something racist by saying all he does is make sounds! I mean, I took the kid in. I was the one who helped him."

"Well," said Mirabel slowly trying to sidestep the looming rage, "I'm not saying that teachers of color are better teachers, I'm just saying that literature often asserts that White teachers have a hard time understanding the experiences of students of color. I mean, Angela Valenzuela, Geneva Gay, and even Sonia Nieto are just a few scholars who have documented this phenomenon. Honestly, as a Latina, I've had that same experience growing up here in the local public schools."

"Ya, ya, ya. I know you must've had some experiences, but," interjects Becka, "I want you to know that I was married to a Hispanic man for 5

years. And for 5 years I was the one who went to his family reunions, and it was they who wouldn't accept me!" From Becka's extremely resentful tone, her use of past tense, and a quick glance at her bare ring finger, Mirabel assumed that marriage with her Hispanic husband had not ended happily.

Not surprised by Becka's insistence to engage a person of color as a symbolic marker of not being a racist, Mirabel continued. "Becka, thank you for sharing your personal life with us. I was not referring to that. Rather, I was simply articulating how ..."

Mirabel was cut off. Becka seethingly glared at Mirabel and scoffed, "I'm no racist. When I was married to my Hispanic husband, I did everything Hispanic. Listen to music, tried to speak Spanish ... for God's sake I have mixed race kids with Spanish last names!"

"Becka, I never called you a racist. I am talking about the importance of teachers of color and how ...," reassured Mirabel.

"... even my last name is still Spanish—Gutiérrez. Trust me, I know what it's like," continued Becka.

"Becky, please!"

EXPOSING WHITENESS

In this scenario, we see several exertions of whiteness in the form of rhetorical moves (Bonilla-Silva, 2013). The first of these moves is Becka's attempt to shut down the conversation by demanding that Mirabel "Don't go there!" Becka continues to exert her whiteness by presuming what is and what isn't racist. She does this by following up with an example of what we are to presume is a teacher of color who is being racist to a student of color and how she was the White savior. Interestingly, Becka does not identify the race of either the Brazilian teacher or the Ethiopian student, and chooses instead to refer to their nationalities. Yet, given the racial tensions in Brazil between Black and White Brazilians, the question of the racial identity of the Brazilian teacher is noteworthy. Though considered White in Brazil—a racial moniker that affords a different racialized experience—Becka homogenizes Latinos and presumes her to be racially, Hispanic.

Within this rhetorical move, Becka makes two presumptions. First, she presumes the Black Ethiopian student is ignorant and helpless (while strategically framing the Brazilian teacher as the racist; not her). She does this by framing the student as without having language and just making noises. The student has no name, no other characterization. Suffice it to say, the Black student is used as a pawn in the story needed only to redirect the true point of the story, which brings us to the second move. Becka then presumes herself to be the White savior by saving the student from the "true" racist: the Brazilian teacher. She then reiterates how it was her who did the good deed and by doing so, helped "the kid" out. This ongoing rhetoric aligns with whiteness in that White teachers are often depicted as saviors coming into urban schools saving urban students of color (Matias, 2013a). By doing this, White teachers are seemingly absolved of any wrongdoing because the wrong doers are often embodied in the urban students of color themselves. This phenomenon positions these White teachers as White saviors, who in turn pathologize Black and brown student bodies as those representing a deficit and needing help. Yet at the same time these children seem ungrateful for their White teachers' presumed selfless acts and do-good-isms (Vera & Gordon, 2003).

Furthermore, when Mirabel offers explication of the importance of understanding the experiences of students of color, Becka then positions herself as one who understands the experiences of people of color by virtue of her marriage to a Hispanic man. Bonilla-Silva (2013) asserts that Whites who excessively find themselves using the fictive friends of color rationale as a way to validate their antiracist stance are in fact promoting color-blind racism. Simply put, people of color, or in this case, Becka's Hispanic husband, are nothing more than a validation sticker they can wear on their imaginary "I'm not a racist card." In fact, Becka's strategic use of her Hispanic husband (a husband of no name), ups the ante a bit in that she likens her personal marriage to the "I have a Black best friend" rhetorical move. Although Becka's past marriage is likely not fictive in the sense that Bonilla-Silva presents, it nonetheless is used as a way to cast off her whiteness through her nuptials with a man of color. Plainly put, whiteness does not rub off when color enters you. This is proven by Thompson and Collier (2006) who argue that White women in interracial marriages still exhibit racism and exert whiteness even within their marriage. Frankenberg (1993) delves into this deeply in her interviews with White women from various backgrounds who take on an assumed knowledge and even faux identity of color when in a romantic relationship with a person of color. Yet, these same women reveal their whiteness through their stereotypical and demeaning impressions of people of color and/or their color-blind stance.

Becka also gives us a glimpse of her true feelings toward people of color as she accuses her ex-husband's family of not accepting her, presumably homogenizing her family to all Latinos. She could have perhaps shown more disdain if she had referred to "them" as "those people," which she got dangerously close to doing. Becka asserts her privilege in whiteness again by claiming she is not a racist, despite not truly understanding what racism is about. This is tantamount to someone claiming to be an oncologist although they don't believe that cancer exists! How can one who claims to not see race, or explains race is not a problem, then go on to define what is and is not racist? This is an example of letting the blind lead the sighted.

The racial battle fatigue settles in with Mirabel when Becka assumes to know what being Latina is all about because she too has a Spanish last name. By doing so Becka reappropriates Mirabel's racialized experiences to something as trivial as blackface, for it is the entitlement within whiteness that makes Becka assume to know the experiences of Mirabel. Important to note, the life experiences of Mirabel do not equal the Guttierez name Becka adopted upon her nuptials. And this act is what causes Mirabel to say "Becky, please." Tired of Becka's constant play of the White race card, Mirabel revolts. That is, when a White person dismisses a discussion of race or co-opts the experiences of people of color, they ultimately reinforce White norms and White supremacism. Though the experience of people of color are valid counterstories that reveal the nuances of race, racism, and White supremacy (Solorzano & Yosso, 2002), they often get cast as "playing the race card," when coming from a people of color. This is seen when Becka responds to Mirabel's incorporation of her Latina experiences by saying, "Ya, ya, ya" instead of truly validating those experiences. Instead, Becka uses her White race card to position herself as the authority on race and Latino experiences. However, as Leonardo (2009) suggests, playing the White race card is often not identified because of the pervasiveness and power of whiteness. Ultimately, Becka a) controls the dialogue of race, b) denigrates Mirabel and her experiences as a Latina, c) belittles the Hispanic experience, d) redefines race, racism, and racists, and e) upholds White supremacy.

"BUT I VOLUNTEERED FOR OBAMA"

"Excuse me, I have to say something! You keep saying that nothing changes and racism and privilege are always the same, but it's changed! I'm so tired of people acting like racism hasn't changed!"

Nadia blinked at Rebecca, the young White woman, whose face was bright red with frustration. Though Nadia was also a White female, she was not surprised by Rebecca's textbook whiteness behavior. Sadly, Nadia had seen it all too often before in her classes, home life, and in society at large. Being it was an intercultural education course, Nadia found it relevant to introduce the concept of race and privilege; no one even mentioned anything about the change that Rebecca was so obviously angry about. Despite this oversight, Rebecca began screaming, "Racism and privilege have changed and are no longer relevant!"

Exhausted by the repetitiveness of Rebecca's emotional display upon the mere utterance of race and White privilege, Nadia could not help but think,

"That's true for her until someone upsets her White complacency." Rebecca, fighting an internal battle and trying to externalize her fight, shot bullets at Nadia through her hardened face and icy, blue-eyed stare. In the corner of her eye, Nadia caught Rebecca violently shaking her head "no" every time Nadia spoke up in class. Feeling targeted now, Nadia wondered whether she should stop participating in the classroom discussion.

Turning around, Nadia noticed how the two students of color quietly squirmed in their seats, seemingly nervous that Rebecca's race-related rage would soon be redirected at them. Wanting to do more as an ally, Nadia took it upon herself to continue to challenge Rebecca. "Rebecca, I notice that you're getting upset. Why is that? Are you so uncomfortable talking about race that you refuse to turn the microscope on you and look at your own whiteness?"

Looking as if she has just had it with Nadia, Rebecca resorted to a passive-aggressive diversionary tactic of whiteness by refusing to examine her own whiteness and deflecting the issue to why talk about whiteness at all. "Look Nadia, why do we have to talk about race and whiteness, again!?! This is an intercultural education course and it has nothing to do with that. We've already talked about that stuff to death last semester. I'm exhausted!"

Nadia sucked in her breath before replying "You're exhausted?! Exhausted by merely talking about race?! What about the people who are forced to face it every day? Look Rebecca, I know you find it so unbearable to talk about race and whiteness for two hours a week, but rest assured you can return to your whiteness the minute you step out of this classroom. So, stop avoiding the question of how you enact whiteness."

Flabbergasted at Nadia's aggressiveness, Rebecca retorts with "Oh ya?! Well I volunteered for Obama's campaign. What about you?"

Nadia, fed up with Rebecca's whiteness, rolls her eyes and exasperates, "Becky, please."

EXPOSING WHITENESS

The first thing we notice in this scenario is the White emotionality exerted by Rebecca. She makes several emotional, defensive statements to divert from ever talking about the issue of her whiteness. In fact, she controls the discourse of whiteness through her passive aggressive remarks to Nadia, a discursive tactic that keeps her White emotionality intact. Matias and DiAngelo (2013) describe this White emotionality as White fragility that results when a White person's position and beliefs on race are challenged by a person of color, or by another White person who is daring to upset the racial contract (Mills, 1997). Within this racial contract, racism and White supremacism are accepted as the status quo. As such, those who broach the subject in ways that unbalance the status quo are met with hostility and great defensiveness. This White fragility relies on the racial comfort of Whites where critiques to whiteness are left unvoiced (DiAnglo, 2011). The consequences of upsetting this White racial complacency can be violent in various ways (Leonardo & Porter, 2010). The threat to White fragility can also provoke what Matias and DiAngelo (2013) describe as a "latent mob mentality." And, in this scenario, we see the students of color squirming in their seats, not because they are surprised by the conversation or emotional outburst, but because they know from experience that this vehemence can quickly turn onto them. However, the vehemence will be more compounded for those two students of color because of the fact that there is often a White majority in college classes. And this realization alone undergirds the creation of a rhetorical White lynch mob mentality.

More evidence of upsetting White fragility can be seen in Rebecca's misplaced argument. Instead of recognizing Nadia's conversational contribution by introducing race and White privilege, Rebecca exerts her whiteness by putting words in Nadia's mouth, claiming that she's tired of hearing that nothing's changed. This "white neurosis" (Matias & DiAngelo, 2013) is when those entrenched in whiteness get so convoluted in the lie of whiteness that they a) hear what they want to hear about race and b) get tongue-tied because they choose to hear what they want to hear, often delivering an illogical statement in a sort of defensive hysteria. Bonilla-Silva (2013) characterizes this behavior as a White defensive mechanism to maintain color-blind racism. In this mechanism, the White speaker gets so lost in a flawed argument that she/he succumbs to fear and emotions, ending up with a White-speak that becomes illogical (at best) and gibberish (at worst).

The next tactic Rebecca then employs is one of closing the conversation altogether. She seems to realize that she has met her match in Nadia, and that Nadia is not going to be intimidated back into a silence or color-blind philosophy (Bonilla-Silva, 2013). Therefore, Rebecca—acting as the discussion dictator—commands that they drop the topic because she (assuming that whiteness makes her the center) has already talked about race and privilege in her previous class. And with this line of reasoning, since Rebecca has talked about it before no one else needs to talk about it now. It should come as no surprise that Rebecca's act of whiteness would be exhausting for her; her short discussion about race gets at the crux of how she is exerting her whiteness on the entire class, a realization that is too much to bear. Additionally, with regard to the narcissism of race, Rebecca then only prefers to talk about the "good intentions" she has (such as working for President Obama's campaign) instead of acknowledging the racially microaggressive impacts she leaves behind.

Notwithstanding, Nadia identifies Rebecca's exertion of whiteness and refuses to acquiesce to it by pointing out that the exhaustion that Rebecca is feeling is minuscule when compared to the racial battle fatigue (Smith, Hung, & Franklin, 2011) that plagues people of color. Racial battle fatigue is the physical, emotional, and psychological exhaustion that plagues people of color as a result of myriad racial microaggressions, confrontations, and violence encountered on a daily basis in a White supremacist society (Fasching-Varner, Albert, Mitchell, & Allen, 2015). Nadia goes further by calling Rebecca out on her tactics. By explicitly describing Rebecca's strategy to evade a conversation on race and why she continues to wriggle out of the dialogue, Nadia makes Rebecca rightfully uncomfortable by placing a mirror in front of her. Because Rebecca is more comfortable within her bubble of whiteness—where she is not questioned on her privilege and how her racial positioning contributes to the marginalization and indeed oppression of people of color—Rebecca exerts her whiteness to refuse to answer the question.

Although the scenario is but a snippet of the reality of White teachers learning about race, we could presume a few endings. One, Rebecca soon after this discussion walks out of the class. This is often seen in antiracist training courses conducted by Jane Elliot (https://www.youtube.com/watch?v=TZKWkhnSb5k). Or, perhaps Rebecca feels entitled to continue arguing with Nadia, hoping that the other White classmates will come to her aid (as seen in Matias, 2014). Or, finally, Rebecca breaks into tears after her final statement, and her White classmates who are socialized to see the weeping White woman as a symbolic marker of extreme pity (Matias, 2013b) begin to comfort her. While providing such comfort, the class exchange daggered-eye glares at Nadia that say, "How could you?"

At any rate, Rebecca pulls out her White alibi (Leonardo & Zembylas, 2013), where she invokes her work and support of Obama, the United States' first Black president, as the reason why she cannot possibly be racist or participate in a racist system. This rhetorical maneuver parallels Becka's strategic insertion of her "Hispanic husband" in the earlier scenario and are both employed as White, neoliberal argument stoppers. Simply put, such a stopper really says, "Don't question me about race! My best friend is Black (Bonilla-Silva, 2013), my husband is Hispanic, my cousin is mixed, I volunteered for Obama!" Of course, even if any of these claims are true (although Bonilla-Silva showed that they are often fiction or exaggerated), they do not mean a thing when engaged for that purpose. For instance, former Clippers basketball owner, Donald Sterling, was involved with a woman of color. Yet, that did not stop him from spewing his hate speech against Black men. Obviously, the strategic employment of one's affiliation to a person of color is nothing more than a racial fetish (Matias, 2015) used to assuage the emptiness of those who adopted the inhumanity of whiteness.

The truth is, most White people have some sort of justification that they use to excuse themselves from being part of the problem of racism and White supremacism, and White women are no exception (Frankenberg, 1993). They too have White alibis (Leonardo & Zembylas, 2013) that are used to convince themselves and others of their righteous intent. But like Swiss cheese, there are holes in these arguments. And these holes, as Thandeka (1999) suggests, are filled with lie after lie, a process that eventually undergirds the White ethnic shame produced in White teachers.

YOU'RE KILLIN' ME, SMALLS: WARNINGS FROM THE "BECKY PLEASE" CROWD

You call this saving education?
When you tell me it's not all about race you tell me to deny my life;
When you tell me to it's more about class you ignore your own white privilege;
When you tell me I'm important but refuse to listen to my story
you deny me my validation;
When you tell me to sit down and listen to the lesson,
you assume you have a lesson to teach;
When you tell me to get out of your class, you deny me a proper education;
When you tell me I need to try harder you deflect your responsibility to do better;
When you tell me I'm just sensitive you choose to protect being white;
When you tell me you care but assume I'm a thug you lie to yourself;
When you tell me you can't teach it because
that's not standards you show me your laziness;
When you tell me to stop talking about race you strategically kill my voice;
When you tell me I don't want to hear about race anymore you oppress me;
When you make me believe you're here to save me you murder our souls.

This poem is an illustrative response to what happens to students of color when White teachers leave their whiteness intact. In fact, as critical race scholars we argue that this same response can be said for people of color, writ large, when dealing with people who subscribe to the whiteness ideology in any field. Whiteness becomes debilitating when White teachers assume they can pick up more strategies and techniques on how to deal with students of color. In fact, the whole notion of "dealing with" students of color is the wrong mindset. As professors, our predominantly White teachers often complain about learning about race, racism, and White supremacy in education particularly because it does not offer strategies on how to "do it right." They ask, "Just give us the strategies so that we can work with students of color." To get at the absurdity of the question we sarcastically mock, "Do you have a checklist to deal with your partners? Do you have a checklist to deal with your mothers? Do you have a checklist to deal with your best friend (not the fictive Black one)?" Simply put, if a White teacher truly wants to engage in a racially just education, she/he must stop believing that a checklist will cure all. As Freire (1993) or hooks (1994) so cogently argue, the humanization process of teaching and learning happens when an educator develops a relationship with his or her students. And in developing any relationship—whether it is lover, friendship, or parent—no checklist is needed. Rather, one needs to deeply invest in cultivating a mutually beneficial relationship. And that is a human dynamic that cannot be captured through some standardized checklist.

Another warning White teachers must take is that no amount of education will prepare them for the journey of teaching and learning if they refuse to begin with the self. That is, instead of fixating their teacher preparation in the hope of accumulating culturally responsive pedagogies, multicultural education, and/or antiracist teaching strategies, White teachers need to begin with an honest self-reflection on their own White selves. Accumulation of strategies is rendered useless if White teachers do not check their whiteness and realize how it impacts their pedagogies, teaching, and learning. Simply dismissing its relevancy and importance is worse. The K-12 schooling system (and we would argue college teacher preparation programs as well) is almost 90% White (NCES, 2012), and yet with all these "strategies" the persistence of the "achievement gap" continues in racially obvious ways. As such, to dismiss the saliency of how race impacts that achievement gap perpetuates systemic racism. In order to move to a more racially just educational system, we must touch upon the disease instead of narrowly focusing on the symptomatic outcomes, such as the racialized achievement gap.

Sadly, despite these statistics and racial realities, society still often overlooks the topic of race, and more specifically that of whiteness and White supremacy, because the mere utterance of those words make White teachers cringe. And in silencing topics of whiteness, society elevates the feeling of cringing above the devastating reality of Black and brown students failing. As educators committed to the academic and personal progress of our students can we not reconsider what is really worth cringing about here? Is it too much to ask and demand an answer to "Why are you cringing over a word?" Because if cringing is the reason for refusing to learn, shouldn't we reconsider who's really doing the teaching? Again, this chapter does not intend to demonize White teachers. Rather, in order to expose the mechanisms of whiteness in teaching and explore how White teachers can be a part of the racially just process, then the issue of whiteness must be directly taught. To that, we know many White teachers who are ever committed to dismantling racism and White supremacy. But for those who are just beginning we say, "Becky, please … learn about yourself first."

AUTHORS' NOTE

To Malina, Noah, Elisa, Benjamin, and Linus. Know that we will do everything to protect you.

REFERENCES

Allen, R. L. (2004). Whiteness and critical pedagogy. *Educational Philosophy and Theory, 36*(2), 121–136.

Bonilla-Silva, E. (2013). *Racism without racists: Color-blind racism and the persistence of racial inequality in America*. Lanham, MD: Rowman & Littlefield.

DiAngelo, R. (2011). White fragility. *International Journal of Critical Pedagogy, 3*(3), 54–70.

Fasching-Varner, K. J., Albert, K. A., Mitchell, R. W., & Allen, C. M. (Eds.). (2015). *Racial battle fatigue in higher education: Exposing the myth of post-racial America.* Lanham, MD: Rowman & Littlefield.

Frankenberg, R. (1993). *White women, race matters.* Minneapolis, MN: University of Minnesota Press.

Freire, P. (1993). *Pedagogy of the oppressed,* (M. B. Ramos, Trans.). New York, NY: Continuum.

Helms, J. E. (1990). *Black and White racial identity: Theory, research, and practice.* Westport, CT: Greenwood Press.

Hooks, b. (1994). *Teaching to transgress.* New York, NY: Routledge.

Leonardo, Z., 2009. Race, whiteness, and education. New York, NY: Routledge.

Leonardo, Z., & Porter, R. K. (2010). Pedagogy of fear: Toward a Fanonian theory of 'safety' in race dialogue. *Race, Ethnicity, and Education, 13*(2), 139–157.

Leonardo, Z., & Zembylas, M. (2013). Whiteness as technology of affect: Implications for educational praxis. *Equity and Excellence in Education, 46*(1), 150–165.

Matias, C. E. (2013a). Check yo'self before you wreck yo'self and our kids: Counterstories from culturally responsive white teachers?... to culturally responsive White teachers! *Interdisciplinary Journal of Teaching and Learning, 3*(2), 68–81.

Matias, C. E. (2013b). On the flip" side: A teacher educator of Color unveiling the dangerous minds of White teacher candidates. *Teacher Education Quarterly, 40*(2), 53–73.

Matias, C. E. (2015). White skin, Black friend: A Fanonian application to theorize racial fetish in teacher education. *Educational Philosophy and Theory.* doi: 10.1080/00131857.2014.989952

Matias, C. E., & Zembylas, M. (2014). "When saying you care is not really caring": Emotions of disgust, whiteness ideology, and teacher education. *Critical Studies in Education, 55*(3), 319–337.

Matias, C. E., Viesca, K. M., Garrison-Wade, D. F., Tandon, M., & Galindo, R. (2014). "What is critical whiteness doing in our nice field like critical race theory?" Applying CRT and CWS to understand the white imaginations of white teacher candidates. *Equity & Excellence in Education, 47*(3), 289–304.

Matias, C. E., & DiAngelo, R. (2013). Beyond the face of race: Emo-cognitive explorations of White neurosis and racial cray-cray. *Educational Foundations, 27* (3/4), 3–20.

Matias, C. E. (2014). "And our feelings just don't feel it anymore": Re-feeling whiteness, resistance, and emotionality. *Understanding and Dismantling Privilege, 4*(2), 134–153.

Mills, C. (1997). *The racial contract*. Ithaca, NY: Cornell University Press.

National Center for Education Statistics. (2012). *The condition of education 2012* (NCES 2012-045). Washington DC: U.S. Department of Education.

Perez Huber, L., Benavides, C., Malagon, M., Velez, V., & Solórzano, D. (2011). Getting beyond the "symptom," acknowledging the "disease": Theorizing racist nativism. In S. R. Harper & S. Hurtado (Eds.), *Racial and ethnic diversity in higher education* (3rd ed., pp. 925–936). Boston, MA: Pearson.

Shannon, S. M. (1995). The hegemony of English: A case study of one bilingual classroom as a site of resistance. *Linguistics and Education*, 7(3), 175–200.

Shannon, S. M., & Escamilla, K. (1999). Mexican immigrants in U.S. schools: Targets of symbolic violence. *Educational Policy, 13*(3), 347–370.

Smith, W. A., Hung, M., & Franklin, J. D. (2011). Racial battle fatigue and miseducation of Black men: Racial microagressions, societal problems, and environmental stress. *The Journal of Negro Education. 80*(1), 63–82.

Solorzano, D. G., & Yosso, T. J. (2002). Critical race methodology: Counter storytelling as an analytical framework for educational research. *Qualitative Inquiry, 8*(1), 23–44.

Thandeka. (1999). *Learning to be white: Money, race, and God in America.* New York, NY: Continuum.

Thompson, J., & Collier, M. J. (2006). Toward contingent understandings of intersecting identifications among selected U.S. interracial couples: Integrating interpretive and critical views. *Communication Quarterly, 54*(4), 487–506

Vera, H., & Gordon, A. (2003). *Screen saviors: Hollywood fictions of whiteness.* Lanham, MD: Rowman & Littlefield.

CHAPTER 7

THE MURKY AND MEDIATED EXPERIENCE OF WHITE IDENTITIES IN EARLY CHILDHOOD

Erin Miller
University of North Carolina, Charlotte

It is a familiar narrative. Over and over, professional literature cites concerns about young White women in teacher education programs as resistant toward learning about race and racism (Gomez, 1996; LaDuke, 2009; Sleeter, 1993; Tatum, 1992, 1994), noncritical of their own racialized identities (Barnes, 2006; Gay, G. & Kirkland, K., 2003; Milner, 2006), and adept at using strategies such as silence, separation and deflection (Case & Hemmings, 2005; Nash, 2013; Nash & Miller, 2015) in conversations about racial inequities. The concerns are well-justified as we consider the consequences when new teachers enter a profession where there is a great need to challenge inequitable schooling practices and policies (Gangi, 2008; Reid & Knight, 2006; Souto-Manning, 2009). Consequently, much has also been written about how teacher education programs might help preservice teachers build knowledge about race and racism (Cochran-Smith, 2000, 2005; Milner, 2003, 2007; Solomon, Portelli, Daniel, &

White Women's Work: Examining the Intersectionality of Teaching, Identity, and Race
pp. 123–144

Campbell, 2005). However, little has been written to provide insights for teacher educators about how White women have been racialized from early childhood. This chapter argues that bringing such information to the forefront in programs of teacher education could support deeper, keener theorizing about White women and the complexities of White women teaching in culturally diverse classrooms, and tells stories about learning to be White providing straightforward examples to help us more clearly recognize the lessons learned by White children who may one day grow into contemporary White women teachers.

Findings from this nine-month ethnographic study offer a careful look at messages of whiteness, which I define as the implicit normalizations of the oppression of persons of color as they are taught and learned in childhood. Relevant to understanding how to address the perceived reticence and resistance of White women who comprise most teacher education programs, these findings make visible the ways that White women teachers may have been socialized into whiteness from early childhood, ways they developed the enculturated and deeply held beliefs that ultimately shaped their embedded adult views about race. Thus, this chapter's focus on the ways young White children are "raced" or the ways they learn whiteness has the potential to shed light on elements in cycles of socialization (Harro, 2000) that lead human beings to develop unexamined racist dispositions. This, in turn, can help us—teacher educators and school leaders—garner insights about White women teachers and teachers of color who have internalized White normalization, as we search for, recognize, face, and interrupt nuanced manifestations of racism in our work with our nation's children.

METHODOLOGY

Research Questions

Using critical ethnography methodologies (Carspeken, 1996; Ellis, Adams, & Bochner, 2011) and pattern analysis techniques (Grbich, 2007) to gather and examine data over a nine-month period of time, I studied the experiences of my three young children (ages 6, 7, and 10) as they constructed, deconstructed, normalized and/or resisted messages of whiteness. I was interested in how young children developed their understandings about race, and whiteness in particular. Specifically, I asked: What can I learn about the dominant discourses that shape three young White children's construction of race, particularly what it means to be White?

Primary Participants and Methods

The primary participants were my three children: Ella (9-years-old), Olivia (6- to 7-years-old), and Max (5-years-old). Because of its focus on White women, this chapter focuses on data from the two girls, Olivia and Ella. Data were collected in many of the places/settings/events in which my children engaged during the course of their day-to-day activities in our hometown of Columbia, South Carolina: the car, dance studios, church, family gatherings, bath time, play at home, etc. The primary methods for data collection were a) audio and videotaped recordings, b) ethnographic field notes, c) photographed artifacts, and d) my researcher's journal.

I chose to study my own children because a) they self-identified as being White, b) they were growing up in a mostly White community (which is representative of the communities of many preservice teachers), and c) I understood the potential for insights (not accessible by other researchers) through my daily and intimate access to their worlds. The study of my own children is situated within a rich tradition of rigorous and highly-regarded parent-child studies (Haddix, 2014; Leopold, 1949; Long, 2004; López-Robertson, 2014; Martens, 1996; Miller, 2014; Piaget, 1974; Weir, 1962), all important contributions to the field of qualitative methodologies and early childhood education "because [they] deal with core process of intimate, unexpected encounters" (Baghban, 2014, p. 149). As with any qualitative work, the insights gained are not posited as generalizable, and while it is important to acknowledge issues of parental power in the study of my children, as a critical ethnographer I recognize that issues of power and voice exist in any research whether parent-child, teacher-student, or adult-adult.

Data Analysis

The data analysis process began as I uploaded audio and video data and field notes and transcribed data using the NVivo 10 software program. Guided by Glasser and Strauss's constant comparison approach (Grbich, 2007), I read and reread the data and developed preliminary categories (patterns and anomalies to those patterns) generating folders to house preliminary themes. I also ran word frequency queries, tree diagrams, and color-coded node strips. As new relationships were formed in the data, categories were collapsed or expanded until I felt I had exhausted my data and was comfortable that the categories were representative of my findings (Agar, 1996). During this process, I also recorded reflective notes in my researcher's journal (Bogdan & Biklin, 2007).

Situated in a New Wave of White Teacher Studies

The concern from which this study was built did not originate in a desire to understand overt racism. I wanted, rather, to know how whiteness is learned in small, usually unnoticed and mundane ways during the early childhood years. I wanted to understand how, beyond explicit racist or antiracist teachings, my children were raced and how we appropriated that learning in our lives. With those understandings, I wanted to better understand what might lead White preservice teachers to seem to express discomfort and resistance in the study of race and education. My hope is that this work will provide a contribution to a new wave of studies of White preservice teachers that moves from merely characterizing White resistance as a manifestation of White privilege (McIntosh, 1988) and focuses on identity as stages (Hardiman, 2001; Helms, 1990; Miller & Fellows, 2007) to a research that emphasizes the complexities of White identifications (Jupp & Slattery, 2010) as connected to life history and an archive of becoming rather than being. As such, I share data from the lives of White children from the stance that they were/are becoming White through particular racialized messages, which I call discourses, in their world.

LITERATURE THAT GROUNDS THIS WORK

This work is grounded in two major assumptions: a) White people in America became White through a complex social ordering system based on social and material exclusions of anyone who was defined as non-White, and b) young children learning to become White are socialized in overt and covert ways into the ways of whiteness.

The Historical Construction of Whiteness

This study is primarily situated in the body of work called whiteness studies as explored as a sociohistorical construction. In conversations about White women teachers, this becomes a salient lens because White women are a part of a larger social milieu and their identities are in a process of being shaped everyday through their participation with their environment. Moving away from static definitions of whiteness helps us understand how White women teachers are continually constructing, deconstructing, and reconstructing themselves in their work in urban education. Thus, attention to the social construction and fluidity of whiteness can prove insightful, beginning with the creation of whiteness itself.

According to Allen (1994), the American White race is an invention of the plantation bourgeoisie who needed a way to excuse the enslavement of Africans. To justify such oppression, this small, elite class readily accepted and perpetuated the existence of a biologically predetermined social ordering system based, in part, on the pseudo-science of craniology, wherein those who came to be known as Caucasian, or originating from the Caucasus Mountains in the present day area of Southeastern Europe and Asia were thought superior to humans from other parts of the world because their skulls were classified as larger and more beautiful than skulls from other parts of the world (Gould, 1993; Hodl, 2002). This theory justified upper-class European economic privilege gained by exploiting and enslaving those who came to be known as non-Caucasians. Realizing the fragility of their dominance, the ruling elite create race as a social division—using the pseudo-science of craniology—and was reinforced with the most rigid distinctions between persons of African and English descent. While other groups (i.e., Irish, Jewish, and Italian immigrants) have not always been considered White (Brodkin, 1998; Ignatiev, 1995; Jacobson, 1999), over time they have been able to assimilate into whiteness and thus enjoy the privileges (if not material, then psychological) of being White.

Contextualizing whiteness in this historical context serves two purposes when theorizing about White women teachers: it offers insights into the social construction of race and it offers possibilities for broader conceptual understandings of race and racism, because White women identities are understood as malleable and contextually defined—that is, what it means to be White is understand by what it means not to be White in a particular context. Specifically related to White women then, I posit that they have been enveloped in socially constructed whiteness from early childhood and that their process of becoming White continues into adulthood as they interact with those who are not White: the majority of children in our nation's urban schools.

Whiteness and Young Children

The second key body of work in which this study is situated is that which looks at the construction of whiteness among young children, including ways that White children are persistently given unconscious messages that whiteness is preferred. Over the years, racial favoritism studies examine that this is at work in young children's lives (Brown, 1995; Clark & Clark, 1939; Katz & Kofkin, 1997). For example, in multiple large, quantitative studies, Aboud (1988, 2003) found that White children between the ages of 3 and 8 consistently matched positive adjectives (i.e., "good" and "kind") with pictures of White people and negative adjectives (i.e., "mean" and cruel") with pictures of African Americans. This study has had similar results across multiple racial contexts. In correlating the White children's racial attitudes to those of their parents, Aboud found no positive correlations. That is to say that the children developed their positive in-group messages and negative out-group messages independent from their parent's professed racial attitudes. Due to these hidden messages, White children, as well as children of color, unconsciously conclude that whiteness equals goodness.

Vendantam (2010) argued that young children expose their racism so clearly because they have not yet learned to overrule racist generalizations that their hidden brain instructs. This idea is consistent with other studies as well. For example in an ethnography of multiracial preschool age children, Ausdale and Feagin (2001) found the children were violently racist despite attending a school that prided itself for its work in multiculturalism; the young children used race as a marker to exclude and ridicule their peers. Vendantam attributed this, in part, to the work and power of the unconscious brain. These hidden racist beliefs are then carried into middle childhood where children are less likely to have multiracial friendships and more likely to solidify, in unconscious and conscious ways, their own whiteness. White children who grow into White women teachers, then, have been deeply socialized to value their own superiority, which impacts the way they—unconsciously or consciously—interact with youth in schools.

A White Researcher's Blind Spot

When I started this study, I worried that indications of racialization might be hard to find in the mundane day-to-day discourses of children. This blind spot is a critical finding to this study. After all, I study whiteness in an effort to address issues of inequity in public education. How could I have considered the possibility that I might not find messages about race? As I began to analyze data, I realized my fears were driven by my own racial naiveté. Because we live in a racially charged, racially stratified society, discourse about race is implicitly constructed, deconstructed, and even interrupted at all times. The racial identities of my children were being formed continuously through big and small interactions with their world, because knowing who they are in American society means understanding that they belong to a particular race. I also realized that who my children are as White people can only be known in a relationship to who they are not: persons of color. Drawing on the work of Toni Morrison (1993), I began to think about the discourses of my children's worlds in terms of discourses of whiteness and blackness. If discourses of whiteness serve to implicitly and explicitly oppress persons of color by perpetuating White supremacy, discourses of blackness serve the same function by perpetuating blackness as inferiority. The two formed a duality of unconsciousness that my children used to construct their understandings of themselves as White. Our developing understanding as raced White people seemed consistent with Morrison's (1993) explanation that, in order to be racially dominant, there must be an "other" to be dominated. Since the process of becoming White does not end in childhood, these discourses continue to operate and to influence the ways White women teach our nation's youth.

WHITE CHILDREN LEARNING WHITENESS

The focus on my children yielded findings too often hidden from those for whom whiteness is normalized. Thus, the findings shared in this section provide specific examples of young children learning whiteness on the road to becoming adults. More detailed discussions of findings can be found in other work (Miller, 2014; Nash & Miller, 2014). The findings presented here demonstrate that messages of normalized whiteness came through in a range of dominant discourses in the lives of my family found in church and Sunday school, dance classes, magazines and catalogs that came through our mail drop, worksheets and texts from school, the images on packages of food on our shelves, the toys with which my children played, and the very neighborhood in which we lived. These messages were, quite literally, everywhere and they were sustained by simultaneous messages that conveyed systematic oppression and degradation of blackness. Blackness was often portrayed in ways that conjured feelings of superiority, fear, pity, or hatred.

In this chapter, I highlight two of the dominant discourses that played roles in the racialization of my children: discourses of overrepresentation and discourses of omission along with the children's appropriation of those discourses as well as their critique of racialized messages. The examples shared here are a few of many, and provide the powerful demonstrations of the insidious nature of whiteness lessons in the lives of young children and the ease with which children appropriate, but also are able to critique, those teachings. Presented here is but a small slice of data. Over time, these and hundreds of other messages of whiteness overlapped in constant, rhythmic and almost indistinguishable ways, their racialization barely noticeable to us, offering insight into how deeply ingrained these racial messages become as children grow into the young White women with whom we work.

Discourses of Overrepresentation

Within the hundreds of examples of texts and images in my children's worlds explored through this study, White people were everywhere despite my efforts to create a world that affirmed people of color. Thus, discourses of overrepresentation became foundational in weaving a story of racial dominance for my children. The messages of whiteness generally came into our home through the mail or through the children's home/school folders that were sent home by their teachers. Over and over our conversations around these served to further embed the belief that White is best, right, most beautiful, most deserving. When my children picked up the magazines that came through the mail slot, for example, and saw the predominantly White people depicted within various activities, they learned to associate being White with having material things that they desired: colorful swimsuits, expensive birthday parties, going on vacations to the beach. Olivia reveals the normalcy through which this occurred as she turned the pages of a catalog:

> Don't you think I should do that for my birthday, cause look at that [showing me the pillowed stools around the table]. Don't you think that's nice? That one [turning to a page with photographs of a pirate-themed birthday party] would be really nice for Max. He gets dressed up like a pirate. Or, he might want to do the shark one. Which one do you think is better?

As she continued, Olivia wrote extended family members into her script: "I thought that would be nice for, like, if you were turning 1years old. I thought that would be nice for Ethan [her 15-month-old cousin]. And that [turning to another page] would probably be nice for Maddie [her 3-year-old cousin]." Although Olivia is saying nothing that indicates her knowledge of the overrepresentation of whiteness in the catalog, it is the very existence of this overrepresentation that she was taking in, a part of her process of becoming White.

The real power in this overrepresentation was that it offered possibility and power to those who were represented, people who looked like my children. Olivia and Ella saw people like themselves reflected over and over in positive ways—children with arms outstretched on a beach in colorful swimwear, shaking hands with important people, laughing as they washed a golden retriever in a grassy backyard, entertaining laughing groups of friends, eating cakes decorated in detail, having tea parties with stuffed animals. As a result, I began to realize that a kind of consciousness was forming for the girls: "I look like this too!" and "This could be me!"

To illustrate how frequently images of White models occurred in the catalogs that came into our house, I randomly gathered one of each of the five clothing catalogs received most often and conducted a frequency count of the number of images of White models and the number of images of models appearing to be of color. Out of a total number of 423 images, 380, or 89.8% were of White models, while only 43, or 10.2% of the total, pictured models of color. The assumption seems clear that the companies chose such an abundance of White models because they wanted to appeal to their White customers, targeting a market that is White and middle to upper-middle class. However, the disproportionate number of White people to persons of color in these catalogs can hardly be accepted as benign marketing. They are rather a gross example of how the lived experiences of White people, in being overrepresented, contribute to their supremacy and construction of dominance.

These messages of overrepresentation were embedded in the daily protocols of our household. When the children opened the pantry door, smiling faces of White people on the packaging of food—Grandma's Molasses, images on cereal boxes, and White Lily flour—greeted them. Images on flyers and promotional materials for campaign ads, restaurant coupons, and recreational spaces that came into our house through our mail slot almost exclusively consisted of an all-White cast. The songs on music radio stations the children asked to sing along with told a White narrative of dominance, such as when Brad Paisley, an artist the children admired, sang, "I bet when my great granddaddy stepped off that ship, he never thought he would have all this."

In another powerful example, of 650 images of human characters on Scholastic fliers that were sent home from school in Ella's folder, 84.2% appeared to be White. Even paperwork from school that contained images of faceless paper dolls had long, wavy, relaxed hair more typically belonging to a White face than a face of color. Although the skin color of these dolls was left up to individual children to create, the appearance of hair alone confounds the idea that the doll might not be White. This wide range of the overrepresentation of White people created a force-field of racism into our lives, an unspoken yet powerful lesson about whose lives were superior. In schools today, teachers, mostly White women, face a barrage of White supremacist curricula that likewise promote discourses of overrepresentation. Since most White women were socialized by these discourses themselves, even noticing this overrepresentation can be a daunting task.

Discourses of Omission

If White people were grossly overrepresented in the textual and visual materials that proliferated the texts that came into our home, a simultaneous omission of persons of color and historical inaccuracies (omitting historical information that did not reify White dominance) were also dominant. I found this in two data sources in particular: the children's school projects and curricula, and artifacts of the holiday season.

In her 4th-grade history curriculum, 9-year-old Ella studied the typically highlighted moments in American history: colonialism, slavery, Westward Expansion, the Civil War, the Roaring Twenties, etc. In school, these events were studied largely through weekly magazines *USA Studies Weekly* (American Legacy Publishing, 2012b) and *South Carolina Studies Weekly* (American Legacy Publishing, 2012a). After reading and discussing these magazines at school, Ella brought them home to continue reading and referencing them. She enjoyed the magazines because they "explained things in ways that kids could understand," and became known as our family's history buff because she was able to recall and discuss historical facts on a moment's notice.

However, her enjoyment and pride in knowledge also meant that she was internalizing discourses of omission as the documents she read presented White dominant and often romanticized and sanitized versions of history grossly omitting important elements of the historical accounts (Loewen, 2007; Zinn, 2003). For example, one of the newspapers on antebellum South Carolina, contained an article about economic growth during this time period and opened with the following two sentences: "Money! Money! Money! The 1800s in South Carolina were years of great wealth known as the antebellum times. Many South Carolinians became rich plantation owners by growing and selling cotton" (American Legacy Publishing, 2011a, Week 10, p. 1). These two sentences belie the facts that only a small percentage of White, wealthy men actually made money by growing cotton and that women, the nonwealthy, and people of color were excluded from this system of privilege; African slaves, who were not even considered human, drove the Southern economy by forced labor without any hope of benefitting from the "Money! Money! Money!" (American Legacy Publishing, 2011a, Week 10, p. 1).

Another example of omission was found in an issue of *U.S. Studies Weekly* (American Legacy Publishing, 2011b, Week 25) which featured an article about life after World War II. The author wrote that "the end of World War II brought a new prosperity to the United States. People had good jobs during the war and saved a lot of money.... Returning soldiers and almost anyone who wanted a job could find one in the factories and distribution channels for these new products" (p. 1). Not mentioned were the postwar racial tensions across the country, the stark economic disparities between White families and families of color, and the sanctioned segregationist policies that denied African Americans opportunities for economic growth and educational attainment (Freund, 2007). The article continued by stating, "War veterans received assistance from the G.I. Bill, which helped them buy a home.... At the end of WWII, Blacks moved from the South, followed by Latinos, to fill the inner cities. Whites moved to the suburbs" (p. 2) without mentioning that, for many veterans of color, the benefits of the G.I. Bill, which provided low-interest home loans, were interrupted by the openly racist Federal Housing Authority, as "institutional racism built into the housing system at the time shut many African Americans and American Indians out of the American dream of home ownership" (Freund, 2012, p. 2).

Discourses of omission abounded throughout other areas of our lives. For example, I wanted to buy the children Advent calendars to mark the days leading up to Christmas. Because of this study, my growing sensitivity to how persons of color are omitted from popular narratives led me to notice that there were no characters of color illustrated in the five advent calendars I could choose from at a local grocery store. I decided to check other stores, hoping to purchase calendars that did not feature an all-White cast of characters. It was an unsuccessful quest because I could not find any Advent calendars in which illustrations of White people did not adorn the front. This was true after countless Internet searches as well. This was not only true for Advent calendars: In displays of books at our nearest book store, White characters were not only dominant, characters of color literally did not exist. In a city where 42.2% of its population is African American, 4.3% is Latino, 2% self-identifies as more than one race, and where the majority of the population is Christian (United States Census Bureau, 2012), this is a striking way that racial oppression works through omission. Like my daughters, White women teachers were likely socialized into these discourses of omission as well, and like my daughters, they were not cognizant of them until those discourses were named. Thus, supporting White women teachers to notice and name these stealthy discourses is a starting point in the quest to support White women to recognize the ways children of color are routinely oppressed in schools.

Reappropriating Whiteness

The fact that everywhere my children turned White people were represented over and over again is not surprising, when considered within a critical framework where whiteness is perpetuated as normal through every day discourse. However, the questions that guided my study were not so much about how hegemony works, but how those normalized racial messages were then used by my children to construct whiteness.

Throughout the study, I watched how the children reappropriated the overrepresentation of whiteness and omission in their own lives every day.

For example, in the hundreds of pieces of artwork I collected from them, drawings of people were prolific. Exclusively they drew White people despite the fact that their worlds are not exclusively White. For example, Olivia drew countless girls in dresses and skirts—all White. She explained that the girls were going to church, going shopping, running errands, or simply modeling new styles—internalizing the normalcy of whiteness. Olivia sometimes used yellow crayons or markers to color in her girls' skin. In a poststudy interview, Olivia said, "I meant for her skin to be white but I could not find the peach color so I just drew it with yellow because that's the closest color." These images of smiling, White girls adorned with butterflies or rainbows were oddly similar to the smiling White girls, also adorned with butterflies and rainbows that she saw on the many, many catalogs that came into our house.

Likewise, when Ella drew pictures depicting people—cultural icons, family and friends, and people who existed in her imagination—they were all White. During one period of time, she drew countless characters from the trilogy, *The Hunger Games* (Collins, 2008). In one of her many drawings of the protagonist Katniss Everdeen, it is apparent that Ella imagined Katniss to be White despite the ambiguity of the book's author on that point. Ella's imagination of Katniss as White was further confirmed after I took her to see the movie based on the book. After seeing the film, the following conversation occurred:

Erin: Was Katniss the way you imagined her to be after you saw her in the movie?
Ella: No, not really.
Erin: How so?
Ella: I thought she would have blond hair.
Erin: Did you always think she would be White?
Ella: Yes, if [the book] would have told us if she were not White.

Ella's comment, "[The book] would have told us if she were not White" is an automatic default into whiteness. Because whiteness was so normalized, so overrepresented in her life, because persons of color were so prolifically omitted from the discourses in her worlds, and because she was accustomed to descriptors used such as "Black girl" or "African American child" when persons of color were discussed, but not when White persons were indicated, Ella assumed that there would be a warning if the book deviated from the assumption of whiteness.

The images of whiteness were so pervasive that the children sometimes reappropriated those messages by assigning White skin to characters in their drawings and stories even when the real-life scenes they depicted included persons of color. For example, Ella danced at a jazz school that I chose, in part, because of its diverse group of dancers and instructors. Approximately 50% of the dancers in this school were students of color and 50% were White dancers. Throughout the course of this study, dance students of color were often highlighted and celebrated by the dance director who put them in leading roles in performance pieces. In December of each year, the studio performed a jazz/hip-hop version of *The Nutcracker* ballet called *The Two Claras*. This was not a typical ballet performance that one might consider to be a representation of White culture. It is infused with contemporary popular music that draws on a variety of genres and musicality from jazz and hip-hop, and is choreographed and directed by a woman of color herself. *The Two Claras* is only loosely connected to the popularized White Russian *Nutcracker* ballet. Despite the fact that, for years, the lead dancers were usually African American or racially mixed dancers, Ella's own drawings of the dance only depicted White dancers. Once again, Ella successfully reappropriated the pervasive nature of whiteness in her life to white-out the dancers of color. When girls like Ella and Olivia grow into White women, they will likely continue to reappropriate whiteness as normal, if they are not carefully taught how their racial lens can blind them to recognizing a reality that eliminates/ignores the experiences of persons of color.

Critiquing Whiteness

The children were not, however, merely silent absorbers of these messages. There were times when they pushed back against them. For example, they learned to question the absence of people of color in images of religious figures and popular cultural figures, such as the all-White images of Jesus at our church. When looking for and not finding the visibility of nondominant cultures, they became enraged and at times, this led to actions like writing and posting letters to websites that advocated for more inclusive school curricula. Thus, within the imbricated nature of multiple identity narratives, my children seemed to both reify and reject the dominance and superiority of whiteness. However, I ultimately concluded that despite my attempts at what I saw to be antiracist parenting, it was not enough to stop the racist discourse that permeated our lives.

DISCUSSION: BECOMING WHITE

Discourses of whiteness and blackness were the backdrop that led to my children's constructions of race. These identity messages were not tidy—at times they were completely contradictory and often competed with each other for dominance. They were also recycled among those of us in our family and the wider world in which we lived. That is, as the world passed messages to us about hegemonic whiteness, we used those messages to construct our own microcosm of larger society, and thus reflected whiteness back out as the norm. In this chapter, I focused primarily on data collected on how my two White daughters were socialized into whiteness and the implications of this for White women teachers. I did not include data I collected on my son because of the unique implications the socialization of girls has to do with White women teachers. Since the majority of teachers in urban schools are White women, looking at the socialization of White girls is imperative. This become particularly more so true when we consider that in schools, White girls are more successful than another subgroup that indicates that White women are doing the best job teaching White girls. If White women are to expand their success with children of color and boys, they must begin to seek the nuanced ways they have been socialized—and thus implicitly enact—to reify whiteness as the norm.

My realization that racial discourses are everywhere, in ways that are no doubt not a revolutionary finding to many persons of color, for whom racial oppression is an ever-present facet of life. However, I have been enculturated into whiteness from infancy, which has successfully taught me a limited/naïve racial consciousness. I have lived, until recently, without ever having to, as Baldwin (1984) writes, "confront the ravage and the lie" (p.180) of my whiteness. I was only able to locate the findings of this study when I recognized that investments into the regime of racism often occur behind the curtain of what is generally accepted as benign discourse—discourse that is so common in White America it is hardly considered by most White Americans as salient or even noteworthy within a paradigm of racism. Thus my study, which was deliberate in its intent to uncover and recognize the many ways that whiteness and blackness shaped the realities of my children, resulted in not only my discoveries as a researcher about just how insidious and embedded those messages were in the intimate spaces of my family's world. What, then, do the insights from this study mean for White preservice teachers?

FROM *BEING* TO *BECOMING*: CHANGING OUR STANCE WITH WHITE WOMEN PRESERVICE TEACHERS

Given the insidious ways whiteness is constructed and reappropriated in the process of becoming White, it is not sufficient to identify our White female students as resistant, racist, or indignant. Imposed characterizations of White students does little to transform oppressive conditions that marginalize urban youth and dehumanize all of us. We must understand that White women are in a continual state of becoming White through discourse messages that dichotomize whiteness and blackness. While I have given examples of this in early childhood as my two girls constructed whiteness, these lessons continue well into adulthood. Thus, I believe it is essential that we begin work with our White female teaching candidates to help them understand the myriad implicit ways that whiteness is at work in the most mundane parts of their life. Drawing on Ignativ and Garvey's (1996) suggestion that a path into whiteness is a treason against humanity, Matias (2015) argues for a racial rehumanization. Likewise, in another work (Miller, 2015) I argue for a rebirth of awareness regarding how racialization occurs. I explore how this could happen in what follows.

Seeing Whiteness in More Than Big Moments

In teacher education, some educators have found success in asking students to reflect on their racial memories (Wasson, & Jackson, 2002), yet in this assignment alone resides the assumption that racialization happens in memorable, sometimes dramatic events. Many times, White students do recall instances where they were not allowed to play with dolls of color or where they were not allowed by their families to love people of color (Nash, 2013; Nash & Miller, 2014). While pivotal, these big moments must have occurred with hundreds of thousands *of daily instances wherein whiteness was constructed without words*, where whiteness crept into young worlds like vapor through the many unnamed and unnoticed discourses of overrepresentation and omission. This is the real authority of whiteness: it is constructed most vehemently when it is unnoticed.

As a White researcher of race, I was naïve to believe that being constructing understanding about race only happened in overt discourse about race. In fact, I was paralyzed by fear when I started my study that would have no data to collect if my children did and I did not openly discuss race. To help our students understand the real clout of racism, then, it is these moments that must be better understand. They must be understood not merely because they represent the complexity of becoming raced, but because they turn our direction to how the world around us, rather than good or bad people in our lives, shapes our racialized understandings of the world. This serves multiple purposes. For one, it prevents us from having to characterize people or events in our own world as "ignorant" or "close-minded." Contemporary scholars (i.e., Lensmire et al., 2013; Sullivan, 2014; Thandeka, 2007) argue that White people may reject learning about whiteness because they fear being divorced from their loved ones or that, in order to confess their White sins, they must be disloyal to their families and other loved ones. Additionally, studying the world, rather than studying our own individual stories alone, helps us circumvent the inevitability of shame and guilt that can lead to resistance or defensiveness. That is, we better understand that our historical narrative and our concurrent contextual landscape have made it nearly impossible not to succumb to racism unless we are intentionally fighting against it. Understanding that an antiracist stance means working together to counter the messages the world sends us in droves strengthens alliances between White teachers of teachers and White preservice teachers and their students, giving heed to Palmer's (1998) caution against the creation of static caricatures of White preservice teacher students, which may serve to elevate our own status as instructors who look "noble comparison to the barbaric young [while placing] the courses of students' problems far upstream from the place where our lives converge with theirs" (p. 41). I argue that a more fruitful line of questioning would be to work with our students to ask, "How does the world socialize us and continue to socialize us into whiteness as normal? Collectively, how might we work together to fight these messages?"

Examining the Ontology of Race With White Women

As a starting point, learning how race came to be is important when working with White women. This is not in an effort to evoke guilt or shame, but rather to demonstrate how, before race was constructed as a social distinction, White people and people of color worked together and they have continued to do so for centuries. White women should be able to identify with White people for whom they are proud for their antiracist efforts, the same way that people of color need affirming and truth telling narratives. When race and racism are more deeply understood in relation to their historical and social constructs, we have more choices in how we approach various interactions in our lives. Instead of asking if particular interactions are about race, as is common in modern-day America, we can assume that every interaction is racially laden, and thus begin to search for the ways racism is at work. These interactions need not be sought out. By simply taking snapshots of daily life, we can make personal choices using our worlds as the basis for racial inquiry and questioning. For example, school assignments, textbooks, picture books, and curricula; daily mail; political campaigns; and day-to-day events all provide structures from which teachers, youth and teacher educators can begin to ask important questions about race and racism. Once lessons including discussions about the notion of racism (what it looks like, feels like, sounds like, and how it was historically constructed for the political and economic gain of Whites) have been explained, children can begin to examine the artifacts and experiences that fill their lives by interrogating the answers to questions such as:

- Where is race and racism in this snapshot or event (political campaign ads, worksheets, dance classes, ball games, drugstores)? How is this event controlled by White people? Why? How did that happen? How does that help us understand the notion of White supremacy?
- How is this snapshot/event located in time in terms of the historical racial antecedents that led to it as it appears today?
- How does this snapshot maintain/fight against White supremacy/racism?
- What needs to be changed structurally for this snapshot to reflect a more just world?

Breaking Down Antiracist Hierarchies

To support these efforts teacher educators must have spaces in their professional lives to dialogue about issues of race and racism. Too often there exists an ethos in colleges and universities that the professors who made it to academia are not bound by racist ideologies, that advanced degrees are symbolic of antiracism. This is not true. Liberation from racism is not a decree of an advanced educational program. If we are to transform teacher education to create spaces for the re-education of prospective teachers, serious attention must be paid to the racial histories left out of our understandings about how we came to be raced. In the process, students should become intimately familiar with the work of scholars from underrepresented groups who have, for centuries, argued for a confrontation of whiteness. Too often, the voices of persons of color exist only on the periphery of teacher education programs, their work subjugated to additional or optional reading lists, rather than located in the essential cannon of every discipline. Townes (2006) expressed these optional reading lists only "rescue the killers" (p. 151), meaning that such lists just reify and provide a place of safety for White scholars and their White students. A starting point could be an examination of required texts. A commitment to maintaining or rejecting White supremacy will likely become painstakingly clear from this one exercise alone.

CONCLUSION

This chapter contends that the lessons learned by White children who may one day grow into contemporary White women teachers are embedded in constant, rhythmic, and almost indistinguishable ways within a dichotomy of whiteness and blackness through typical socialization in their worlds. Thus, I argue that helping White women see that, although they make individual choices that are racist or antiracist every day, they likely learned to be White from early childhood in unrecognized ways and continue to become White every day in those same unrecognized ways. Specific classroom strategies such as working collectively with White women to examine how whiteness works in mundane ways, considering the ontology of race and racism with White women, and avoiding false hierarchies of antiracism that prevent teacher educators and school leaders from examining how whiteness works in their own teaching can all led to a more productive and generative space for urban education. Furthermore, leading White women through a search of the invisibility through every day discourses in their worlds is a powerful assault against whiteness because this recognition attacks whiteness in its most powerful stronghold: normalcy. These attacks on whiteness are necessary to lead the racial rehumanization that must be on the forefront of our agenda in urban education.

REFERENCES

Aboud, F. (1988). *Children and prejudice*. Cambridge, MA: Basil Blackwell.

Aboud, F. (2003). The formation of in-group favoritism and out-group prejudice in young children: Are they distinct attitudes? *Developmental Psychology, 39*(1), 48–60.

Agar, M. (1996). *The professional strange: An informal introduction to ethnography* (2nd ed.). San Diego, CA: The Academic Press.

Allen, T. W. (1994). *The invention of the White race: Racial oppression and social control.* New York, NY: Verso.

American Legacy Publishing. (2011a). Antebellum South Carolina. *South Carolina Studies Weekly: A weekly newspaper for young students of South Carolina history, 7*(2, Week 10), 1–4.

American Legacy Publishing. (2011b). Life in the 1950s. *U.S. Studies Weekly: A weekly magazine for young students of U.S. history, 5*(3, Week 25).

Ausdale, D. V., & Feagin, J. (2001). *The first R: How children learn race and racism.* Lanham, MD: Rowman & Littlefield.

Baghban, M. (2014). Looking backward in order to look forward: The enduring contribution of parent research. In B. Kabuto & P. Martens (Eds.), *Linking families, learning, and schooling: Parent researcher perspectives.* New York, NY: Routledge.

Baldwin, J. (1984). On being White and other lies. In D. Rodeger (Ed.), *Black on white: Black writers on what it means to be White.* New York, NY: Schocken.

Barnes, (2006). Preparing preservice teachers to teach in a culturally responsive way. *The Negro Educational Review, 57*(1/2), 85–100.

Bogdan, R., & Biklen, S. K. (2007). *Qualitative research for education: An introduction to theory and methods* (5th ed.). Boston, MA: Pearson.

Brodkin, K. (1999). *How Jews became White folks and what that says about race in America*. New Brunswick, NJ: Rutgers University Press.

Brown, R. (1995). *Prejudice: Its social psychology*. Cambridge, MA: Blackwell.

Carspecken, P. (1996). *Critical ethnography in educational research: A theoretical and practical guide*. New York, NY: Routledge.

Case, K. A., & Hemmings, A. (2005). Distancing strategies White women preservice teachers and antiracist curriculum. *Urban Education, 40*(6), 606–626.

Clark, K., & Clark, M. (1939). The development of consciousness of self and the emergence of racial identification in Negro preschool children. *Journal of Social Psychology, 10*, 591– 599. Retrieved April 15, 2011, from http://psychclassics.yorku.ca

Cochran- Smith, M. (2000). Blind vision: Unlearning racism in teacher education. *Harvard Educational Review, 70*(2), 157–190.

Cochran-Smith, M. (2005). The new teacher education: For better or for worse? *Educational Researcher, 34*(7), 3–17.

Collins, S. (2008). *The hunger games*. New York, NY: Scholastic.

Ellis, C., Adams, T. E., & Bochner, A. P. (2011). Autoethnography: An overview. *Historical Social Research, 16*(4), 273–290.

Freund, D. M. (2007). *Colored property: State policy and White racial politics in suburban America*. Chicago, IL: University of Chicago Press.

Gangi, J. M. (2008). The unbearable whiteness of literacy instruction: Realizing the implications of the proficient reader research. *Multicultural Review, 17*(1), 30–35.

Gay, G., & Kirkland, K. (2003). Developing cultural critical consciousness and self-reflection in preservice teacher education. *Theory Into Practice, 42*(3), 181–187.

Gomez, M. L. (1996). Prospective teachers' perspectives on teaching "other people's children." In K. Zeichner, S. Melnick, & M. L. Gomez (Eds.), *Currents of reform in preservice teacher education* (pp. 109–132). New York, NY: Teachers College Press.

Gould, S. J. (1993). American polygyny and craniometry before Darwin. In S. Harding (Ed.), *The racial economy of science: Toward a democratic future*. Bloomington, IN: Indiana University Press.

Grbich, C. (2007). *Qualitative data analysis: An introduction*. Thousand Oaks, CA: Sage.

Haddix, M. (2014). Preparing teachers to teach other people's children while homeschooling your own: One Black woman scholar's story. In B. Kabuto & P. Martens (Eds.), *Linking families, learning, and schooling: Parent researcher perspectives*. New York, NY: Routledge.

Hardiman, R. (2001). Reflections on White identity development theory. In C. L. Wijeyesinghe & B. W. Jackson (Eds.), *New perspectives on White racial identity development: A theoretical and practical anthology* (pp. 129– 52). New York, NY: New York University Press.

Harro, B. (2000). The cycle of socialization. In M. Adams, W. Blumenfeld, C. R. Castaneda, H. Hackman, M. Peters, & X. Zuniga (Eds.), *Readings for diversity and social justice* (pp. 15–21). New York, NY: Routledge.

Helms, J. E. (1990). *Black and White racial identity: Theory, research, and practice.* Westport, CT: Greenwood.

Hodl, K. (2002). The Black body and the Jewish body: A comparison of medical images, *Patterns of Prejudice*, *36*(1), 17– 34.

Ignatiev, N. (1995). *How the Irish became White*. New York, NY: Routledge.

Jacobson, M. F. (1999). *Whiteness of a different color. European immigrants and the alchemy of race*. Cambridge, MA: Harvard University Press.

Jupp, J., & Slattery, P. (2010). Committed White male teachers and identifications: Toward creative identifications and a "second wave" of White identity studies. *Curriculum Inquiry, 40*(3), 454–474.

Katz, P. A., & Kofkin, J. A. (1997). Race gender and young children. In S. Luthar, A. Burack, D. Cicchetti, & J. R. Weisz (Eds.), *Developmental psychopathy: Perspectives on adjustment, risk, and disorder* (pp. 51–74). New York, NY: Cambridge University Press.

Laduke, A. E. (2009). Resistance and renegotiation: Preservice teacher interactions with and reactions to multicultural education course content. *Multicultural Education, 16*(3), 39–44.

Lensmire, T., Mcmanimon, S., Tierney, J., Lee-Nichols, M., Casey, Z., & Lensmire, A. (2013). McIntosh as synecdoche: How teacher education's focus on White privilege undermines antiracism. *Harvard Educational Review, 83*(3), 410–431.

Leopold, W. F. (1949). *Speech development of a bilingual child* (Vol. 3). New York, NY: AMS Press.

Loewen, J. (2007). *Lies my teacher told me: Everything your American history textbook got wrong*. New York, NY: Simon & Schuster.

Long, S. (2004). Passionless text and phonics first: Through a child's eyes. *Language Arts, 81*(5), 41.

López-Robertson, J. (2014). My gift to you is my language: Spanish is the language of my heart. In B. Kabuto & P. Martens (Eds.), *Linking families, learning, and schooling: Parent researcher perspectives.* New York, NY: Routledge.

Martens, P. (1996). *I already know how to read: A child's view of literacy.* Portsmouth, NH: Heinemann.

Matias, C. E. (2015). White skin, Black friend: A Fanonian application to theorize racial fetish in teacher education. *Educational Philosophy and Theory.* doi: 10.1080/00131857.2014.989952

McIntosh, P. (1988). White privilege and male privilege: A personal account of coming to see correspondences through work in women's studies. In P. H. Collins & M. L. Anderson (Eds.), *Race, class and gender: An anthology* (pp. 70–81). Belmont, CA: Wadsworth.

Miller, A., & Fellows, K. (2007). Negotiating White racial identity in multicultural courses: A model. In L. Cooks & J. Simpson (Eds.), *Dis/placing race: Whiteness, pedagogy, performance*. (pp. 49–66). Lanham, MD: Rowman & Littlefield.

Miller, E. (2014) Discourses of whiteness and blackness: An ethnographic study of three young children learning to be White. *Ethnography and Education, 10*(2), 137–153.

Miller, E. T. (2015). Race as the Benu: A reborn consciousness for teachers of our youngest children. *JCT* (Online), *30*(3), 28.

Milner, H. R. (2003).Teacher reflection and race in cultural contexts: History, meanings, and methods in teaching. *Theory into Practice*, *42*, 173–180.

Milner, H. R. (2006). Preservice teachers' learning about cultural and racial diversity: Implications for urban education. *Urban Education*, *41*(4), 343–375.

Milner, H. R. (2007). Race, narrative inquiry, and self-study in curriculum and teacher education. *Education and Urban Society*, *39*(4), 584–609.

Morrison, T. (1993). *Playing in the dark: Whiteness and the literary imagination*. Cambridge, MA: Harvard University Press.

Nash, K., & Miller, E. (2015) Reifying and resisting racism from early childhood to young adulthood: Implications for early childhood education. *The Urban Review*, *47*(1), 184–208.

Nash, K. T. (2013). Everyone sees color: Toward a transformative critical race framework of early literacy teacher preparation. *Journal of Transformative Education*, *11*(3), 151–169.

Palmer, P. J. (2010). *The courage to teach: Exploring the inner landscape of a teacher's life*. New York, NY: John Wiley & Sons.

Piaget, J. (1974). *To understand is to invent: The future of education*. New York, NY: Grossman.

Reid, K., & Knight, M. (2006). Disability justifies exclusion of minority students: A critical history grounded in disability studies. *Educational Researcher*, *35*(6), 18–23.

Sleeter, C. E. (1993). Advancing a white discourse: A response to Scheurich. *Educational Researcher*, *22*(8), 13–15.

Solomon, P., Portelli, J., Daniel, B., & Campbell, A. (2005). The discourse of denial: How white teacher candidates construct race, racism, and 'white privilege.' *Race, Ethnicity and Education*, *8*(2), 147–169.

Souto-Manning, M. (2009). Negotiating culturally responsive pedagogy through multicultural children's literature: Towards critical democratic literacy practices in a first grade classroom. *Journal of Early Childhood Literacy*, *9*(1), 53–77.

Sullivan, S. (2014). *Good white people: The problem with middle-class white anti-racism*. Albany, NY: State University of New York Press.

Tatum, B. D. (1992). *Why are all the Black kids sitting together in the cafeteria: And other conversations about race*. New York, NY: Basic Books.

Tatum, B. D. (1994). Teaching White students about racism: The search for White allies and the restoration of hope. *Teachers College Record*, *95*(4), 462–476.

Thandeka. (2007). *Learning to be white: Money, race, and God in America*. New York, NY: Continuum.

Townes, E. M. (2006). *Womanist ethics and the cultural production of evil*. New York, NY: Palgrave Macmillan.

United States Census Bureau. (2012). *Quick facts*. Retrieved from http://quickfacts.census.gov/qfd/states/45/4516000.html

Vendantam, S. (2010). *The hidden brain: How our unconscious minds elect presidents, control markets, wage wards, and save our lives*. New York, NY: Spiegel & Grau.

Wasson, D. H., & Jackson, M. H. (2002). Assessing cross-cultural sensitivity awareness: A basis for curriculum change. *Journal of Instructional Psychology, 29*(4), 265–276.

Weir, R. H. (1962). *Language in the crib.* The Hague, the Netherlands: Mouton.

Zinn, H. (2003). *A people's history of the United States: 1492–present* (3rd ed.). White Plains, NY: Pearson Longman.

PART III

DISENTANGLING RACE AND WHITENESS TO BETTER ENSURE CULTURALLY RESPONSIVE INSTRUCTION

CHAPTER 8

"NICE WHITE LADIES"

Race, Whiteness and the Preparation of a More Culturally Responsive Teacher Workforce

Chezare A. Warren
Michigan State University

Lloyd Matthew Talley
University of Pennsylvania

INTRODUCTION

> *"Inner-city high schools are a dangerous place. Where hope has lost out to hate. Where your homework isn't about math, it's about staying alive. 'At this school, if you're Black, Latino, or Asian, you will get shot, and that's a fact!' Only one thing can make these kids learn. A Nice White Lady."*

This excerpt from the MADtv sketch titled "Nice White Lady,"[1] though exaggerated, poses an intriguing conundrum. Well-meaning White women enter urban schools armed with visions of teaching divorced from the social, political, and cultural realities of where they teach. Eurocentric notions of success drive their passion to help "disadvantaged," "at-risk"

White Women's Work: Examining the Intersectionality of Teaching, Identity, and Race
pp. 147–175

youth whose circumstances preclude them from any chance at achieving meaningful life outcomes. They are good people whose admirable intentions position them to do little more than maintain systems of White dominance. Not surprising, since the abolition of slavery as a state-supported economic institution in the 1860s, White women (e.g., missionaries) were put in positions to "save" and "civilize" Black youth and children of color (Anderson, 1988). Still, today White women, and most persons preparing to teach in urban settings, are ill-equipped to adopt points of view that support their capacity to negotiate professional decisions that lead to evidence of culturally responsive teaching. At the same time, mainstream images of diverse youth attending urban schools construct them as thugs, uneducable, anti-intellectual, and academically disengaged until a nice White lady comes in to save the day.

This chapter is not an attempt to demonize or exceptionalize White women who choose to teach students of color. Instead, the substance of this chapter is anchored by one question: *What replicable knowledge and ideological stances are there to be learned from White women who have demonstrated evidence of their effectiveness serving racially and ethnically diverse youth in urban school settings?* We have identified and reviewed a series of empirical research studies that depict White female teachers as multidimensional—women with flaws and strengths, varying trajectories, interests, aspirations, and competencies. By reviewing this work, we then cataloged trends in behavior and teacher learning that emerged across the studies useful for clarifying how White women might be better prepared to demonstrate evidence of culturally responsive teaching.

Our aim by authoring this chapter is to push back against monolithic caricatures of White, female teachers that portray them as suburban-bred, middle to upper class, hyperprivileged, unassuming, colorblind, "savior" types who have "good intentions," and love youth of color enough to rescue them from the trappings of poverty (Lensmire & Snaza, 2010; Milner, 2011; Sleeter, 2001). Portrayals like these, similar to that of Erin Gruwell whose story was popularized in the movie *Freedom Writers* (Amy Little in the *MADtv* sketch), Louanne Johnson (Michelle Pfeiffer's character in *Dangerous Minds*), or even Ms. Cobb from Oprah Winfrey Network's *Blackboard Wars* docu-series, offer little hope. These caricatures also do not provide instructive insight for developing a replicable approach needed to better equip and/or professionally develop White women[2] to be effective teachers as a race minority in urban schools serving predominantly students of color. In the next section, we provide an overview of what it means to become culturally responsive and the significance of recognizing race and whiteness in the process.

CULTURALLY RESPONSIVE TEACHING AND "NICE WHITE LADIES"

Nice White Lady: Why won't you let me teach you?

Black Female Student: Cause you a White lady! You don't know me.... What you think is going to happen here? You think you gon' inspire me? You think you gon break through my tough girl act and teach me the beauty that's inside? You think you gon make me do and feel things that I ain't never have, never had before.... Well you wrong! We fightin for our lives in these streets!

Nice White Lady: [Hands Black female student a composition journal] Write that down!

The Black female character in this excerpt questions the nice White lady's intention. The nice White lady approaches the circumstance with a presumption of contempt and discombobulation. She only wants to help the Black female student. She does not quite understand why this young lady would dare reject her benevolence. There is clear dissonance in their points of view. Again, though satirical in nature, the encounter mirrors the experiences of many urban youth. The Black female student in the above scenario has had experience with other nice White ladies. Her monologue denotes a pattern in behavior observed in prior interactions with other White women teachers. She articulates in no uncertain terms how their goals diverge from her own and how the teacher's priorities are divorced from her lived realities. To watch this *MADtv* exchange is comical, but the themes are eerily familiar to the nature of interactions many White women have each day with students of color in urban settings. Satire is only funny because of its relationship to the truth. Culturally responsive teaching is intended to remedy this interpersonal disconnect between teachers and students. It is a professional framework or *instructional orientation* that builds on and appreciates, rather than eliminates, cultural difference. Evidence of cultural responsiveness in a teacher's practice likely minimizes interactions like the one featured above.

The language of culturally responsive teaching gets thrown around quite a bit by practitioners in discourse about how to best meet the academic needs of, and connect interpersonally with, urban youth. Fergus, Noguera, and Martin (2014) found in their study of seven urban single-sex schools serving predominantly boys of color that there was little evidence of culturally responsive teaching practice even though this was the instructional orientation touted by each of the school's administrators and teachers. This determination was made in large part because of the lack of academic success and the failure of specific lessons to deliver the intended learning objectives. Moreover, practitioners tend to struggle when asked to articulate the processes involved in enacting a culturally responsive teaching praxis beyond the mere integration of diverse images and examples into different classroom lessons. In the first author's personal experience as a classroom teacher turned instructional leader and now as a teacher educator, he has found it challenging to identify individuals who can adequately describe the dimensions of cultural responsiveness and the skills required to translate culturally responsive teaching theory to practice. Similarly, it is difficult to imagine one's self as culturally responsive while at the same time failing to adopt students' and families' *perspectives of culture*, and *perceptions of cultural*, to frame decision making across the range of professional instructional tasks.

The branch of multicultural education (Banks & Banks, 2004) known as *culturally responsive teaching* (Gay, 2010, 2013) provides the theoretical foundation needed to support White women's capacity to more effectively educate racially diverse youth. This orientation insists teachers teach diverse students "*through* their own cultural filters" (Gay, 2013, p. 50, italics in original). In other words, teachers must competently affirm the cultural genius and culture-specific needs of individual students using students' own various cultural frames of reference. The use of culturally responsive teaching in this chapter also incorporates an orientation that Paris (2012) champions as "culturally sustaining" pedagogy (CSP). He asserts that culturally sustaining pedagogy aims to "support young people in sustaining the cultural and linguistic competence of their communities while simultaneously offering access to dominant cultural competence" (Paris, 2012, p. 95). He emphasizes that teachers not use students' culture simply as a modality to assimilate them toward standard White racial and cultural norms. Cultural responsiveness involves establishing learning atmospheres that build on, maintain, and extend the cultural brilliance young people bring to school. A culturally responsive teaching orientation includes using culture as a bridge to support diverse students' access to academic content. Culturally sustaining pedagogy insists that one's pedagogical practice privileges the home lives of diverse students by ensuring a student's culture supports content knowledge acquisition, *and* that content knowledge honors students' cultural heritage. Simply put, teachers aiming to be culturally responsive must learn to enact instructional strategies that support maintenance of students' own cultural norms, home language, character traits, and forms of personal expression.

Naming the Role of Race and Racial Socialization in Becoming Culturally Responsive

The capacity of a teacher to demonstrate cultural responsiveness hinges on their acknowledgment of race as both socially constructed and navigated within the school building (Nasir, 2012). Teachers must also be exceedingly aware of the role they play in the racial socialization of their students (Stevenson, 2014). Second only to families, teachers serve as one of the major socializing forces in the lives of their pupils; they facilitate the immersion and enculturation of their students to the social norms and conventions of the world beyond their communities. They have a power to orient the mindsets of their students. This power to direct and define the worldviews of minority students must not be abused. In a racial world, acknowledging these dynamics is critical to the achievement and well being of minoritized students. Teachers both explicitly and implicitly advance their own individual perspectives of morality, achievement, deservingness and justice within classrooms through the many interactions they have with young people. Therefore, aside from the explicit curricular aims of culturally responsive pedagogy, we must acknowledge the utility and potential consequences of race in the lives of students and the role that teachers play in negotiating this dynamism.

Research on the development of racial identities in youth of color suggests that positive racial identity development and racial/ethnic socialization are imperative to positive youth outcomes in a variety of contexts (Friend, Hunter & Fletcher, 2011; Hughes et al., 2006; Sellers, Caldwell, Schmeelk-Cone, Zimmerman, 2003; Wang & Hugley, 2012; Yip, 2014). Positive racial identity development is efficacious in both academic and mental health outcomes. Alternatively, scholars suggest that the development of Anglo-orientations is predictive of depressive symptoms in Latino youth (Derlan et al., 2014) and the development of colorblind racial ideologies in students of color is detrimental to both psychosocial and academic outcomes (Holoien & Shelton, 2011; Oyserman, 2013; Oyserman, Harrison, & Bybee, 2001; Umaña-Taylor, 2014). Recognizing the power that teachers have in the socialization of students is increasingly important. Consequently, ignoring the impact of teachers' own racial ideologies can weaken the achievement and health outcomes of diverse students.

Creating a culturally responsive learning environment must push back against the tendency to acculturate students to be more White. This aim sits at the core of the Black female student's lament in the excerpt above, and the real-life refusal embodied by students of color in urban school settings around the United States. A fundamental function of culturally responsive teaching is to respect and build upon the cultural and linguistic diversity students bring to school. Still scholars have found that teachers can call themselves culturally responsive and still hold deficit perspectives of youth (Garcia & Guerra, 2004; Valencia, 2010; Villegas & Lucas, 2003; Warren & Hotchkins, 2015). To that end, becoming culturally responsive is bolstered by a teacher's capacity to *see* race, racial identity development, and racial socialization as important lenses for understanding culture.

Learning to See Race, Racism, and Whiteness in Pursuit of Cultural Responsiveness

Whiteness has an invisible, but palpable impact on student outcomes, education policy, and practice (DeCuir & Dixson, 2004; Dixson, 2003; Sleeter, 2001). Culturally responsive teachers are aware that whiteness severely limits his or her ability to effectively acquire or comprehend students' points of view (Hinchey, 2006; Leonardo, 2009; Young & Rosiek, 2000). Banks (1995) contends knowledge is manufactured based on the confluence of one's observations in a context and the subjectivity of the observer. No judgments a White teacher makes about culture are without bias or prejudices connected to his or her own racial identity. Therefore, learning how practicing White female teachers negotiate, or have negotiated, the reality of race and whiteness in their work with students of color is essential for nuancing how White women are prepared and professionally developed to demonstrate evidence of cultural responsiveness in their own teaching.

Ladson-Billings (2001) persuasively argues that much more work has to be done to understand the nature and context of one's pedagogy. In other words, as Ladson-Billings (1994/2009) and others (Foster, 1997; Gonzalez et al., 2005; Hollins, 1996/2008, 2012; Irvine, 1991, 2002; Siddle Walker, 1996; Valenzuela, 1999) have asserted, there is a tangible skill set, dispositions, and conceptions of knowledge about cultural difference that effective teachers of Black and Latino students possess. For White women, it is essential that they become explicitly aware of how whiteness shapes the way they see the world, particularly for informing their "good intentions" to teach students of color in communities of color. This is especially true when they may have had little to no prior interaction with people of color before their first teaching assignment.

Moreover, being aware of one's White racial identity and whiteness is significant because these two constructs influence how White women (mis)perceive students' skills, behavior, and capacity to accomplish academic-related tasks. Racialized understandings of what is good, normal, and appropriate relative to student learning outcomes set the stage for teacher perceptions and beliefs about students' cultural differences and expectations for these students' school performance (Dixson, 2003; Downey & Pribesh, 2004; Ferguson, 2003; T. C. Howard, 2010). Researchers find that White teachers tend to view and evaluate Black students' behavior and competence more negatively than White students (Downey & Pribesh, 2004; McGrady & Reynolds, 2013), as early as the first 2 years of formal schooling (Sbarra & Pianta, 2001). Students of color who are misunderstood or whose actions are misinterpreted by a teacher are constantly being judged unfairly by Eurocentric standards of achievement that fail to acknowledge how schooling is racialized. This is the opposite of what culturally responsive teaching is supposed to accomplish.

Tyler, Boykin, and Walton (2006) found significant differences in 62 "European American" teachers' perceptions of Black students' classroom motivation and achievement when compared to White children. The study's participants overwhelmingly favored students who displayed behavior characteristics and preferences for learning akin to Eurocentric norms and themes. Full consideration of students' learning habits and abilities is not realized without significant attention to their culture and cultural preferences (Foster, Lewis, & Onafowora, 2003; Gay, 2010; Lee, Spencer, & Harpalani, 2003). Simply put, race and whiteness unconsciously dictate how teachers *see* their work. It cannot be expected that White women will do a good job of considering and interpreting student cultural intelligence, a necessary function of culturally responsive teaching, without explicit attention to the impact of race privilege, hegemony, and whiteness on shaping their perceptions and perspectives of racial diversity.

In sum, cultural responsiveness is personal work that begins with a teacher's understanding of self in relationship to others who are culturally different. It is not possible for a White female teacher to enact a culturally responsive teaching practice as put forward here without duly acknowledging and tending to her own racial history, biases, stereotypes, racial socialization, and race-laden prejudices. A critical examination of one's teaching practice facilitates exposure to and replacement of deficit perspectives that characterize cultural difference as a threat, rather than a benefit (Valencia, 2010). White teachers' engagement with and acknowledgment of the issues and challenges race and whiteness pose to the pedagogical process begin in teacher education, but must progress throughout the course of her career (McAllister & Irvine, 2000; Sleeter, 2001). It would be useful to know more about the specific challenges White women face when attempting to making cultural responsiveness a priority (Ladson-Billings, 2006; Landsman, 2001; Marx, 2006), and to learn from those challenges to make recommendations for how to better prepare them for work with diverse student populations.

THEMATIC LITERATURE REVIEW

We conducted a thematic literature review. The review is categorized as a "conceptual literature review" (see Kennedy, 2007, p. 139). Conceptual literature reviews are systematic, yet more general and open ended. They are meant to unpack meanings associated with a particular concept without rigid boundaries for what counts when attempting to make meaning. Kennedy (2007) argues, "At some point, the balance of benefit between systematic and conceptual reviews tips back toward conceptual reviews, for in their lack of 'system,' they have the flexibility to address the complexity of the substantive issues we care about" (p. 146). This chapter is meant to explore what can be learned from studies of White women teachers that place emphasis on the ways that race and whiteness influence, intersect, or inform their professional practice with students of color.

The task of spotlighting insights for better preparing White female teachers to be culturally responsive educators was complex in terms of developing research study selection criteria. Hence, we began by searching out literature with specific themes that alluded to the centrality of race for in-service White female teacher's professional decision making and interactions with stakeholders of color (i.e., children/youth, family, and community members). The studies chosen for review expound on student outcomes to varying degrees. Outcomes are telling of a teacher's effectiveness. Student outcomes that include evidence of their academic success, cultural competence, and social and political awareness are indicators of the impact of a culturally relevant, or culturally responsive teacher (Ladson-Billings, 1994/2009). Also, we searched out studies that somehow spotlighted evidence of White female teachers who help students to "maintain [their] heritage ... and value cultural and linguistic sharing across difference" (Paris, 2012, p. 95). Again, race and whiteness had to be an explicit aspect of the analysis in each study selected for review.

In an attempt to "define a literature" as Kennedy (2007) admonishes, and to abstain from an overly biased and value-laden selection of works to review, there were several other criteria used to narrow the literature reviewed for inclusion here. First, the literature chosen had to be recent. Recent is defined as works first published or rereleased in the year 2000 through the present. It makes sense to use work written in the last decade to make claims about being culturally responsive for today's student. Second, White female teacher participants' actual behavior, disposition, and/or practice with students had to be the focus of the research inquiry, not just their beliefs or attitudes about a topic related to culture, diversity, multiculturalism, race, or whiteness. Sleeter (2001) notes that a majority of the literature base regarding the preparation of White teachers for multicultural classroom settings addresses their attitude toward and lack of knowledge about multiculturalism and diversity. Too few studies document the strategies and experiences that make practicing White female teachers successful in multicultural school environments. Also, we wanted to scrutinize findings *not* conflated with the narratives or experiences of male teachers, or teachers of a different race. In other words, the studies we reviewed had an explicit focus on White women teachers, not White teachers.

A third criterion was that we only reviewed studies that feature the work of practicing classroom teachers or former classroom teachers, as opposed to preservice teachers. Studying teachers' superlative practices *and* their shortcomings are essential to helping future teachers or novice teachers. Therefore, using the examples of teachers who have persisted in teaching beyond the first few years offers insights that studying early career teachers do not. It was also beneficial to survey literature that explores the multidimensionality of White women who have chosen to teach in schools where they are the race minority. Lastly, if there were numerous works written by the same author, we chose the most recent work to review.

Table 8.1 is an overview of the empirical studies chosen for review. The table includes each paper's bibliographic reference, research question(s), demographic information of the teachers featured in each study, and the most important findings from the study. The works are arranged in the table in order from oldest to most recent. The table is followed by a brief discussion of the overlapping methods of data analysis, interpretation, and reporting used in the reviewed studies.

CULTIVATING A MORE CULTURALLY RESPONSIVE TEACHER WORKFORCE

There were a few key commonalities relative to an understanding of race and whiteness amongst the women in each of the studies reviewed for the chapter. The women had to at some point acknowledge racial difference as significant for informing *how* they negotiated their work, and that White privilege was an impediment as long as they allowed it to be that way (DeCuir & Dixson, 2004; Dixson & Rousseau, 2006; T. C. Howard, 2010; Ladson-Billings & Tate, 1995). Also, these White women learned to describe, to some degree, how whiteness shaded her ability to see and understand students' points of view (Leonardo, 2009). These realizations many times only came after a result of having numerous failures when navigating interactions with students and families of color. Seeing race when you have never had to see it is not something you learn to do from a textbook. These women learned by having to interact with others who were different. They made mistakes and learned to levy their vulnerabilities as an asset to their development.

Three salient themes related to the women's *dispositions*, or intersecting beliefs, knowledge, and skills used to make professional decisions with the

Table 8.1. Conceptual Literature Review Entries

Reference	*Description*	*Teacher Participant Demographics*	*Brief Summary of Relevant Key Findings*
Paley, V.G. (2000). *White teacher* (2nd ed.). Cambridge, MA: Harvard University Press.	Personal narrative or memoir of one White female teacher who candidly reflects on her process of discovering and ultimately working to dismantle her own racism as a teacher of racially diverse students. The school, an integrated elementary school, in a predominately White, middle-class neighborhood is the site of this critical memoir that unpacks how to recognize and address one's own prejudices of racially different students.	Vivian Paley. Preschool and kindergarten teacher with more than 35 years teaching experience. Taught in suburban and rural classroom settings.	"I have … discovered that all the children have more in common with one another than any one of them has with me. The major source of incongruity is between their thinking and mine." (p. 136). Paley learned to recognize systemic and institutional racism through a critique of her own racial "blind spots." Her prejudices as a White woman were made evident through her day-to-day interactions with her students and families of color. Each interaction pushed her to surveil her own teaching to ensure that every student who walked through her door had equal chance of being maximally successful. Conversely, she identifies with her students because she too has been seen as an "outsider" for her Jewish heritage, and thus, she "understand[s] the need to be seen exactly as [you] are and to be accepted and valued" (p. 131). This realization helped Paley to acknowledge how she used generalized racial group labels in pejorative ways when describing individual students like "the Black girls"; different from how she addressed White students. As opposed to taking the more difficult approach and learning their names, interests, and individual human characteristics outside of the students' race.
Johnson, L. (2002). My eyes have been opened: White teachers and racial awareness. *Journal of Teacher Education*, *53*(2), 153–167.	Life history qualitative study of six White female teachers identified as "aware of race and racism." The methods, that incorporate interview, "a drawing of their racial identity" (document analysis), and classroom observation explore how teachers' perceptions are shaped by interaction with their students of color.	Teachers' names were not given. They range in age from 36–63 with professional teaching experience between 4 years and over 30. Students included Native American youth.	"Few outward signs of multiracial images, multicultural children's literature, or multicultural curriculum materials" were apparent or available across the classrooms to the mostly students of color being taught (p. 161). Teachers talk a lot about understanding race and being aware of the mechanics of race. However, there was little evidence that their awareness had any significant bearing on how they negotiated interactions with students. From their interactions, they tended to note cultural difference, but it is unclear how their interpretation of that difference influenced their instructional decision making, for the good or the bad. Furthermore, the teachers were offered little support by the administration in their school to engage in multicultural education practices.

Harding, H. (2005). City girl: A portrait of a successful White urban teacher. *Qualitative Inquiry*, *11*(1), 52–80.	Author uses portraiture to describe and “chronicle one White teacher’s journey to becoming a ‘successful’ teacher of inner city students of color” (p. 54). Through observations and multiple in-depth interviews, this study aims to understand how one White female teacher defines success and the various factors informing her pedagogy and practice with Black and Latino students.	Jennifer Black. A 30-year-old National Board certified White female sixth-grade middle school English/language arts teacher.	“Success can exist within extreme contradictions.” (p. 78). White teachers must develop “spheres of cultural congruence” with students that “acknowledge the possibility that successful cross-racial teaching can coexist with confusion about personal social location” (p. 75). Jennifer’s self-identification as a “city girl” facilitates positive interactions with her students of color. Of her various identities (e.g. White, thirty-something, female, single etc.), her identity as urban leads when it comes to negotiating interactions with her students and their families. An “urban category” allows her to claim a “shared culture” with her students that they both value and validate. She capitalizes on their shared culture to create a classroom space that regularly integrates students’ urban, cultural experiences and expressions. This identity does ask her to compromise her whiteness, which admittedly, has been challenging for her at various points throughout her career. One thing that ultimately makes her successful is her ability to recognize the limitations of her whiteness, incorporate student home culture, and “explicitly teach the culture of power” (p. 77).
Parson, E. C. (2005). From caring as a relation to culturally relevant caring: A White teacher’s bridge to Black students. *Equity & Excellence*, *38*(1), 25–34.	Case study examination of one White female teacher’s negotiation of whiteness in an attempt to enact in “culturally relevant care.” The author studies this woman’s teaching practice to investigate how “aspects of engrossment, receptivity, and reciprocity” (p. 27) from Nel Nodding’s (1984, 1992) work is enacted in her interactions with her students of color.	Angel. A fourth-grade teacher with 8 years of teaching experience who teaches in a high resourced and diverse elementary school. The school has 50% low-income students who were bused to school in response to the recent desegregation order.	“The first aspect of culturally relevant caring is engrossment, which is a state in which caregivers are fully attentive to and act in the best interest of the cared-for … followed by receptivity, a nonjudgmental acceptance of the cared-for and a vision of the best possible outcome for the recipient of care” (p. 27). Engrossment disrupts White teacher’s dominant racial norms of care by challenging the teacher to see the circumstance or condition from the student’s perspective more often. Student’s congruent reciprocity of care, both for the teacher and one another, is a key indicator of the effectiveness by which the teacher has demonstrated evidence of care for the student(s). Modeling by teachers, practice, and fluid dialogue between students and teachers around the tensions of demonstrating culturally relevant care are key to developing one’s self as a culturally relevant care-giver. “The culturally relevant caring of the students for one another may have been expressed in more ways if Angela had discussed with the students her actions and the reasons for those actions” (p. 31).

(Table continues on next page)

Table 8.1. (Continued)

Reference	*Description*	*Teacher Participant Demographics*	*Brief Summary of Relevant Key Findings*
Cicetti-Turro, D. (2007). Straight talk: Talking across race in schools. *Multicultural Perspectives*, *9*(1), 45–49.	Commentary and personal reflection of one White woman's experience teaching and building a relationship with her Black female colleague. The features the challenges of opening up and maintaining the lines of communication between White faculty and faculty of color in K–12 schools around issues of race, racism, and diversity.	Danielle Cicetti-Turro. A 1st year White female teacher teaching a self-contained classroom of African American boys labeled "emotional and behavior disordered"	"Through her [the teacher participant's Black female colleague] silence however, she was speaking to me. She was imploring me to be sure I was ready to listen, to hear, to feel, to accept what she had to say as valid before asking her anything again" (p. 49). The burden of talking across race rests on White teachers. People of color cannot be expected to simply teach White teachers everything they need to know about race and racism. Talking and cultivating substantive relationships across race require that White people earn the respect and trust of their colleagues and students of color—something that is done over time and demonstrated through the White teacher's persistence in the workplace and capacity to be taught.
Marx, S. (2008). Popular White teachers of Latina/o kids: The strengths of personal experiences and the limitations of whiteness. *Urban Education*, *43*(1), 29–67.	Year long phenomenological qualitative study in an urban high school with a majority Latino student population and 100% White teachers. Author examined how four White women related to students, the ways they do not relate, and the influences of their Whiteness on how they relate.	Nikki Starr, Mickey Currey, Jane Alexander, and Rose Green. Four White female teachers selected by their students, administration, and staff for their ability to "relate" well to students. Their professional teaching experience ranged between 12 and 32 years.	"The teachers represented in this article were exemplary in many ways. Their students admired them greatly. However, just a few pointed questions revealed the many ways they were unable to relate to their students of color and the many ways that racism influenced their misperceptions of these students" (p. 61). Each of the teachers with the exception of one failed to recognize and overcome the effects of Whiteness on their teaching; including most prominently, the teachers' negative beliefs and deficit perspectives of students' home lives and culture. They related to students through the parallels of tragedy, trial, and pain as personal life experiences. This allowed them to separate the student from their culture. That is, use a colorblind ideology to guide instructional and interactional decision-making, which as a result positioned them to negatively judge students' home lives and actively acculturate them to dominant ways of thinking, acting, and being. On the contrary, one teacher referred to as "Ms. Currey" in the article, "was able to construct multifaceted, complex images of her students' realities and to gather the help of others to help her cross racial barriers in relating to her students" (p. 61).

Garza, R. E., & Garza, E. (2010). Successful White female teachers of Mexican American students of low socioeconomic status. *Journal of Latinos and Education*, *9*(3), 189–206.	Phenomenological study of four White female urban elementary school teachers' professional teaching practices, as influenced by their perceptions of social justice, equity, and excellence. Methods include interview and classroom observation.	Velma, Kim, Miriam, and a fourth unnamed participant. Four White women identified for their "effectiveness" with Mexican American students and who go "above and beyond" for students.	"The participants were relentless in their efforts to incorporate students into a society of 'good citizens.' The sooner the students learned to operate in the 'White way of knowing,' the sooner they as well as their teachers were deemed successful" (p. 205). The teachers primarily taught to the standardized test objectives because this demonstrated the standard success their school district valued. The teachers denigrate students' home cultures by insisting on their assimilation to the standard English and the systematic devaluing of their primary Spanish language. The teacher's ascribe "good" citizens by emphasizing they become more patriotic and loyal to their country. These women made many of their instructional decisions based on deficit perceptions of their Mexican students.
Yoon, I. H. (2012). The paradoxical nature of whiteness-at-work in the daily life of schools and teacher communities. *Race, Ethnicity, and Education*, *15*(5), 587–613.	Case study research of a small study group comprised of White women teachers intent on addressing equity issues in their school. Critical discourse analyses are used to interrogate the dissonance in teacher beliefs, intentions, and actions or behavior. Study group was formed around the reading and discussion of *The Freedom Writers Diary* as a method for better understanding teachers' own practices.	A group of White women, but namely one "focal teacher" (p. 594) named Sarah. First-grade teacher with 5 years teaching experience. Active member of her school's equity team.	"Through contradictions between intentions and actions: conversations were deracialized.... White individuals compared their beliefs to those of White individuals, but shied away from taking responsibility for challenging problematic statements. Sarah ... drew unspoken boundaries around what kind of feedback [she] gave [in her classroom], focusing on affirmation rather than considering the implications" of students' racial and ethnic diversity for how they interacted and communicated with her and one another (p. 607). Sarah facilitated conversations and student interactions relative to race difference and racial identity development in the classroom without ever referring to herself as privileged or "raced." These interactions were an extension of her all White female teacher study group where "teachers did not talk about their own identities as White women or question their own and each other's privilege or participation in racism. Instead, teachers positioned themselves in nonracial and culturally neutral terms, positioning students as generically 'different'" (pp. 607–608).

(Table continues on next page)

Table 8.1. (Continued)

Reference	*Description*	*Teacher Participant Demographics*	*Brief Summary of Relevant Key Findings*
Brown, A. (2013) Waiting for superwoman: White female teachers and the construction of the "neoliberal savior" in a New York City public school. *Journal for Critical Education Policy Studies, 11*(2), 123–164.	This ethnographic study explores the "White female savior" trope and its intersections with the neoliberal ideology and discourse in a contemporary traditional New York City public high school. The author scrutinizes the teaching practice and stakeholder interactions of four White female teachers to understand how these womens' pedagogy adopts, reinforces, or rejects mainstream depictions of White women who teach urban youth.	Ms. Easton and Ms. Smith (Composite characters who represent the four White female teachers). Secondary teachers identified by parents, students, and colleagues as "effective pedagogues" and whose students "demonstrate evidence of learning in their classes" (p. 133).	Ms. Joseph "ironically ends up embodying another version of the savior through her adherence to a definition of neoliberal social justice … she sees her place at the school as doing the impossible: Saving students from a socioeconomic crisis that already exists" (p. 153). Ms. Easton "critiques the model of the school, and critiques the politics of her colleagues … her pedagogy is emblematic of self-reflective and critical race, gender, and class politics, and she recognizes her activist work as serving her own interests as well" (p. 153–154). These two teachers' streams of consciousness are arrayed on a continuum of social, political, and racial awareness. Their degree of awareness impacts her pedagogy in distinct ways including how she does or does not decide to act in response to the proliferation of the oppressive, deficit-laden, neoliberal agenda in her school. The women's professional decision-making is largely influenced by their personal agenda, or subjective conception of "social justice teaching.

Warren, C. A. (2014). Towards a pedagogy for the application of empathy in culturally diverse classrooms. *The Urban Review, 46*(3), 395–419.	Qualitative multimethod study that combined qualitative and quantitative methodology. Study examined White female teachers' conceptions of empathy and its utility for helping them effectively negotiate academic, behavioral, and social/relational interactions with Black male students. Student-teacher interactions were studied to better understand empathy as a professional disposition of teachers identified as culturally responsive.	Four White female high school teachers in one school district on the periphery of a large, urban metropolis. Their professional teacher experience ranges between 7 and 16 years.	"Teachers who have little to no experience in communities of color benefit greatly from the social and cultural perspectives students provide through interaction with them" (p. 414). "The teachers in this study have no issue acknowledging that they are White women initially unfamiliar with many of the students' lived realities, however, they did struggle with the reality that they did not treat all students the same.... A teacher's awareness and explicit acknowledgment that they are different from students is essential" (p. 415). Empathy is an activity that includes adopting students' point of view, interpreting that point of view, and then applying that point of view to negotiate various interactions with them. Evidence of the teachers' success demonstrated their keen attention to student feedback, which in turn informed their subsequent interactions with students. Empathy facilitates the establishment of positive classroom communities and trusting relationships with students. Also, empathy helps teachers to intervene proactively to prevent students' academic attrition. Finally, empathy was found most useful for improving each teacher's willingness to take risks and negotiate flexible interactions with their Black male students.

youth of color they served emerged in this review. *Shared humanity, negotiating good intentions,* and *empathy* surface as important factors for better preparing White women to become culturally responsive educators. We explore their relevance to extant literature and what the literature reviewed teaches us about the importance of their cultivation when considering the aims of culturally responsive teaching. The chapter closes with some brief reflections and recommendations for teacher educators and researchers.

Shared Humanity

Interests in music, and in some cases, mutual trauma and tragedy are each points of congruity between White female teachers' life experience and their students. These serve as bridges to a shared humanity that closes gaps in difference posed by identity markers such as race. Ford and Sassi (2014) contend in their comparative case study of a White and Black teacher's style of authority, that White teachers' relationships with students of color do not go far enough and that they have to "counteract the tendency to privilege whiteness in the classroom" by *cultivating alliances* with students (p. 25). Teachers' partnerships with students with the explicit goal of identifying where they are alike is useful, but not without acknowledging how race makes them different, and then learning to see those differences as an asset to the relationship-building process. Efforts such as these further humanize the teaching and learning process for youth.

The language, gestures, mannerisms, learning preferences, and prior knowledge of both teachers and students are racially coded. Still, when White teachers are able to find and highlight overlaps between their own humanity and that of their students, culturally responsive teaching can commence. Milner (2010) describes how White teachers in his study found parallel experiences through divulging personal stories and other meaningful instructional texts that gave students something to "hold on to" during instruction (p. 69). Students have to see themselves and their experiences represented in the official curriculum. They also have to feel their cultural difference is valued. Warren and Lessner's (2014) "family business" describes an approach White women can take to get to know students on their terms. It also creates a classroom environment that allows the teacher to be vulnerable. It is in the vulnerability that teachers and students' humanity can be made visible. Learning where and how human experiences, emotions, aspirations etc. converge with teachers happens through multiple student-teacher interactions.

Negotiating Good Intentions: Acknowledging the Hidden Nature of Racism and Whiteness

Several of the studies demonstrate how these White women's good intentions to improve the schooling outcomes of diverse students got lost early in their careers. They learned that without active resistance to deficit-laden, pejorative, subversive perspectives and perceptions of diverse students, they were actually only reproducing the oppression they hoped to alleviate. White women teachers were identified by various stakeholders as "effective" or "successful" teachers of Black and Latino students in Brown (2013), Marx (2008), and Warren's (2014) studies. Yet, it was found that they also tended to construct students as at risk, without cultural capital, and in need of their "saving." Dismantling whiteness as a process of becoming culturally responsive includes using studies like the ones reviewed in this chapter (Table 8.1) to demonstrate how easy it is to call one's self culturally responsive without ever attending to the privileged ways that "culture" and race are constructed by White teachers (Picower, 2009; Sleeter, 2004; Warren, 2015).

Lynn and Parker (2006) conclude in their review of critical race studies in education research that more work is needed to uncover "the hidden costs of racism" (p. 283). The invisibility of whiteness, for example, makes recognizing its harmful effects extremely difficult. Whiteness veils a White teacher's ability to recognize the multiple ways their attitudes, beliefs, and cultural perceptions disadvantage students of color. Addressing matters of passive racism, in particular, is key in helping White female teachers to think differently about themselves in relationship to the types of learning experiences they provide.

Empathy

Not only did the women in the studies reviewed have to learn how their good intentions potentially limited their awareness of race and whiteness, they also had to pursue steps to acquire student and families' points of view of culture. Adopting an individual's social or cultural perspective is conceived as the act of applying empathy, or *perspective taking* to be more specific (Barr, 2011; Davis, 1994; Warren, 2014). Again, it was through teachers' routine interactions with students and families of color that they came to understand and position race in their work. Winners of the 2012 "Teaching Tolerance Culturally Responsive Teaching" awards administered by the Southern Poverty Law Center cite the importance of learning to see the world through student's eyes, and the relevance of anchoring the curriculum in students' lived realities (*Education Week*, 2014).

Similarly, Gay (2013) insists every aspect of a teacher's work with culturally diverse students in an effort to orchestrate culturally responsive learning depends on a teacher's capacity to filter their professional decisions through students' points of view. It is a specific racialized experience and lens that is absolutely necessary for framing and negotiating all professional teacher tasks.

Scholars in multicultural education argue that teachers utilize empathy to adopt professionally informed social and cultural perspectives of students, raise academic expectations, and demonstrate culturally congruent forms of care (Dolby, 2012; T. C. Howard, 2010; Ladson-Billings, 2006; McAllister & Irvine, 2002; Milner, 2010). Warren (2014) argues that each subsequent interaction teachers have with students should build on knowledge of students acquired in previous interactions. Every interaction provides the space for teachers to make pedagogic adjustments that respond to the culturally specific needs of youth to accomplish the goals of culturally responsive teaching as laid out in the beginning of this chapter. Student feedback in the form of behavioral and academic outcomes is pivotal for helping teachers adjust their expectations, interactional style, and the impact of their instructional interventions (Ferguson, 2003; Gorman, 2011; Hoban & Hastings, 2006; Warren, 2014). When knowledge of students is applied to negotiate interactions, students' critique or validation is a form of evidence of their response to the teacher's actions. The teacher's use of person-level knowledge of students and knowledge of the broader social context inform professional and personal adaptations they make when negotiating interactions. These interactions are ultimately the building blocks that produce outcomes characteristic of culturally responsive teaching (Warren, 2013). Still, just as Ullman and Hecsh (2011) warn, there are risks associated with teachers' application of empathy in their work with students of color, and those risks must be carefully calculated.

The capacity to apply empathy can be linked to several sentiments of the White women featured in the studies reviewed for this chapter. Some of the authors cite developing "spheres of cultural congruence" (Harding, 2005, p. 78), engaging in "a nonjudgmental acceptance of the cared-for" (Parsons, 2005, p. 27), and/or "constructing multifaceted, complex images" of students of color (Marx, 2008, p. 61) as significant in helping these White women teachers to be successful with their students of color. The women understand that connecting meaningfully with students and families of color requires getting to know them *on their terms*. By doing so, the women practice centering the cultural perspectives of students in every aspect of instructional planning, implementation, and assessment. Doing this, as opposed to constructing students of color from privileged, racially hegemonic, or liberal viewpoints, likely improves the types of assumptions, interpretations, and responses White women teachers have of the needs of racially diverse youth.

RECOMMENDATIONS

Taken together, learning to make the classroom more humane, empathizing with youth, and becoming aware of race and racism are important steps forward for shaping priorities in preparing and professionally developing "nice White ladies" to become culturally responsive pedagogues. The remaining sections help to better understand some strategies teacher educators, teacher preparation programs, and researchers might consider when attempting to concretize the steps needed to achieve the aforementioned aims. Cultural immersion and mentorship are key to supporting a teacher's capacity to cultivate empathy. Moreover, understanding meritocracy, racial illiteracy, and managing racial stress are also useful for developing White women's capacity to see race and whiteness more clearly, and its relationship to organizing a culturally responsive learning environment.

Cultural Immersion

Cultivating empathy includes engagement in cultural immersion experiences. Immersion experiences like those in McAllister and Irvine's (2002) study may include touring and spending significant time in the communities of color where White female teachers are planning to teach. These are not "drive thru" experiences where White teachers look out of the window and gawk at poor kids and communities. Teachers in McAllister and Irvine's study at least 30 hours in places of worship and other culturally specific communities of practice. They went to work with families, ate dinner in their homes, and engaged in culturally specific activities. All of this in spaces where the teacher's privilege and power mattered least, where for many of them, they were the "minority." These experiences have the potential to provide White teachers with perspectives that counter majoritarian stories about racially diverse students from poor communities (see Dixson & Rousseau, 2006). Effective White teachers understand how these contexts influence one's pedagogy and they negotiate power and privilege to ensure the most favorable outcomes for students of color (Banks & Banks, 2004; Delpit, 1995/2006, 2012; G. Howard, 2006; McAllister & Irvine, 2000). Experiences like these prompted the practicing teachers in McAllister and Irvine's study to recognize the significance of empathy to successfully responding to and communicating with students across racial and cultural difference. They also give teachers access to the social, cultural, historical, and political context that paint the social landscape from which students emerge. Prolonged engagement and partnership with communities through individual and/or institutionally initiated efforts gives voice to the experiences of students of color.

Mentorship

Similarly, immersion experiences might include the mentorship of White teachers by people of color (e.g., other teachers of color, students' parents, community members, etc.). Cicetti-Touro's (2007) mentorship by Ms. Watkins was significant in moving her practice forward with students of color. Relationships with older more experienced teachers of color, community members, or even students would be highly beneficial for giving White teachers, and any teacher, the opportunity to understand students who are of a different race or culture. Delpit (2012) in her latest book problematizes how White female teachers, like those who matriculate through Teach for America, would have benefitted from the mentorship of the veteran Black teachers they replaced in the public schools of New Orleans post-Hurricane Katrina. Mentorship by individuals who are intimately connected to the communities where White women will teach potentially disrupts ill-informed good intentions and privileged assumptions. Being smart, having earned a degree from a top-tier university and a well-to-do socioeconomic background is inadequate for effectively responding to the problems of failing schools.

Additionally, teachers in Lawrence and Tatum (1997) and Marx and Pray (2011) discuss the benefit of apprenticeship programs similar to McAllister and Irvine (2002) for helping White people to shift: (a) their social and cultural perspectives of racial difference; or b) considerations for classifying behavior as normal or aberrant. Leonardo (2002) contends, "Whiteness constructs history as separate racial details without coherence" (p. 40), but that "participation [in whiteness] is very much within the realm of choice and whites have been able to speak against the dehumanizing structures of racism even against their own immediate interests" (p. 35). For many White people growing up in a White world, their acceptance of whiteness is a consequence of their upbringing—never before having to be challenged by or confront the evils of racism. Once they realize whiteness is a threat to their own well-being, many will still invest in it for the sake of holding onto what little power they perceive they may possess. Mentorship, including peer mentorship, is one way to help White female teachers deal explicitly with blind spots in their reasoning about race, racism, and race relations.

Misconceptions of Merit and Racial Illiteracy

In the process of beginning to help White Female teachers to address their racial blind spots, teacher education and professional development must help them to also critically examine their beliefs about American meritocracy. A majority of the reviewed studies have a recurrent focus on racialized conceptions of merit, which undergird the pervasiveness and justification of the participants' deficit orientations. Milner (2009) harkens us to recognize that there exists a prevailing "myth of meritocracy" (p. 121) in American life, especially within the domain of schooling. Teachers' conception of their privileged status as justified and normal biases their interactions with culturally different students. Assumptions that suppose privilege and inequity are solely the result of individual choices and not structural forces are common in color-blind racial perspectives, facilitate these misconceptions. Several authors (Brown, 2013; Milner, 2009; Yoon, 2012) suggest that critical engagement of American economic policy and philosophical governing principles are necessary to aid White female teachers in dismantling their preconceived meritocratic ideals. This critical engagement with merit recenters the conversation from deficit-oriented thinking about Black and Brown students to the paradoxical nature of American rhetoric and American reality. Reluctance on behalf of school-level staff to embrace or support this strategy of consciousness development creates a volatile environment for students because it suggests learning preferences that diverge from the mainstream are deviant and aberration that needs to be corrected. This is a problem that the institution has to tackle directly.

For many White Americans, race is a burden of the marginalized. Across the lifespan White Americans are severely undersocialized on matters of race and structural inequality (Lesane-Brown, 2005; Pahlke, Bigler, & Suizzo, 2012). White parents tend to most often socialize their children using colorblind or colormute racial ideologies (Hughes et al., 2006). We come to understand that many of these teachers have been actively living in concert with colorblind and colormute racial ideologies since early childhood. Whether intentional or not, we must recognize that many White female teachers have not had to grapple with the notions of race and inequity. Lack of engagement with these concepts throughout their lives is further exacerbated by the ubiquitous discomfort in American society about dialoguing on issues of race. This circumstance foregrounds the necessity for these teachers to engage in the process of developing not only race consciousness but also racial literacy (Stevenson, 2014). Stevenson (2014) suggests that teachers not only develop a more lucid understanding of race but also the ability to navigate racial encounters. Actively assessing and confronting their own racial illiteracy and working toward developing antiracist White identities (Michael, 2014) improves White female teachers' ability to navigate the racial milieu which is readily present in urban schools.

Racial Stress

Understanding racial stress as an ever-present dynamic in the lives of White female teachers is an essential function in developing a more racially literate teaching force. Compounded with the stress that teachers face as a result of the profession an additional layer of racial stress (Coleman & Stevenson, 2013; Stevenson, 2014), can pervade the lives of White female teachers who struggle with their own racial illiteracy (Bentley-Edwards et al., in press). This stress has been shown to impede teachers' classroom management practices as well as their stress coping mechanisms (Bentley-Edwards et al., in press). Managing this stress is an active process that can be encouraged by the facilitation of a racial community of practice (Lave & Wenger, 1991) in which educators have an ongoing critical dialog about race within their schools. The facilitation of these dialogues can be inherently uncomfortable for teachers. Boler, Zembylas, and Tryfonas's (2003) argues that discomfort is emotional labor that is often encountered in understanding difference. It is necessary. While the discomfort may be unsettling for the teachers who experience it during this process, this discomfort should not be confused with insecurity. Michael (2014) suggests that safety in having racial conversations should not be conflated with comfort. This distinction allows teacher educators and administration to disentangle the 'discomfort is unsafe narrative' that often exists in racial dialogue.

CONCLUSION

Administrator: Forget it, these are minorities. They can't learn, and they can't be educated.

Nice White Lady: With all due respect sir, I'm a White lady. I can do anything.

Though ironic, we echo the nice White lady's sentiments. White ladies can do anything, when they have adequate preparation. There are numerous

White female teachers who have learned how to do their work in a way that is humane and affirming of the cultural diversity students of color bring to the urban classroom. Learning from their work, rather than making excuses for the failure of White women to be effective in these settings, constitutes a professional imperative. Ultimately, disrupting the abysmal student outcomes of U.S. public schools to provide an adequate education to racially diverse students includes reinscribing the critical role teachers play, and their preparation to demonstrate evidence of cultural responsiveness. Nothing in the literature or labor trends suggest more people of color or men are entering the teaching profession (Toldson, 2013). Spotlighting White female teachers and the tensions race and whiteness impress upon their work exposes some of the necessary steps the field needs to take to improve the likelihood of their success, both at teaching students of color as well as helping those students to maintain a strong sense of self and connection to their home cultures.

The conclusions drawn from the review of literature and the recommendations provided in this chapter are noteworthy for underscoring the pragmatic significance of culturally responsive teaching for today's learners. This chapter is simply a point of departure for a more nuanced empirical research agenda that more clearly establishes the relevance of race, whiteness, and one's racial identity development to improving how we prepare White women, who mean well, to be culturally responsive teachers. Moreover, research must be done that includes the intersectionality of race with gendered and feminist analyses. In the meantime, efforts at helping nice White ladies demonstrate evidence of cultural responsiveness must take up the ever-present task of doing more than just adding to their personal knowledge of race and whiteness. The preparation of a more culturally responsive teacher workforce necessarily includes challenging White women's complicity in maintaining dominant White racial norms in schools and equipping them with the tools to resist becoming simply another "nice White lady."

NOTES

1. Video for the *MADtv* "Nice White Lady" sketch can be found on YouTube at https://www.youtube.com/watch?v=JaewfHk9KiA
2. The underlying premise of this paper is that the teacher's racial identity is central to his or her development as culturally responsive. Experiences accorded to one's race, whiteness, and racial socialization must be accounted for in contemporary research, curriculum, and programs of study meant to improve White women's capacity to be effective teachers in classrooms where they are the race minority.

REFERENCES

Anderson, J. D. (1988). *The education of Blacks in the south*, 1860–1935. Chapel Hill, NC: The University of North Carolina Press.

Banks, J. A. (1995). The historical reconstruction of knowledge about race: Implications for transformative teaching. *Educational Researcher, 24*(2), 15–25.

Banks, J., & Banks, C. A. M. (2004). *Handbook of research on multicultural education* (2nd ed.). San Francisco, CA: Jossey-Bass.

Barr, J. J. (2011). The relationship between teachers' empathy and perceptions of school culture. *Educational Studies, 37*(3), 365–369.

Bentley-Edwards, K. L., Stevenson, H. C., Thomas, D. E., Adams-Bass, V. N., & Coleman-King, C. (in press.) Teaching scared: Pre-service teacher appraisals of racial stress, socialization and classroom management self-efficacy. *Teaching and Teacher Education*

Boler, M., Zembylas, M., & Tryfonas, P. (2003). Discomforting truths: The emotional terrain of understanding differences. In P. P. Trifonas (Ed.), *Pedagogies of difference: Rethinking education for social justice* (pp. 110–136). New York, NY: Routledge.

Brown, A. (2013). Waiting for superwoman: White female teachers and the construction of the "neoliberal savior" in a New York City public school. *Journal for Critical Education Policy Studies, 11*(2), 123–164.

Cicetti-Turro, D. (2007). Straight talk: Talking across race in schools. *Multicultural Perspectives, 9*(1), 45–49.

Coleman, S., & Stevenson, H. C. (2013). The racial stress of membership: Development of the faculty inventory of racialized experiences in schools. *Psychology in the Schools, 50*(6), 548–566.

Davis, M. H. (1994). *Empathy: A social psychological approach*. Boulder, CO: Westview Press.

DeCuir, J. T., & Dixson, A. D. (2004). "So when it comes out, they aren't that surprised that it is there": Using critical race theory as a tool of analysis of race and racism in education. *Educational Researcher, 33*(5), 26–31.

Delpit, L. (2006). *Other people's children: Cultural conflict in the classroom* (2nd ed.). New York, NY: The New Press. (Original work published 1995)

Delpit, L. (2012). *"Multiplication is for White people"—Raising expectations for other people's children.* New York, NY: The New Press.

Derlan, C. L., Umaña-Taylor, A. J., Toomey, R. B., Updegraff, K. A., Jahromi, L. B., & Flores, L. I. (2014). Perceived discrimination and ethnic affirmation: Anglo culture orientation as a moderator among Mexican-origin adolescent mothers. *Child Development, 85*(4), 1357–1365.

Dixson, A. (2003). When race matters: Examining race-conscious education policy and practice. *Educational Researcher, 32*(8), 39–43.

Dixson, A., & Rousseau, C. K. (Eds.). (2006). *Critical race theory in education: All God's children got a song*. New York, NY: Routledge.

Dolby, N. (2012). *Rethinking multicultural education for the next generation: The new empathy and social justice*. New York, NY: Routledge.

Downey, D., & Pribesh. S. (2004). 'When race matters: Teachers' evaluations of students classroom behaviors. *Sociology of Education*, 77, 267–282.

Education Week. (2014). Teaching Tolerance Honors Culturally Responsive Teaching award winners. Retrieved from http://www.edweek.org/tm/events/teachingtolerance/resources_2013.html?intc=thed

Fergus, E., Noguera, P., & Martin, M. (2014). *Schooling for resilience: Improving the life trajectory of Black and Latino boys*. Cambridge, MA: Harvard Education Press.

Ferguson, R. F. (2003). Teachers' perceptions and expectations and the Black-White test score gap. *Urban Education, 38*(4), 460–507.

Ford, A. C., & Sassi, K. (2014). Authority in cross-racial teaching and learning: (Re)considering the transferability of warm demander approaches. *Urban Education, 49*(1), 39–74.

Foster, M. (1997). *Black teachers on teaching*. New York, NY: New Press.

Foster, M., Lewis, J., & Onafowora, L. (2003). Anthropology, culture, and research on teaching and learning: Applying what we have learned to improve practice. *Teachers College Record, 105*(2), 261–277.

Friend, C., Hunter, A., & Fletcher, A. (2011). Parental racial socialization and the academic achievement of African American children: A cultural-ecological approach. *Journal of African American Studies, 15*(1), 40–57.

Garcia, S. B., & Guerra, P. L. (2004). Deconstructing deficit thinking working with educators to create more equitable learning environments. *Education and Urban Society, 36*(2), 150–168.

Garza, R. E., & Garza, E. (2010). Successful White female teachers of Mexican American students of low socioeconomic status. *Journal of Latinos and Education, 9*(3), 189–206.

Gay, G. (2010). *Culturally responsive teaching: Theory, research, and practice* (2nd ed.). New York, NY: Teachers College Press.

Gay, G. (2013). Teaching to and through cultural diversity. *Curriculum Inquiry, 43*(1), 48–70.

Gonzalez, N., Moll, L., & Amanti, C. (Eds.). (2005). *Funds of knowledge: Theorizing practices in households, communities, and classrooms*. Mahwah, NJ: Erlbaum.

Gorman, J. C. (2011). *The association between grades preK-12 student achievement and differentiated instructional strategies in the anytown township school district explored through units of study* (Doctoral dissertation). Retrieved from http://dspace.rowan.edu/bitstream/handle/10927/126/gormanj-d.pdf?sequence=4

Harding, H. (2005). "City girl": A portrait of a successful White urban teacher. *Qualitative Inquiry*, 11(1), 52–80.

Hinchey, P. H. (2006). *Becoming a critical educator: Defining a classroom identity, designing a critical pedagogy*. New York, NY: Peter Lang.

Hoban, G., & Hastings, G. (2006). Developing different forms of student feedback to promote teacher reflection: A 10-year collaboration. *Teaching and Teacher Education, 22*(8), 1006–1019.

Hollins, E. R. (2008). *Culture in school learning: Revealing the deep meaning* (2nd ed). New York, NY: Routledge. (Original work published 1996)

Hollins, E. R. (2012). *Learning to teach in urban schools: The transition from preparation to practice*. New York, NY: Routledge.

Holoien, D. S., & Shelton, J. N. (2012). You deplete me: The cognitive costs of colorblindness on ethnic minorities. *Journal of Experimental Social Psychology, 48*(2), 562–565.

Howard, G. (2006). *We can't teach what we don't know: White teachers, multiracial schools* (2nd ed.). New York, NY: Teachers College Press.

Howard, T. C. (2010). *Why race and culture matter in schools: Closing the achievement gap in America's classrooms*. New York, NY: Teachers College Press.

Hughes, D., Rodriguez, J., Smith, E. P., Johnson, D. J., Stevenson, H. C., & Spicer, P. (2006). Parents' ethnic–racial socialization practices?: A review of research and directions for future study, *Developmental psychology, 42*(5), 747–770.

Irvine, J. J. (1991). *Black students and school failure: Policies, practices, and prescriptions*. New York, NY: Praeger.

Irvine, J. J. (2002). *In search of wholeness: African-American teachers and their culturally specific classroom practices*. New York, NY: Palgrave.

Johnson, L. (2002). "My eyes have been opened": White teachers and racial awareness. *Journal of Teacher Education, 53*(2), 153–167.

Kennedy, M. M. (2007). Defining a literature. *Educational Researcher, 36*(3), 139–147.

Ladson-Billings, G. (2001). Unpacking culture, teaching and learning: The power of pedagogy. In W. Watkins, J. Lewis, & V. Chou (Eds.), *Race and education: The roles of history and society in educating African American students* (pp. 73–88). Boston, MA: Allyn & Bacon.

Ladson-Billings, G. (2006). Yes, but how do we do it? Practicing culturally relevant pedagogy. In J. Landsman & C. W. Lewis (Eds.), *White teachers/diverse classrooms: A guide to building inclusive schools, promoting high expectations, and eliminating racism* (pp. 29–42). Sterling, VA: Stylus.

Ladson-Billings, G. (2009). *The Dreamkeepers: Successful teachers of African American children* (2nd ed.). San Francisco, CA: Jossey-Bass. (Original work published 1994)

Ladson-Billings, G., & Tate, W. F. (1995). Toward a critical race theory of education. *Teachers College Record, 97*(1), 47–68.

Landsman, J. (2001). *White teacher talks about race*. Lanham, MD: Rowman & Littlefield.

Lawrence, S. M., & Tatum, B.D. (1997). White educators as allies: Moving from awareness to action. In M. Fine, L. C. Powell, L. Weis, & L. Mun Wong (Eds.), *Off White: Readings on race, power, and society* (pp. 333–342). New York, NY: Routledge.

Lave, J., & Wenger, E. (1991). *Situated learning: Legitimate peripheral participation*. Cambridge, MA: Cambridge University Press.

Lee, C. D., Spencer, M. B., & Harpalani, V. (2003). "Every shut eye ain't sleep": Studying how people live culturally. *Educational Researcher, 32*(5), 6–13.

Lensmire, T. J., & Snaza, N. (2010). What teacher education can learn from Blackface Minstrelsy. *Educational Researcher, 39*(5), 413–422.

Leonardo, Z. (2002). The souls of White folk: Critical pedagogy, Whiteness studies, and globalization discourse. *Race Ethnicity and Education, 5*(1), 29–50.

Leonardo, Z. (2009). *Race, Whiteness, and education*. New York, NY: Routledge.

Lesane-Brown, C. L. (2005). The comprehensive race socialization inventory. *Journal of Black Studies, 36*(2), 163–190.

Lynn, M., & Parker, L. (2006). Critical race studies in education: Examining a decade of Research on U. S. schools. *The Urban Review*, 38(4), 257–290.

Marx, S. (2006). *Revealing the invisible: Confronting passive racism in teacher education*. New York, NY: Routledge.

Marx, S. (2008). Popular White teachers of Latina/o kids: The strengths of personal experiences and the limitations of Whiteness. *Urban Education, 43*(1), 29–67.

Marx, S., & Pray, L. (2011). Living and learning in Mexico: Developing empathy for English language learners through study abroad. *Race, Ethnicity, and Education, 14*(4), 507–535.

McAllister, G., & Irvine, J. J. (2000). Cross cultural competency and multicultural teacher education. *Review of Educational Research, 70*(1), 3–24.

McAllister, G., & Irvine, J. J. (2002). The role of empathy in teaching culturally diverse students: A qualitative study of teachers' beliefs. *Journal of Teacher Education, 53*(5), 433–443.

McGrady, P. B., & Reynolds, J. R. (2013). Racial mismatch in the classroom: Beyond Black-White differences. *Sociology of Education, 86*(1), 3–17.

Michael, A. (2014). *Raising race questions: Whiteness and inquiry in education*. New York, NY: Teachers College Press.

Milner, H. R. (2009). What does teacher education have to do with teaching? Implications for diversity studies. *Journal of Teacher Education, 61*(1–2), 118-131.

Milner, H. R. (2010). *Start where you are, but don't stay there: Understanding diversity, opportunity gaps, and teaching in today's classrooms*. Cambridge, MA: Harvard Education Press.

Milner, H. R. (2011). Good intentions are not enough: Doing what's necessary to teach for diversity. In J. Landsman & C. W. Lewis (Eds.), *White teachers/diverse classrooms: Creating inclusive schools, building on students' diversity, and providing true educational equity* (2nd ed., pp. 56–73). Sterling, VA: Stylus.

Nasir, N. (2012). *Racialized identities: Race and achievement among African American youth*. Palo Alto, CA: Stanford University Press.

Oyserman, D. (2013). Not just any path: Implications of identity-based motivation for disparities in school outcomes. *Economics of Education Review, 33*, 179–190.

Oyserman, D., Harrison, K., & Bybee, D. (2001). Can racial identity be promotive of academic efficacy? *International Journal of Behavioral Development, 25*(4), 379–385.

Pahlke, E., Bigler, R. S., & Suizzo, M. A. (2012). Relations between colorblind socialization and children's racial bias: Evidence from European American mothers and their preschool children. *Child Development, 83*(4), 1164–1179.

Paley, V. G. (2000). *White teacher* (2nd ed.). Cambridge, MA: Harvard University Press.

Paris, D. (2012). Culturally sustaining pedagogy: A needed change in stance, terminology, and practice. *Educational Researcher, 41*(3), 93–97.

Parson, E. C. (2005). From caring as a relation to culturally relevant caring: A White teacher's bridge to Black students. *Equity & Excellence, 38*(1), 25–34.

Picower, B. (2009). The unexamined Whiteness of teaching: How White teachers maintain and enact dominant racial ideologies. *Race, Ethnicity, and Education, 12*(2), 197–215.

Sbarra, D. A., & Pianta, R. C. (2001). Teacher ratings of behavior among African American and Caucasian children during the first two years of school. *Psychology in the Schools, 38*(3), 229–238.

Sellers, R. M., Caldwell, C. H., Schmeelk-Cone, K. H., & Zimmerman, M. A. (2003). Racial identity, racial discrimination, perceived stress, and psychological distress among African American young adults. *Journal of Health and Social Behavior, 44*(3), 302–317.

Siddle Walker, V. (1996). *Their highest potential: An African American school community in the segregated south.* Chapel Hill, NC: The University of North Carolina Press.

Sleeter, C. E. (2001). Preparing teachers for culturally diverse schools: Research and the overwhelming presence of Whiteness. *Journal of Teacher Education,* 52(2), 94–106.

Sleeter, C. E. (2004). How White teachers construct race. In G. Ladson-Billings & D. Gillborn (Eds.), *The RoutledgeFalmer reader in multicultural education: Critical perspectives on race, racism, and education* (pp. 163–178). Abingdon, England: RoutledgeFalmer.

Stevenson, H. C. (2014). *Promoting racial literacy in schools: Differences that make a difference*. New York, NY: Teachers College Press.

Toldson, I. A. (2013). Race matters in the classroom. In C. W. Lewis & I. A. Toldson (Eds.), *Black male teachers: Diversifying the United States' teacher workforce* (pp. 15–21). Bingly, England: Emerald.

Tyler, K. M., Boykin, A. W., & Walton, T. R. (2006). Cultural considerations in Teacher's perceptions of students classroom behavior and achievement. *Teaching and Teacher Education*, 22, 998–1005.

Ullman, C., & Hecsh, J. (2011). These American lives: Becoming a culturally responsive teacher and the 'risks of empathy.' *Race, Ethnicity, and Education, 14*(5), 603–629.

Umaña-Taylor, A. J., Quintana, S. M., Lee, R. M., Cross, W. E., Rivas-Drake, D., Schwartz, S. J., Seaton, E. (2014). Ethnic and racial identity during adolescence and into young adulthood: An integrated conceptualization. *Child Development, 85*(1), 21–39.

Valencia, R. R. (2010). *Dismantling contemporary deficit thinking: Educational thought and practice.* New York, NY: Routledge.

Valenzuela, A. (1999). *Subtractive schooling: U.S.-Mexican youth and the politics of caring*. Albany, NY: State University of New York Press.

Villegas, A. M., & Lucas, T. (2002). *Educating culturally responsive teachers: A coherent approach.* Albany, NY: State University of New York Press.

Wang, M. T., & Huguley, J. P. (2012). Parental racial socialization as a moderator of the effects of racial discrimination on educational success among African American adolescents. *Child Development, 83*(5), 1716–1731.

Warren, C. A. (2013). The utility of empathy for White female teachers' culturally responsive interactions with Black male students. *Interdisciplinary Journal of Teaching and Learning, 3*(3), 175–200.

Warren, C. A. (2014). Towards a pedagogy for the application of empathy in culturally diverse classrooms. *The Urban Review, 46*(3), 395–419.

Warren, C. A. (2015). Conflicts and contradictions: Conceptions of empathy and the work of good intentioned White female teachers. *Urban Education, 50*(5), 572–600.

Warren, C. A., & Hotchkins, B. K. (2015). Teacher education and the enduring significance of "false empathy." *The Urban Review, 47*(2), 266–292.

Warren, C. A., & Lessner, S. (2014). "Who has family business?" Exploring the role of empathy in student-teacher interactions. *Perspectives on Urban Education, 11*(2), 122–131.

Yip, T. (2014). Ethnic identity in everyday life: The influence of identity development status. *Child development, 85*(1), 205–219.

Yoon, I. H. (2012). The paradoxical nature of Whiteness-at-work in the daily life of schools and teacher communities. *Race, Ethnicity, and Education, 15*(5), 587–613.

Young, M. D., & Rosiek, J. (2000). Book reviews: *Interrogating Whiteness*. *Educational Researcher, 29*(2), 39–44.

CHAPTER 9

THE EVIDENCE OF THINGS *NOT* SEEN?

Race, Pedagogies of Discipline, and White Women Teachers

Kevin Lawrence Henry, Jr.
University of Arizona

Chezare A. Warren
Michigan State University

A PRECURSOR: THE CHRONICLE OF THE UNSAVED CHILD

She pulled the drawer out of the dark mahogany desk and ravaged its contents for the near empty bottle of Tylenol. She popped two pills in her mouth as she pensively waited for her 4th-grade class to return from lunch on a particularly hot spring day. Elizabeth, a White woman around 22 years old and recent college graduate of the prestigious Friedman University in Oxford, Massachusetts, was a transplant to New Atlantis. This was a city she'd known of but had never visited prior to her move here this past summer. Elizabeth was fascinated by the vibrancy of New Atlantis. The humidity cloaked itself onto your being with unforgiving force. The rhythm with which

White Women's Work: Examining the Intersectionality of Teaching, Identity, and Race
pp. 177–199

language seemed to flow off the tongues of the locals, and the food with its intoxicating aromas and flavors nurtured Elizabeth's past, present, and future. Elizabeth was in love with New Atlantis. She was certain this was her new home.

Elizabeth often spends her lunch period, when she's not on duty, thinking about how it is she ended up as an elementary school teacher ... in New Atlantis ... at an "urban school" ... teaching African American and now an increasing number of Latinx kids. She always thought she'd be an advertising executive. And in truth, after she is finished with her second year of teaching she intends to apply to a MBA program at her alma matter with plans to return to New Atlantis to enter the business sector. Elizabeth has always loved children. So that most certainly was one of the reasons she decided to teach. As a leader of the College Democrats, she also settled that "these 'at-risk' Black kids in New Atlantis desperately need me." Her assertion is the result of images being flashed across her television of the city's devastation following the flooding caused by breaches in New Atlantis's levees. Elizabeth felt so sorry for "those people." Two years later during her senior year of college, she would finally be given a chance to make a difference in the lives of "those people." A recruiter from Schooling For Them (SFT), an alternative teacher placement program, approached her at a College Democrats meeting asking if she'd be willing to join their teaching corps. She quickly agreed and was pushed through the application process because of her good grades and campus leadership. Nonetheless, it seemed as if her life nor her 6-week summer training institute had adequately prepared her for being a teacher.

The bell indicating lunch was over [and] was met with the boisterousness of 1,000 trumpets. Elizabeth quickly lifted her head hoping it was a dream, but knowing it wasn't, walked to meet her students in the cafeteria. As she approached their table, the laughter and smiles of the children quickly dissipated. "Stand up!" Elizabeth sternly said. "Let's go. We have work to do." The children's smiles slowly faded with every step Elizabeth took nearer. They had become quite familiar to what they perceived to be Elizabeth's harsh demeanor. Demands such as these were no longer painful. Pain had been supplanted by numbness. However, though not often—but one should say often enough in the eyes of teachers and administrators—students would bend the rules of compliance. They, too, needed to breathe, preferring childhood and its accompanying antics and playfulness to a somnambulating zombie-ism.

The students walked through the school in a single file line, adorned in cotton white polo shirts with the school name and emblem just above the heart. Some wore khaki pants starched just two degrees less hard than cardboard, while others' pants resembled that of crinkled filler paper used for gifts or shipping. Some students' uniforms were simply perfection, or in other words, they complied with the uniform code with scrupulous detail—black belts, black socks, and black shoes, and only that color, lest an infraction be given. Their petite hands were to their sides. They walked the line the school literally had built into the floor. Lines like these were never found in New Atlantis' elite schools, nor was the eerie, deafening silence that cocooned the hallways. The students arrived to their classroom named after Elizabeth's alma mater. As the students walked in, their little 4th-grade bodies began to fill the desks.

The classroom's walls were a bright aureolin yellow. Motivational messages from people the children did not know were in each quadrant of the room. And of course, every flag or picture or statistic of Elizabeth's former school decorated the classroom with presumed authoritarian hope. This, after all, was what the youth needed, according to the school's administration: images of colleges. This unequivocally would inspire "these" children.

Elizabeth stood firmly over her students as they fumbled to ready themselves for class. As Elizabeth looked at the clock situated between two quotes, she realized time was quickly passing. Patrolling the aisles to indicate to students time was of the essence, she announced, "It's time to take out our pencils as we will be taking our timed math portion in anticipation for the Astroid Test!" None of the students "anticipated" the Astroid Test. In fact, they dreaded the test. How often would students capitulate to these frequent testing demands? How often would they go along to get along? How often did the anxiety of passing the test race through their minds? This was supposedly for their own good. Tests that obliterated relevance and threw responsiveness to the wind. These tests were important and essential, according to everyone whose voice was heralded as truth: politicians, philanthropist, business leaders, and the reformers for whom Elizabeth worked. Teachers needed data. Data proved teachers were efficient. And efficiency is good. Unless it's bad data. In the case of teachers like Elizabeth, bad data really meant bad students. Elizabeth never really questioned the rationality of high-stakes testing as the modus operandi of justice, as the new arm of the Civil Rights Movement, or the futility of her almost totally teacher-centered, zero-tolerance pedagogy and the narrowing of curricular content.

With that version of the truth in hand, Elizabeth prompted her students to turn to page 40 in their workbooks. Many students complied instantaneously to the orders. Wayne, however, was moving slower than his colleagues.

"Wayne, don't you think you need to be moving faster? Elizabeth questioned disapprovingly.

Wayne sat silently, never looking up at Elizabeth. Thumbing through the pages, clearly en route to page 40. However, he had not made it there yet. Elizabeth frustrated with Wayne asked again. This time more harshly, edging closer to his desk. "Wayne, don't you think you need to be moving faster?" Wayne looked Elizabeth in the eyes and responded, "I'm doing it,

Miss..." Before Wayne could finish his sentence Elizabeth took the booklet from his hands and opened it to page 40. "There. Now you're where I need you to be Wayne." Wayne, visibly embarrassed and offended, stood up, pushing himself up from his desk and chair. He said, "Ms. S, that's not fair!" With tears welling in his eyes, Wayne threw his pencil to the ground and sat back down. Elizabeth took this act as defiance. Punishable defiance. After her initial interpretation of his behavior as defiance, Elizabeth thought: "Well, if he'd throw a pencil, what might be next ... the workbook, a chair, his desk?" Elizabeth, a towering woman in comparison to her students, at the speed of light, was back to Wayne's desk. "Wayne this is unacceptable. You are unacceptable." In that moment, Elizabeth proclaimed. "And because of this you will need to have a moment away from civilization. Get up, now!"

All students dreaded being torn away from "civilization" as Elizabeth called it. It was Elizabeth's behavioral intervention. Elizabeth thought, "This will teach him and others to follow directions and to listen to me." The closet in the back of the room, away from the class is where the uncivilized belong. Out of sight. Out of mind. Wayne, whose feet, now two anvils, reluctantly walked to the closet. While the closet was large, it was still, nonetheless, a closet. He sat silently as his classmates bubbled in a's, b's, c's, d's, and e's on their scantrons. Wayne sat quietly, thinking about how much he hated school, of how he longed for a different kind of education. One hour had passed and his classmates were still bubbling in answers. By this time Wayne had fallen asleep.

Elizabeth, walking up and down the aisles of her classroom, heard a knock on her door. Moving quickly to the door, it was one of the custodians, Richard, a stout, older African American man with salt-and-pepper locks to his shoulder. He told her to gather her class and prepare for evacuation: There was a gas leak in the school. As Richard was telling Elizabeth this, the principal of the school came on the intercom and told teachers it was a "code 4"—mandatory evacuation. Elizabeth quickly gathered her students, telling them to walk in a single file line to the designated space across from the school. Students quickly prepared for the drill. As they were departing from the room. Brittany tried to alert Elizabeth of who had been forgotten. "Oh Ms. S is everything ok?" Elizabeth responded calmly, "Yes, Brittany. We just have to take a little break. But let's pay attention because we don't want to miss something important, do we?" "But Ms.—" Before Brittany could finish her statement, Elizabeth 'shhh-ed' her and reminded her to follow directions and pay attention or she would have to attend detention after school and be given the "punish packet."

About 30 minutes had passed and the gas leak still could not be contained. It was then that Elizabeth realized ... she realized the very terrible reality that was upon us. Elizabeth had forgotten about Wayne. She had forgotten he was stowed away, being "civilized" by being removed from "civili-

zation." Elizabeth ran past everyone, screaming and pointing toward the stately school "He's in there! He's in my room." Thoughts of Wayne flooded her mind. She inaudibly uttered a version of "What have I done? Oh my God. Oh my God. My God ... my God." Streams of tears rolled down her face as she, her assistant principal, and the firefighters entered her classroom. By then it was too late, much too late, as Wayne was no longer with us: suffocated by that which could not be seen.

INTRODUCTION

We use storytelling in an attempt to maintain a sense of fidelity to critical race theory (CRT) in not just substance, but also in form. Derrick Bell (1995) notes, "Critical race theory writing and lecturing is characterized by frequent use of the first person, storytelling, narrative, allegory ... and the unapologetic use of creativity" (p. 899). This chronicle provides readers with a context for understanding the ways in which racialized suffering exists within a stratified society, and more precisely how inequity is manifested on a micro level through student discipline (Dumas, 2014; Ladson-Billings, 2006). Being cast away, or separated from the group as a discipline measure is common in charter schools where strict student behavioral norms are established as a precursor to learning. This chronicles pushes us to think about the consequences of educational malfeasance that is deemed as normal, natural, and standard. This scenario is necessarily histrionic with the resulting death of Wayne from Elizabeth's disciplinary malpractice. Our use of hyperbole and symbolism is meant to illuminate how the futures of youth are too often easily imprisoned and "celled" by those fixated on power, and more precisely the enactment of "power over" (Duncan, 2000; Winn, 2010). This is a reality far too many African American youth face daily.

We are symbolically referring to spirit murdering in this chronicle. It happens to African American youth, the result of discipline practices that fail to consider how schooling is racialized and the ways race shades teacher interpretations of student behavior. The consequences of such color-blind discipline include an evisceration of hope, agency, counterhegemonic practices, and in some instances the lives of Black and Latinx youth. As Patricia Williams (1987) comments, racism is so insidious, so "deeply painful and assaultive as to constitute" what she calls *spirit murder* (p.129). Racism is an essential element of spirit murdering. Williams offers,

> Spirit murder, or disregard for others whose lives qualitatively depend on our regard ... [produces] a system of formalized distortions of thought. It

> produces social structures centered around fear and hate; it provides a tumorous outlet for feelings elsewhere unexpressed. (pp. 151–152)

Spirit murdering, which is inherently a process of devaluation and abjection, is part of the racial grammar of our society. It is illustrative of the way exclusionary discipline is wielded against students of color in public schools around the United States. It's embedded in our mental and institutional structures and is affiliated with racial domination (Bernstein, 1977; Bonilla-Silva, 2012).

The incomprehensibility of racist acts, such as spirit murdering in the way that Black students are disciplined in school, is twinned with domination blindness, both of which facilitate the reproduction and maintenance of White supremacy. As Bonilla-Silva (2012) notes, racial grammar "structures cognition, vision, and even feelings on all sort of racial matters. This grammar normalizes the standards of White supremacy as the standard for all sort[s] of social events and transactions" (p. 173). In our era of colorblindness, "race" is often said to not be seen, yet communities of color palpably feel the effects of racism. Issues of racial disparities and disproportionalities run amuck in our schools.

White women teachers dominate the profession making up nearly 80% of the teaching force. They may operate in what Leonardo and Boas (2013) call "the White racial army." That is to say, these teachers may unintentionally work in service of and allegiance to whiteness in their practice without attention to the ways they interact with youth of color. While White women teachers are not the sole reason for racial disparities in schools, nor should they be scapegoated in an effort to overlook larger structural issues that buoy these disparities, they are in a position to arbitrate the impact of oppressive school practices that politicians, policymakers, and neoliberal reformers refuse to address. White women teachers who do not actively work to dismantle White dominance are implicated in processes of spirit murdering for youth of color in schools.

We argue in this chapter that spirit murdering is an accumulative process made manifest in schools by White women teachers when they unconsciously act in ways that suggest Black and brown students are seen as "problems" to be fixed. Students of color are disproportionally suspended and expelled, and too often overreferred for placement in special education. Their resistance in school is a cry out for change and justice. Schools too often erase home cultures, and reservoirs of knowledge are starved to maintain a steady diet of information needed to pass standardized tests. It is this climate that is most characteristic of neoliberalism. We use New Orleans as a site to examine these troubling pedagogic trends. Most importantly, we aim to explore how race is implicated in White woman's discipline practices and their role in reproducing educational inequality.

NEW ORLEANS, NEOLIBERALISM, AND WHITE WOMEN EDUCATORS

New Orleans is heralded by education reformers as the model for school reform and achievement growth, despite claims that illuminate the fabrication of such academic growth (Buras, 2012, 2014). Key to the notion of success in New Orleans is its effective enshrining and embodiment of market, neoliberal values. The proliferation of charter schools and new "innovative talent" (i.e. White, mostly women, alternatively certified, and placed through programs such as Teach for America or teachNOLA) who acquiesce to and are supporters of narrow, high-stakes accountability regimes are the touted markers of success. Significantly, the linkage between charter schools, teachers, and high-stakes testing in New Orleans is illustrative of the racial politics and pedagogies of reform in New Orleans.

Before exploring racial politics at the classroom level, it is crucial to understand the precursors to the New Orleans public school district's characterization. The schools were constituted as "academically unacceptable" on state achievement tests. The definition of academically unacceptable shifted from a cutoff score of 60 to just below the state average of 87.4. This allowed for the creation of charter schools in a special district named the Recovery School District. Former Governor Kathleen Blanco signed Executive Orders 58 and 79, which eliminated the need to consult and obtain votes of community members, parents, and educators who would be impacted by the converting of a traditional neighborhood public school into a charter school. This further removed African Americans from the democratic process. It was an expedient measure to "mute" communities already impacted by racialized political unresponsiveness.

Moreover, the racial demographics of teachers in the district shifted drastically. The predominantly African American teaching force was fired en mass, marking one of the largest displacements of African American educators since *Brown v. Board of Education*. These teachers were replaced with a vast majority of White teachers associated with Teach for America (TFA) or Teach NOLA, a similar alternative program (Buras, 2014; Dixson, Royal, & Henry, 2013). African American veteran educators in New Orleans were scapegoated as the problem for the struggling school system. Their bodies and collective cultural and pedagogical knowledge were seen as superfluous to the restructuring of New Orleans education. The New Orleans case demonstrates how the state has asserted power to replace

African American teachers—individuals with strong roots in the community—with more emphasis on standardized testing and new brigades of White women teachers presumed competent enough to be effective teachers of African Americans. No evidence existed to the latter. Yet, TFA teachers were given carte blanche access to New Orleans' schools and students. These teachers were constructed to the mainstream as the ideal educator.

The elimination of traditional public schools and the influx of White, overwhelmingly female teachers, who support market-based approaches to educating students of color has become the (hegemonic) way of (teaching) life in New Orleans. Teachers become cogs in a well-oiled machine designed to ignore race and cultural difference as an important aspect for negotiating amiable interactions with stakeholders in communities for which many White teachers are unfamiliar. These market-based charter schools are fixated on strict standards for behavioral control and fascinated with "standards" testing accountability regimes, corporate management techniques, the proliferation of "choice" (à la charter schools), and alternative teacher preparation and placement programs, such as Teach for America (Apple, 2006; Lipman, 2011).

This racialized neoliberal project in education ultimately feels like the suffocating of student creativity and the enactment of punitive pedagogies. Punitive pedagogies range from the use of zero-tolerance approaches for school discipline to the erasure of culturally responsive curriculum and teaching approaches. Sondel's (2013) work on TFA educators in New Orleans best illustrates this point. Sondel (2013) illuminated what she called *pedagogies of compliance* among White TFA teachers, locating their teaching on grids of rules, regulations, punishments, reordering of student cultures, and colonizing curriculum. These teachers zealously concerned with standardized testing and data inadvertently recentered whiteness and reproduced racial inequalities.[1] While these White women teachers have not set the policy, they have performed it. As Leonardo and Boas (2013) remind us, "with respect to White women, although they may not call the shots, they often pull the trigger" (p. 315). "Trigger happy" White women teachers, who may be well-intentioned, still commit the act of spirit murder via acts of complicity, dispositions of whiteness, and false-empathetic logics (Mills, 2007; Picower, 2009; Warren, 2015; Warren & Hotchkins, 2015). Punitive pedagogies provide very restrictive possibilities for creating an education worthy of our students, and broader considerations of human freedom and liberation.

Discipline Trends in Louisiana

According to a report from the Louisiana Department of Education, during the 2013–2014 academic year, while African American children made up less than half (44%) of the student body population, they accounted for 63% of in-school suspensions, 67% of out-of-school suspensions, and 68% of expulsions (Louisiana Department of Education, 2015). Even more disturbing in some New Orleans charters more than 25% of the student body is suspended at least once. In some charter schools, the numbers are even more appalling. For instance, during the 2012–2013 academic year, Carver Collegiate and Carver Preparatory suspended 69% and 61% of their student bodies (respectively), while Sci Academy and Joseph S. Clark suspended 58% and 46% of the student bodies (respectively; Dreilinger, 2014). These numbers provide evidence of the ways Louisiana schools and teachers are culpable in what the NAACP Legal Defense and Educational Fund (2005) states, "removes children from mainstream educational environment[s] and funnel[s] them into a one-way path toward prison" (p. 2). It is then no surprise that according to a 2014 report by the United States Justice Department that Louisiana ranks highest among states incarcerating (Carson, 2014). Yet, underneath these dismal statistics is the reality that criminality is always already inscribed on the Black body and already envisioned in the American imaginary. So, even minor offenses that simply require some care get perceived as a bigger challenge than they are by teachers who lack empathy for their students.

PUNITIVE PEDAGOGY IN THE CITY THAT CARE FORGOT

In this section, we consider the racial dispositional reasoning of two novice, White female teachers, Claire and Grace. Our aim is to illuminate how these teachers' particular reasoning about their students of color translate into discipline practices that implicate Claire and Grace in spirit murdering. As such, these teachers' dispositions and practices aid in reproducing racialized educational inequality. At the time of the interviews, both Claire and Grace were first-year teachers in New Orleans. They both were recent transplants to New Orleans, placed in charter schools via the alternative teaching program, Teach for America. While both Claire and Grace do have good intentions and understand their work to be part of the rebuilding of New Orleans, the following vignettes suggest their lack of criticality with respect to how race actually hinges on notions of cultural deprivation.

"Because That's All They Know": Claire's Perspective on Student Discipline

KLH: So, why do you think students act up?

Claire: Because that's all they know ... that's all they've seen. They have friends and family members who don't really value education and they don't value it either. I'm trying to tell you, Kevin, they misbehave because that's how they roll.

KLH: So what can you do as a teacher?

Claire: It's really out of my hands. If there is no support at home, what can I really do? [pause] Those that want to learn will learn. Those that act up … I won't allow to get in the way of those who want to learn.

KLH: And how do you intend to do that?

Claire: I put them out.

The previous conversation between the first author and Claire (pseudonym, as are all names), who teaches in a charter school serving a predominantly Black student body who are 100% free and reduced lunch, took place in the fall of 2014. Claire's comments are insightful, inasmuch as they expose how punitive pedagogies emerge in far too many of our schools. Claire's confident declaration as to why students "act up" is indicative of a lack in understanding of, and a lack of empathy for, her students. This logic makes sense on the surface, but fails to consider the intersections of race and poverty for shaping a family's priorities. For instance, it may be that the number of hours (and jobs) that a parent works limits the amount of free time or time they can take off to show up for parent-teacher conferences.

The implications for Claire's punitive pedagogy and the clear-cut, overly simple approach to dismissing a student are profound. In this instance, we see how easily her Black students are thrown away and pushed out. Students who do not comply with Claire's vision of "good" behavior are quite literally excused. They are out of sight/site and out of mind. Her commonsense approach does not consider the impact of oppressive institutional norms and practices, nor does it account for a child's own opinion and social perspective of their circumstance(s) that lead them to act in particular ways. Moreover, Claire's response to Kevin's questions, similar to Elizabeth's posture in the chronicle at the beginning of the chapter, fails to offer a critical race understanding of the ways Claire's beliefs and interpretations further oppress youth of color. If she was considering race, she would be reminded of national trends in Black students' overrepresentation for exclusionary discipline, and think twice before so easily "putting" a kid out of class. Claire does not see herself as responsible for how her students act in class. On the contrary, there are volumes of research to suggest that how teachers interact with youth has tremendous consequences on the classroom climate and student engagement (Irvine & York, 1995; Pianta, Hamre, & Allen, 2012). Indeed, it is through teachers' actions that some children are left behind and pushed out, given full "permission to fail." Claire's actions beg the question: Who will survive in our classrooms and under what conditions?

Claire's deficit disposition regarding the students, their families, and culture ultimately strains the interactions between Claire and her students and has a deleterious impact on the instruction—or lack thereof—she attempts to deliver to students. This disposition is rooted in the logics of White dominance that allow Claire to leave her practices unexamined and unchallenged. Claire never questioned her positionality and the ways in which power and dominance operates through her, or how these actions of hers implicate her in larger processes that dispossess students of color. While Claire deems teaching all of her students out of her hands, she squarely places the responsibility of educating her students solely in the hands of their communities. As opposed to creating an environment that is supportive, restorative, and affirming, Claire relies on deficit notions situating student misbehavior as a communal characteristic.

In Claire's instance, her engagement in spirit murdering weakens her ability to connect with students and engage in culturally relevant teaching. If we recall that spirit murdering is the outward manifestation of both dysconscious and conscious racisms, then harsh disciplining practices for African American and Latinx youth do not seem untenable (King, 1991). In fact, spirit murdering practices of devaluation and disregard, undergirded by "distortions of thought" about African American and Latinx urban youth, transform these youth into avatars to be fixed and emptied into (Freire, 2008). Attempts to discipline students into submission are motivated by desires for students to comply with testing regimes inasmuch to demonstrate adequate progress, and thus the utility of charter schools and TFA for saving Black and Latinx youth. What this does, however, is create environments where teachers are less able to engage in culturally relevant pedagogies. Teachers such as Claire place a laser-like focus on student achievement via standardized tests and acts of compliance. Culturally relevant pedagogies require that teachers not only authentically engage with their students' cultures, but that they learn to see the value and power in students' cultures thereby helping to "sustain" students' cultures (Paris, 2012; Paris & Alim, 2014). At its core, culturally relevant pedagogies build and strengthen relationships among teachers and students—not forcing narrow notions of compliance or extraction. Claire's acquiescence to and performance of such punitive logics makes it difficult for her to see her students beyond numbers on a spreadsheet, let alone their race and racialized experiences.

Unfortunately, Claire's behavior does not deviate from the norm. She did not say that she prefers students who misbehave to be suspended. However, chances are this is the trajectory they are on in New Orleans's charter schools. As Arcia (2006) notes, there is a disproportionate impact on students of color when schools rely on exclusion from the classroom as a central disciplinary strategy. Wayne, an African American male teacher from New Orleans who works at one of the charter schools (operated by a majority of White female TFA teachers), comments when discussing discipline policies at his school, "[Y]ou really can't make this stuff up, man. They would suspend students if they skipped a detention." Kevin asked, slightly surprised, "Are you serious?" Wayne responded, "Dead serious. Suspended if they skipped a detention. This is ridiculous; it really makes no sense." Wayne's comments about the capricious discipline polices in schools are only echoed by the data that illuminate these racial disparities.

Saving "Grace"... From the Future of the Present: Or, the Road to Hell is Paved With Good Intentions

> I don't have to tell you what crime is like in New Orleans. And you already know how terrible students were doing academically pre-Katrina. It's pretty clear that the more education you have, the less likely you are to go to jail or commit crimes. We want to educate our students and deter them from crime. It's that simple.

Grace, like Claire, works in a school that serves an overwhelmingly African American population with nearly all of her students on free and reduced lunch. Grace's comments reflect the perspectives of many newly minted (White women) educators in New Orleans. Her role and work is twofold: saving Black bodies from themselves by way of schooling and saving herself from those Black bodies (i.e. the future criminal). Grace's linking of schooling, or rather the lack there of, to criminality is an important jump because it situates her as a salvific benefactor and her students as "always already" delinquent. Trust and safety are void in Grace's imaginary. Grace's reading and gaze of her students is of the potential of their criminality, not of their innocence or for that matter their normalcy as youth. The goal becomes to narrowly educate students out of their presumed criminality.

Morris (2005) discusses the role of harsh disciplinary practices being based on the perceptions of a student's race. The purpose of disciplining students is a mechanism to "rework the behavior and appearance of students so their bodies display acceptable, normative comportment" (p. 27). In the case of *J.W. v. Louisiana Board of Elementary and Secondary et al.* (2010), the plaintiff, known as J.W., a student at one elementary charter school in New Orleans, was handcuffed and shackled to chairs for minor violations of school rules. A settlement agreement was reached, however, the psychological and physical damage had already been done. These tactics are a way to change the future by working on the present; a preemptive move rooted in fear to stop a criminality that has yet to exist. These practices traumatize Black youth who have already endured violence against their being as perpetrated by the state, schools, and educators. These acts of spirit murdering slowly erode young people's desire to be affiliated with schools and the teachers that oppress them.

White women teachers, who may be well intentioned yet desirous of conforming their students to meet idealized norms and standards of whiteness espoused by privately run public schools (i.e. charters), are engaging in spirit murdering by way of cultural erasure. In the case of New Orleans, White women teachers who are unfamiliar with the culture of the "chocolate city" and are unwilling to take the requisite steps to engage in culturally relevant pedagogy do a disservice to their students. More importantly, contrary to Grace's deficit linking of criminality with Black youth pre-Katrina, in the time before she arrived to "save" the "ravaged" city, all Black youth in New Orleans are not criminals. In fact, they have been criminalized by a system and individuals who cannot see these youth's highest potential.

Critical race theorists discuss the notion of whiteness as property, situating whiteness as something that has material and symbolic benefits/privileges for its holders, as well as something that can be transferred, like other forms of property (Ladson-Billings & Tate, 1995). Subtle linkages of blackness with criminality and lack of educability casts aspersions on blackness. Grace does just that while also positioning herself and other White female teachers as "saviors." The damage to the reputation and status of Black youth can be contrasted with the positive identity characteristics that Grace and her colleagues hold. Importantly, however, redemption is available for Black students who fit the mold that Grace and others have constructed for idealized students. Their reputation can be saved, if only they adhere to the norms of whiteness. In such instances, whiteness is transferred and students are rewarded for their conformity (Ladson-Billings & Tate, 1995).

MAKING RACE SEEN IN THE PRACTICE OF STUDENT DISCIPLINE

The vignettes of Claire and Grace illustrate the often-subtle ways White women teachers in New Orleans engage in the accumulative process of spirt murder. Claire and Grace's narratives help us to understand that good intentions are not enough. More precisely, these teachers' limited understanding of race and racism, their students' cultures, and humanizing pedagogies thwart approaches to challenge inequality. The narrow understanding of factors that constitute students' cultures, as well as the constant control and disciplining of African American students, cooperate to reproduce racial inequality.

The voices of students in New Orleans are an important index for understanding a critique of punitive pedagogies and an impetus for considering alternate ways of teaching. The perspectives of some students in New Orleans suggest that discipline policies created, supported, and enacted by White women teachers tend to do more harm than good, despite lofty rhetoric. On November 20, 2013, a group of students from Carver Collegiate and Carver Prep organized against what they deemed as unfair treatment in their schools. These two schools were operated by Collegiate Academies, a charter management organization. The students held a walkout and protest. They provided a list of demands to the Collegiate Academies board of directors and administrators. Some students were suspended, while others were pushed out for speaking their minds. We will quote, at length, some of the demands the students made.

> We get disciplined for anything and everything. We get detentions or suspensions for not walking on the taped lines in the hallway, for slouching, for not raising our hands in a straight line. The teachers and administrators tell us this is because they are preparing us for college. But walking on tape doesn't' prepare us for college. It trains us for the military or worse for jail. If college is going to be like Carver, we don't want to go to college.
>
> We get suspended for trying to ask why we must do certain things—teachers consider this to be "disrespectful" and it is the most common reason we get suspended from school. Sometimes teachers take things as disrespect, when they aren't meant to be disrespectful. Asking questions about why something is done a certain way shouldn't be considered as disrespect. We want to know why we have to do these things. We want answers, and suspending us for asking questions isn't an appropriate response.
>
> We want a discipline policy that doesn't suspend kids for every little thing. Suspensions should only be used for [a] very serious matter. We want a discipline policy that keeps kids in school, learning.
>
> We don't have any say into school policies. We can't explain ourselves. We also get talked to like we are little kids, or sometimes like animals. We want our teachers to treat us with respect, and we want to have a say in the school policies.
>
> The teachers don't connect with us or where we come from. There are no Black teachers.
>
> Some of the teachers are racially insensitive. None of the teachers are from New Orleans. They can't relate to us, our neighborhoods, or our community. They have no respect for our customs and culture, and simply want to make us more like them without understanding us and our background.

These counternarratives by students provide an incisive critique of the dominant narrative of charter schools in New Orleans and the complicit role White women teachers play in spirit murdering. Many of these teachers engage in the normative practices of their institutions, accepting the ordinariness of maintaining control of African American bodies. Their stated good intentions to serve African American students is impaired by institutional and cultural blinders. Unfortunately, the experiences of these youth are a testament to the suffering and anti-Black regard many youth around the United States face daily as they struggle to maintain hope, faith, and dreams of justice in the midst of its illusiveness. Their subjugation is standard operating procedure. And that subjugation is made possible by a hegemonic rationality that renders them "like animals" to be tamed and controlled so that the larger project of "educating" them can happen. In fewer words, these Black boys and girls are dehumanized regularly.

The critiques these youth offer illuminate the lack of empathy their teachers and school administrators have for them. Empathy has been found to likely improve the capacity of teachers to engage in culturally relevant teaching (Peck, Maude, & Brotherson, 2015; McAllister & Irvine, 2002; Warren, 2014). By empathy we mean the capacity of teachers to see life through the eyes of youth. Cultivating a sensitive understanding of students' schooling experiences as the student is experiencing school, rather than projecting onto them how they might (or should) be experiencing school from limited privileged viewpoints, can shift one's pedagogy in countless ways. Yet, the harsh policies and the utter disconnect these students accentuate bespeaks of a more insidious dispositional reality in which White female teachers have distorted perceptions of their students.

We argue that it is the responsibility of school leaders, professional preparation, and professional development programs to emphasize the significant role of race and racism on teaching, and the function of an institution for enacting policies that make students feel important, affirmed, and valued. Ferguson (2001) made clear in her discussion of Black masculinity and school discipline practices that perceptions and dispositions play a significant role in creating disproportional disciplining of Black male students. She insists,

> As "not-children," their behavior is understood not as something to be molded and shaped over time, but as the intentional, fully cognizant actions of an adult. This means there is already a dispositional pattern set, that their behavior is incorrigible, irremediable. Therefore, the treatment required for infractions is one that punishes through example and exclusion rather than through persuasion and edification, as is practiced with young White males. (Ferguson, 2001, p. 9)

While Ferguson's (2001) discussion focuses on Black and White males, one can see the connection to African American children writ large, regardless of sex. The harsh policies enacted upon students is both an indictment against charter schools in New Orleans and the workers within them. White female teachers, as the students argue, are unable to see their students' humanity and understand their cultural practices, which leads to misunderstandings and suspensions for "every little thing." White female teachers reproduce these inequalities in their schools by having a "lack of knowledge about the Black children in their classrooms" (Ferguson, 2001, p. 90). Our aim in this chapter is to raise awareness, and to insist that readers take up these issues as serious for improving the quality of schooling provided to youth of color.

DISCUSSION AND POSSIBILITIES: MOVING BEYOND SPIRIT MURDER

We believe that White female educators do what they believe is best for students. Yet, the narratives of Claire and Grace demonstrate the need for White women teachers to move beyond doing what is best for kids and becoming active agents in dismantling racial inequality. This has to be a priority of their preparation to teach in communities of color. One way this is done is by challenging the deficit dispositions they hold of their students through critical explorations in the ways race and culture is acknowledged in perceptions of behavior. Many White women teachers tacitly engage in spirit murdering before they even realize it. This chapter aimed to foreground how enwhitened regimes of discipline become spirit murdering and the ways racial prejudice manifests itself in institutional practices related to discipline as facilitated by its agents (i.e., teachers).

Simple acts such as removing students from school do little to improve students' educational attainment. Practices such as this one likely worsen students' schooling experience. As Gregory, Skiba, and Noguera (2010) highlight, "Suspended students may become less bonded to school, less invested in school rules and coursework, and subsequently less motivated to achieve academic success" (p. 60). This instantiation of spirit murdering is rooted in racism. Spirit murder abrades our students' humanity and chisels away their identities. The students' demands in the quotes shared in this chapter highlight the need for teachers and administrators who are enemies of White supremacy, and who see the value in students' cultures, to do something more. The White women teachers and instances we have detailed illuminate how racial inequality is reproduced though acquiescence to neoliberal logics. One mechanism for White women teachers to counteract the racial stratification and suffering existing in their schools and classrooms is to utilize culturally relevant practices.

MAKING CULTURALLY RELEVANT PEDAGOGY A PRIORITY

We offer culturally relevant pedagogy as an important and useful alternative for ameliorating discipline practices that further oppress, manipulate, and marginalize youth of color. This is especially true in the hundreds of charter schools and other privately operated K-12 educational institutions similar to those in New Orleans that lean on very stringent discipline practices, steeped in philosophies of human control, to create better learning conditions. A focus on White women teachers without attention to the institutions that equip them with, and reward their use of, punitive disciplinary approaches is negligent. We described the philosophies of just two White women teachers practicing in predominantly Black schools, but in doing so intended to demonstrate how their school is implicated in shaping, rewarding, and underscoring such philosophies. With these data made visible, we emphasize the importance of White women's responsibility to advocate for practices and policies in their school that humanize youth of color. When teachers work together and form coalitions with youth, families, and communities, they are better prepared to push back against manifestations of racial subjugation in their buildings. On the contrary, the greatest evidence of any teacher's resistance will be their teaching effectiveness. We have laid out the issue of racialized discipline in this chapter as a means for helping the reader to identify and name the problems they may notice in schools serving high populations of low-income youth of color. Now, we transition to offer a culturally relevant pedagogy as a way to think about microchanges that can lead to broader institutional reform.

Culturally relevant pedagogy is centered on three mutually related concepts—academic achievement (student learning), cultural competence, and sociopolitical consciousness (Ladson-Billings, 1994, 1995). Importantly, those who are interested in developing culturally relevant practices must develop empathy and care for their students; it a necessary element (Warren, 2014).[2] Culturally relevant teaching is first a humanizing effort to challenge White dominance and regimes of truth. As such, teachers see, understand, and value students and their cultures. This process helps to supplant dispositions, norms/practices, and curricula that erode students' humanity and neglect their funds of knowledge. Culturally relevant teaching challenges the way power operates with its attempts to control bodies and ethnic epistemologies.

Moreover, culturally relevant teachers hold high expectations of their students and themselves. They see education much more expansively than standardized test scores. Their students must develop and maintain cultural competence and linguistic, literate, and cultural plurality; experience academic success; and develop a critical consciousness. Moreover, restorative pedagogies aim to create radical healing spaces that aim to transform trauma and pain to purpose and hope. These restorative pedagogies denounce zero-tolerance and punitive policies and they aim to make schools and classrooms sites of peacemaking/keeping, restoration, empathy, and relationship building. Lastly, teachers and schools should consider the root causes of behavior problems and create processes for students to have an active role in discipline policies such as circle processes, peer mediation, or youth court (Gay, 2000; Hill, 2009; Ladson-Billings, 1995; Paris & Alim, 2014; Pranis, 2005; Winn, 2013). What is provided in the following, when taken together, will aid White female teachers in developing culturally relevant practices.

Develop a Critical Consciousness of Inequality (and Continually Do So)

The onus will be on White female educators to educate themselves about White supremacy and other forms of oppression that impact the lives of our youth, as well as their own lives. This book is one great resource. This work is necessarily iterative and on-going. No one book or class or conference can give educators the tools necessary to unpack their privilege and work to dismantle racial injustice. Because racism evolves and morphs, finding comfort in moments when one thinks it's dead, educators must remain vigilant. Being a culturally relevant educator is a lifelong project (Duncan-Andrade & Morrell, 2008; Matias, 2013).

Engage in Strategic Deployments of Whiteness for Justice

This is where the notion of praxis is essential. Building off one's critical knowledge of inequality, actually doing the work of dismantling White privilege, is essential to this project. This includes utilizing one's White privilege for justice, as opposed to hoarding it. Deploying whiteness for justice may include advocating for our students in faculty meetings, professional developments, or elsewhere; or holding a colleague accountable for practices and speech that reproduce inequality. One must also advocate for institutional polices that actively address racial disparities (Lawrence & Tatum, 1997; Leonardo, 2002).

Teaching What You Know

Beyond learning about racial inequality, learn about the beauty, complexity, and strength of your students' cultures and communities. Educators could attend events, communicate with various community organizations and stakeholders, talk with students and families, or develop reading groups (Gay, 2000; Howard, 1999; Ladson-Billings, 1995).

Develop Self-Reflexivity

Turning the mirror on oneself can be particularly hard. Yet, this is essential for educators who are committed to racial justice. Cultivate an understanding of the ways in which your identity is raced, constructed, and privileged. Additionally, critically analyzing your everyday classroom practices is crucial. Think about how and why certain students are supported in your class while others are not. Consider the types of practices that reinforce inequities (Evans-Winters, 2011; Michie, 1998, 2005; Milner, 2010).

CONCLUSION

In this chapter, we aimed to make visible the racialized realities of charter schools in New Orleans, particularly by focusing on the dispositions and practices of White women teachers in enacting pedagogies of punitive discipline. As such, we have attempted to illustrate the undergirding, the often invisible logics that can result in spirit murdering of African American and Latinx students. The rationalities and discipline practices of the White women teachers in this chapter aid in the reproduction and conservation of racial inequality. Dispositions rooted in deficit logics that erase our students' home cultures, as well as focus almost exclusively on standardized testing, create environments that marginalize and exclude students of color in urban contexts, and ultimately lead to spirit murder. Spirit murder is an accumulative process of dehumanization, and in this case punitive disciplinary practices that devalue, disregard, and remove students from educative spaces. Spirit murder is also linked to "distortions of thought" by White female teachers who tacitly internalize and perform whiteness. While these White female teachers may desire to improve the educational and life chances of their students, they inadvertently add to racial disproportionalities by acquiescing (or creating) institutional practices that constrict culturally diverse students and construct them as "at-risk" and deviant. Teachers can be the first line of defense against punitive pedagogies that result in spirit murder. White women teachers can begin the necessary work of dismantling racism by being much more attentive to the quality of their interaction with youth of color, and the utility of those interactions for making school a place where youth thrive intellectually, socially, and emotionally. This chapter has been an effort to raise awareness in hopes of emphasizing the significance of a more critical, humanizing disposition that challenges inequitable discipline policies and practices.

We do not claim the strategies included in this chapter to be the precise summing up, or the silver bullet, of educational reform. Moreover, while these efforts can certainly improve and impact the educational experiences of youth in urban spaces, we must also think of our educational reforms in conjunction with other justice centered efforts. Seeing the aforementioned efforts linked to urban job creation programs, eliminating homelessness and housing instability, the eradication of the prison-industrial complex, adequate health care, quality food, and access to transportation all create more possibilities. Indeed, these are humble unconcluding remarks. We say unconcluding because this work is always in perpetual motion. There is no finality to justice work. Our students may change, our circumstances my shift, our strategies may morph, yet our commitment to ensuring humanizing pedagogies and justice must remain constant. These efforts begin first by acknowledging the way racialized oppression works, then striving to make sure it doesn't.

NOTES

1. Wayne Au's (2007) work reminds us that one of the limitations of high-stakes testing is that "curricular content is narrowed to tested subjects, subject area knowledge is fragmented into test-related pieces, and teachers increase the use of teacher-centered pedagogies" (p.258). White women teachers associated with TFA, as a whole, have ushered in an era of narrowed pedagogies that are culturally irrelevant and nonresponsive to students of color. See Au (2015) for a more nuanced examination of how high-stakes testing has been a mechanism of White supremacy.
2. Warren's (2014) work that illustrates the development of empathy in teachers revolves around the notions of perspective taking and empathic concern. As Warren notes, "Perspective taking may include the implementation of activities, strategies, rituals, and polices meant to obtain first person, micro-level knowledge of students.... Empathic concern encompasses teacher behaviors that communicate a mutual sharing of emotion, feeling, or experience with students" (p. 412). In Warren's study, teachers engaged in various acts that strengthened their teaching and rela-

tionship with students. One central theme was the value of student voice. These teachers built trust with their students in order to learn the various cultural and social perspectives of students. They utilized such knowledge to inform instruction.

REFERENCES

Apple, M. W. (2006). *Educating the "right" way: Markets, standards, God, and inequality* (2nd ed.). New York, NY: Routledge.

Arcia, E. (2006). Achievement and enrollment status of suspended students: Outcomes in a large, multicultural school district. *Education and Urban Society, 38,* 359–369.

Au, W. (2007). High-stakes testing and curricular control: A qualitative metasynthesis. *Educational Researcher, 36*(5), 258–267.

Au, W. (2015). High-stakes testing: A tool for White supremacy for over 100 years. In B. Picker & E. Mayorga (Eds.), *What's race got to do with it? How current school reform policy maintains racial and economic inequality,* (pp. 21–43). New York, NY: Peter Lang.

Bell, D. (1995). Who's afraid of critical race theory? *University of Illinois Law Review, 1995,* 893–910.

Bernstein, B. (1977). *Class, codes, and control* (Vol. 3). London, England: Routledge & Kegan Paul.

Bonilla-Silva, E. (2012). The invisible weight of whiteness: The racial grammar of everyday life in contemporary America. *Ethic and Racial Studies, 35*(2), 173–194.

Buras, K. (2012). "It's all about the dollars": Charter schools, educational policy, and the racial market in New Orleans. In W. Watkins *The assault on public education: Confronting the politics of corporate school reform* (pp. 160–188). New York, NY: Teachers College Press.

Buras, K. (2014). *Charter schools, race, and urban space: Where the market meets grassroots resistance.* New York, NY: Routledge.

Carson, E. A. (2014). *Prisoners in 2013.* U.S. Department of Justice Office of Justice Programs, & United States of America. Retrieved from http://www.bjs.gov/content/pub/pdf/p13.pdf

Dixson, A. D., Royal, C., & Henry, K. L., Jr. (2013). School reform and school choice. In H. R. Milner, IV, & K. Lomety (Eds.), *Handbook of urban education* (pp. 474–503). New York, NY: Routledge.

Dreilinger, D. (2014). *Strict collegiate academies are working to eliminate suspensions.* Retrieved from: http://www.nola.com/education/index.ssf/2014/10/strict_collegiate_academies_ch.html

Dumas, M. J. (2014). "Losing an arm": Schooling as a site of Black suffering. *Race Ethnicity and Education, 1*(1), 1–29.

Duncan, G.A. (2000). Urban pedagogies and the celling of adolescents of color. *Social Justice* 27(3), 29–42.

Duncan-Andrade, J. M. R., & Morrell, E. (2008). *The art of critical pedagogy: Possibilities for moving from theory to practice in urban schools.* New York, NY: Peter Lang.

Evans-Winters, V. E. (2011). *Teaching Black girls: Resiliency in urban classrooms.* New York, NY: Peter Lang.

Ferguson, A.A. (2001) *Bad boys: Public schools in the making of Black masculinity.* Ann Arbor, MI: University of Michigan Press.

Freire, P. (2008). *Pedagogy of the oppressed* (30th ed.). New York, NY: Continuum

Gay, G. (2000). *Culturally responsive teaching: Theory, research, and practice.* New York, NY: Teachers College Press.

Gregory, A., Skiba, R. J., & Noguera, P. A. (2010). The achievement gap and the discipline gap: Two sides of the same coin? *Educational Researcher, 39*, 59–68.

Hill, M. L. (2009). *Beat, rhymes, and classroom life: Hip-hop pedagogy and the politics of identity.* New York, NY: Teachers College Press.

Howard, G. R. (1999). *We can't teach what we don't know: White teachers, multicultural schools.* New York, NY: Teachers College Press.

Irvine, J. J., & York, D. E. (1995). Learning styles and culturally diverse students: A literature review. Retrieved from ERIC database. (ED382722)

King, J. E. (1991). Dysconscious racism: Ideology, identity, and the miseducation of teachers. *Journal of Negro Education, 60*(2), *133–146.*

Ladson-Billings, G. (1994). *The dreamkeepers: Successful teaching for African-American students.* San Francisco, CA: Jossey-Bass.

Ladson-Billings, G. (1995). Toward a theory of culturally relevant pedagogy. *American Educational Research Journal, 31*, 465–469.

Ladson-Billings, G. (2006). They're trying to wash us away: The adolescence of critical race theory in education. In A. D. Dixon & C. K. Rousseau (Eds.), *Critical race theory in education: All God's children got a song*, (pp. v–xiii).

Ladson-Billings, G., & Tate, W. F. (1995). Toward a critical race theory of education. *Teachers College Record*, *97*(1), 47–68.

Lawrence, S. M., & Tatum, B. D. (1997). White educators as allies: Moving from awareness to action. In M. Fine, L. Weiss, L. Powell, & M. Wongs (Eds.), *Off/white: Readings on race, power, and society* (pp. 333–342). New York, NY: Routledge.

Leonardo, Z. (2002). The souls of White folk: Critical pedagogy, whiteness studies, and globalization discourse. *Race Ethnicity and Education, 5*(1), 29–50.

Leonardo, Z., & Boas, E. (2013). Other kids' teachers: What children of color learn from White women and what this says about race, whiteness, and gender. In M. Lynn & A. D. Dixson (Eds.), *Handbook of critical race theory in education* (pp. 313–324). New York, NY: Routledge.

Lipman, P. (2011). *The new political economy of urban education: Neoliberalism, race, and the right to the city.* New York, NY: Routledge.

Louisiana Department of Education. (2015). *Response to senate concurrent resolution 134 of the 2014 regular session.* Retrieved from http://www.boarddocs.com/la/bese/Board.nsf/files/9SDTDG76DCA3/$file/AF_6.1_SCR_134_Response.pdf

Matias, C.E. (2013). Check yo'self before you wreck yo'self and our kids: Counter-stories from culturally responsive white teachers? ... to culturally responsive white teachers! *Interdisciplinary Journal of Teaching and Learning, 3*(1), 68–81.

McAllister, G., & Irvine, J. J. (2002). The role of empathy in teaching culturally diverse students: A qualitative study of teachers' beliefs. *Journal of Teacher Education, 53*(5), 433–443.

Michie, G. (1998). *Holler if you hear me: The education of a teacher and his students.* New York, NY: Teachers College Press.

Michie, G. (2005). *See you when we get there: Teaching for change in urban schools.* New York, NY: Teachers College Press.

Mills, C. W. (2007). White ignorance. In S. Sullivan & N. Tuana (Eds.), *Race and epistemologies of ignorance* (pp. 11–38). New York, NY: State University of New York Press.

Milner, H. R., IV. (2010). *Start where you are, but don't stay there: Understanding diversity, opportunity gaps, and teaching in today's classrooms.* Cambridge, MA: Harvard Education Press.

Morris, E. W. (2005). Tuck in that shirt! Race, class, gender, and discipline in an urban school. *Sociological Perspectives, 48*, 25–48.

NAACP Legal Defense and Educational Fund, Inc. (2005). *Dismantling the school-to-prison pipeline.* Retrieved from http://www.naacpldf.org/publication/dismantling-schoolprison-pipeline

Paris, D. (2012). Culturally sustaining pedagogy: A needed change in stance, terminology, and practice. *Educational Researcher, 41*(3), 93–97.

Paris, D., & Alim, H. S. (2014). What are we seeking to sustain through culturally sustaining pedagogy? A loving critique forward. *Harvard Educational Review, 84*(1), 85–100.

Peck, N., Maude, S., & Brotherson, M. (2015). Understanding preschool teachers' perspective on empathy: A qualitative inquiry. *Early Childhood Education Journal, 43*(3), 169–179.

Pianta, R. C., Hamre, B. K., & Allen, J. P. (2012). Teacher-student relationships and engagement: Conceptualizing, measuring, and improving the capacity of classroom interactions. In S.L. Christenson et al. (Eds.), *Handbook of research on student engagement*, (pp. 365–386). New York, NY: Springer.

Picower, B. (2009). The unexamined Whiteness of teaching. *Race, Ethnicity and Education, 12*(2), 197–215.

Pranis, K. (2005). *The little book of circle processes.* Intercourse, PA: Good Books.

Sondel, B. (2013). *Raising citizens or raising test scores: Ideology and pedagogy in post-Katrina charter schools* (Unpublished doctoral dissertation). University of Wisconsin, Madison, WI.

Warren, C. A. (2014). Towards a pedagogy for the application of empathy in culturally diverse classrooms. *The Urban Review, 46*(3), 395–419.

Warren, C. A. (2015). Conflicts and contradictions: Conceptions of empathy and the work of good-intentioned White female teachers. *Urban Education, 50*(5), 572–600.

Warren, C.A., & Hotchkins, B. K. (2015). Teacher education and the enduring significance of "false empathy." *The Urban Review, 47*(2), 266–292.

Williams. P. J. (1987). Alchemical notes: Reconstructing ideals from deconstructed rights. *Harvard Civil Rights Civil Liberties Law Review, 22*, 401–434.

Winn, M. T. (2010). "Betwixt and between": Literacy, liminality, and the celling of Black girls. *Race Ethnicity and Education 13*(4), 425–447.

Winn, M. T. (2013). Toward a restorative English education. *Research in the Teaching of English, 48*(1), 126–135.

ABOUT THE CONTRIBUTORS

ABOUT THE EDITORS

Dr. Stephen D. Hancock is an associate professor of multicultural education in the Department of Reading and Elementary Education at UNC Charlotte where he also serves as the assistant director of the Urban Education Collaborative. He is an international visiting professor at the Pedagogische Hocshule in Ludwigsburg, Germany, where he teaches courses in diversity and globalization. Dr. Hancock's research interest supports the culture of reading for young children, constructive academic relationships in multiethnic classrooms, image and identity of teachers, and critical autoethnographic research methodologies and theory. His work has been published in *Urban Education, Teacher Education and Practice, The Journal of Curriculum and Pedagogy,* and *The Harvard Educational Review.*

Dr. Chezare A. Warren is an assistant professor in the Department of Teacher Education at Michigan State University. He teaches courses in race and education, urban teacher preparation, and elementary mathematics methods for diverse learners. He has more than a decade of professional experience as a public school educator and school administrator in Chicago. Dr. Warren's research interests include urban teacher preparation, culturally responsive teaching, and critical race theory in education. His work has been published in outlets that include *The Urban Review, Urban Education, Journal of Negro Education, Race, Ethnicity, and Education,* and *the Interdisciplinary Journal of Teaching and Learning.*

ABOUT THE AUTHORS

Keisha L. Bentley-Edwards is an assistant professor of general internal medicine and the director of the Health Equity Working Group for the

Cook Center on Social Equity at Duke University. She is a developmental psychologist who focuses on the racial experiences of youth. She is particularly interested in how the messages we give children and adolescents about race and racism influence racial cohesion, interpersonal relationships and academic outcomes. Dr. Bentley-Edwards studies how cultural strengths can be used to buffer the negative effects of discrimination, bullying, and community violence. Although most of her work focuses on African American children, she also studies the racial conversations that occur in White families and with White practitioners. Dr. Bentley-Edwards was recently awarded a Robert Wood Johnson New Connections grant to study the bullying experiences of African American children.

Amy Brown is an educational anthropologist and a faculty member in the Critical Writing Program at the University of Pennsylvania. Her work focuses on race, gender, and the impacts of privatization on public institutions. She brings not only her postsecondary teaching experience, but also 5 years of experience as a teacher in New York City public secondary schools to her scholarship. Her book, *A Good Investment? Privatization and Professional Performance in an Urban Public School*, is currently under contract with the University of Minnesota Press. Dr. Brown holds a PhD in social anthropology from the University of Texas at Austin.

Colleen H. Clements is currently a researcher in the Department of Curriculum and Instruction at the University of Minnesota. She specializes in cultural studies in education, and the social and political contexts of education and educational policy. Her work is primarily concerned with a critical examination of idealized White femininity as a racialized identity within White, hetero-normative, patriarchal U.S. society and its relation to teaching in both formal and informal learning spaces, as well as its effects in the realm of educational policy. She is coauthoring a forthcoming book with her colleagues, Angela Coffee and Erin Stutelberg.

Angela C. Coffee is a PhD candidate in critical literacy and English education in the Department of Curriculum and Instruction at the University of Minnesota. An English and writing teacher of adult learners, she is profoundly interested in the relationship between language and power. Her research examines stories of teaching and learning through their complex entanglements with race, class, gender, and sexuality.

Chonika Coleman-King received her PhD in teaching, learning, and curriculum from the University of Pennsylvania. Prior to pursuing doctoral studies, she worked as an elementary school teacher in Title I schools bordering the District of Columbia. Dr. Coleman-King has also served as a consultant to a range of organizations concerned with the academic success and development of children and youth of color including low-income urban schools, wealthy private independent schools, and other nonprofit organizations. Dr. Coleman-King is the author of *The (Re-)Making of a Black American: Tracing the Racial and Ethnic Socialization of Caribbean American Youth*. She is currently an assistant professor of urban-multicultural education at the University of Tennessee, Knoxville. Chonika and her husband are raising two children and spend their free time engaging them in new and meaningful experiences.

Kenneth J. Fasching-Varner is the Shirley B. Barton Endowed Associate Professor of Education in the College of Human Sciences and Education at Louisiana State University. Varner's interests center on the intersection of race, culture, and language. The author of more than 40 peer-reviewed publications, Varner challenges normative positions on whiteness and White privilege calling for more critical and direct engagement with racism in academic forums.

Marcie E. Frazier is a graduate student at Louisiana State University in the College of Human Sciences and Education's School of Education. A native of Springfield, Illinois, she received her undergraduate degree from Benedictine University in elementary education. She has been working in urban public schools in Illinois and Louisiana for the past 6 years. Frazier's research interests are culturally relevant pedagogy, race, and language.

Kevin Lawrence Henry, Jr. is an assistant professor of educational policy and practice in the College of Education at the University of Arizona. Kevin's research and teaching primarily revolves around the social contexts and political sociology of education with a particular emphasis on urban education reform and policy (market-based/neoliberal educational policies/school choice), social stratification, and counterhegemonic practices/pedagogies and theories (critical race theory, feminist theories, and queer of color critique). His scholarship has been published in *Educational Policy*, *Journal of Social Studies Research*, *Handbook of Urban Education*, and elsewhere.

Melvin (Jai) Jackson is an assistant professor at Zayed University in the United Arab Emirates with various teaching appointments in the University College. He received both his bachelor's and master's degrees from Appalachian State University and his doctorate from Louisiana State University and A&M College. His research focuses on race and education, higher education in the Middle East and Northern Africa, and leadership in higher education.

Sarah Lee teaches first grade at Friends Select School. The daughter of Korean immigrants who came to the United States in the late 1970s, Sarah grew up in California and Delaware experiencing the complexities of being bicultural. Sarah, who is a certified reading specialist in the state of Pennsylvania, holds a bachelor's degree in elementary education from the University of Pennsylvania and a master's degree in multicultural education from Eastern University. As a living embodiment of both Korean and American cultures, Sarah continually explores the nuances of what it means to live "in-between" two worlds.

Timothy Lensmire is an associate professor in curriculum and instruction at the University of Minnesota. His work explores the possibilities and problems of various critical pedagogies and how White people learn to be White in our White supremacist society. His current research seeks to theorize whiteness and White racial identities, as part of a larger effort to mobilize White people to take up antiracist and social justice work.

Cheryl E. Matias is an assistant professor in educational foundations at the University of Colorado Denver. Her research employs feminism of color to deconstruct the emotionality of whiteness in urban teaching and motherscholarship. A former teacher in South Los Angeles and Bedford–Stuyvesant, Brooklyn, she earned her bachelor's from the University of California San Diego, teaching credential at San Diego State University, and her master's from California State University, Long Beach. She earned her doctorate at UCLA with an emphasis in race and ethnic studies in education. She is a motherscholar of twins, a Lakers fan, and bachata ballroom dancer.

Ali Michael is the director of P-12 consulting and professional development for the Center for the Study of Race and Equity in Education at the University of Pennsylvania and the director and cofounder of the Race Institute for K-12 Educators. She is the coeditor of *Everyday White People Confront Racial and Social Injustice: 15 Stories* (2015, Stylus Press) and *The Guide for White Women who Teach Black Boys* (forthcoming, Corwin Press). Ali sits on the editorial board of the international peer-reviewed journal *Whiteness and Education*. Ali lives in Philadelphia with her partner, Michael, and their two children.

Erin Miller is an assistant professor of reading and elementary education at the University of North Carolina, Charlotte. Her research interests include investigations of racial identity with young children both within and outside of formal school experiences.

Benterah C. Morton spent 12 years in K-12 education as a middle and high school teacher and an elementary school principal. Morton's interests are linked to the supports provided by teachers and school leaders to provide equity in opportunity for all students. He focuses on exploring the supports provided to culturally and linguistically different students. Morton is a graduate of Louisiana State University and A&M College with a PhD in curriculum and instruction.

Naomi W. Nishi is a doctoral student in the School of Education and Human Development at the University of Colorado Denver. Naomi has worked in or with higher education for more than a decade, including serving as an instructor at the University of Denver for 7 years. She is currently a faculty development professional in research development for CU Denver. Her research focuses on building racial inclusivity in the higher education classroom. Her theoretical approach is based in critical whiteness studies and critical race theory. Naomi is also a mother to two crazy boys.

Cecilia Ramirez holds a BA and an MS from the University of Pennsylvania, where she studied sociology, urban studies, international policy, nonprofit leadership, and entrepreneurship. Through the Teach for America program, Cecilia taught fourth grade in the South Bronx. After obtaining her master's degree, Cecilia started and currently runs a consulting company that helps businesses and nonprofits with governance, marketing, and events. She is also a public speaker for teachers and students on issues of race, poverty, empowerment, and identity development. Cecilia is a native New Yorker and has lived in Philadelphia, Massachusetts, Spain, and France. She currently lives in New York City with her partner, Jesse, and son, Oliver.

Naomi Reed is a social anthropologist and postdoc in the African American studies department at UCLA. Her work focuses on whiteness, race, and studying up methodologies. She has done extensive research on upper-class White communities and educational institutions in the United States and hopes to expand this work into a comparative project dealing with racial epistemologies among "White" American Jews and their relationship to Jews of color. Dr. Reed holds an MA in social sciences from the University of Chicago and a PhD in social anthropology from the University of Texas at Austin.

Erin Stutelberg is a PhD candidate in critical literacy and English education in the Department of Curriculum and Instruction at the University of Minnesota. Formerly a high school English teacher, her current work in teacher education focuses on understanding the racialized, gendered, and classed experiences of secondary English teachers. In collaboration with beginning teachers, she is pursuing feminist research methodologies to access and analyze embodied memories of teaching and learning; and collectively theorize, challenge, and reconstruct the stories of our teacher bodies.

Lloyd Matthew Talley is a PhD student in the Applied Psychology and Human Development division of the University of Pennsylvania's Graduate School of Education. His research interests include: racial and ethnic socialization, racial literacy, culturally relevant social and emotional learning, and intervention design and implementation. He is also a graduate researcher at the Racial Empowerment Collaborative at Penn GSE.

52570101R00124

Made in the USA
San Bernardino, CA
24 August 2017